Reader's Guide
to
OSCAR WILDE

Reader's Guide to OSCAR WILDE

W. Cormier

CENTRUM PRESS
NEW DELHI-110002 (INDIA)

CENTRUM PRESS
H.O.: 4360/4, Ansari Road, Daryaganj,
New Delhi-110 002 (India)
Ph.: 23278000, 23261597

B.O.: No. 1015, Ist Main Road, BSK IIIrd Stage
IIIrd Phase, IIIrd Block,
Bangalore - 560 085 (India)
Tel.: 080-41723429
Visit us at: www.centrumpress.com

Reader's Guide to Oscar Wilde

First Edition, 2009

ISBN 978-93-80106-89-2

PRINTED IN INDIA

Printed at Balaji Offset, Delhi.

Contents

Preface

In the centre of the room, clamped to an upright easel, stood the full-length portrait of a young man of extraordinary personal beauty, and in front of it, some little distance away, was sitting the artist himself, Basil Hallward, ... "I hate them for it,"cried Hallward. "An artist should create beautiful things, but should put nothing of his own life into them. We live in an age when men treat art as if it were meant to be a form of autobiography. We have lost the abstract sense of beauty. Some day I will show the world what it is; and for that reason the world shall never see my portrait of Dorian Gray."

Ever the aesthete, Wilde himself was profoundly affected by beauty and lived and dressed flamboyantly compared to the typical Victorian styles and mores of the time. He was often publicly caricatured and the target of much moral outrage in Europe and America. His writings such as *Dorian Gray* with homoerotic themes also brought much controversy for him but he was part of the ever-growing movement of 'decadents' who advocated pacifism, social reform, and libertarianism. While many vilified him, he was making his mark with style and wit and enjoyed much success with many of his plays.

Wilde was lauded by and acquainted with many influential figures of the day including fellow playwright George Bernard Shaw, American poets Walt Whitman and Henry Wadsworth Longfellow, and English author and social critic John Ruskin. His works have inspired countless fellow authors, have been translated to numerous languages, and have been adapted to the stage and screen many times over. Fiction by Wilde includes *The Canterville Ghost* (1887), *The Happy Prince and Other Tales* (1888), *The Portrait of Mr. W. H.*

(1889), *A House of Pomegranates* (1891), *Lord Arthur Savile's Crime* (1891), and *Intentions* (essays, 1891). His plays include *Vera, or the Nihilists* (1880), *The Duchess of Padua* (1883), *Lady Windermere's Fan* (1892), *A Florentine Tragedy* (*La Sainte Courtisane* 1893), *A Woman of No Importance* (1893), *Salomé* (1894), *An Ideal Husband* (1895), an.. *The Importance of Being Earnest* (1895).

After school Wilde settled in London and continued to write poetry; his first collection simply titled *Poems* was published in 1881. That same year he set off on a long tour of America and Canada to deliver lectures on aestheticism. He arrived back in Europe in 1883 and while not further lecturing lived in Paris, France. In 1884 Wilde married Constance Mary Lloyd (1858-1898) with whom he would have two sons; Cyril (1885-1915), who was killed during World War I, and Vyvyan (1886-1976), who would become an author, penning his memoir *Son of Oscar Wilde* (1954) and publishing *Oscar Wilde: A Pictorial Biography* in 1960. The Wildes settled in Chelsea, London where Oscar continued to write and work for such magazines as the *Pall Mall Gazette* and became editor of *Woman's World* in 1887.

In 1891 Wilde met English poet Lord Alfred Douglas "Bosie" (1870-1945), son of John Douglas, 9th Marquess of Queensberry (1844-1900). It was the beginning of a tumultuous relationship that would cause many problems for Oscar and eventually lead to his downfall. Alfred had a tempestuous relationship with his father which did not help matters. He disapproved of his son's lifestyle and when he learned of his openly living with Wilde, he set out to defame Wilde. For the opening performance of *The Importance of Being Earnest* in 1895 at St. James's Theatre in London the Marquess planned to publicly expose and humiliate Wilde. Oscar took legal steps to protect himself against the 'brute' but he ultimately won a case whereby Wilde was charged with "gross indecency" for homosexual acts.

Chapter 1

Introduction

Oscar Fingal O'Flahertie Wills Wilde (16 October 1854 – 30 November 1900) was an Irish playwright, poet and author of numerous short stories and one novel. Known for his biting wit, he became one of the most successful playwrights of the late Victorian era in London, and one of the greatest celebrities of his day. Several of his plays continue to be widely performed, especially *The Importance of Being Earnest.*

As the result of a widely covered series of trials, Wilde suffered a dramatic downfall and was imprisoned for two years hard labour after being convicted of "gross indecency" with other men. After Wilde was released from prison he set sail for Dieppe by the night ferry. He never returned to Ireland or Britain.

BIRTH AND EARLY LIFE

Oscar Wilde was the second son born into an Anglo-Irish family, at 21 Westland Row, Dublin, to Sir William Wilde and his wife Jane Francesca Wilde (née Elgee) (her pseudonym being Speranza). Jane was a successful writer, being a poet for the revolutionary Young Irelanders in 1848 and a life-long Irish nationalist.

Sir William was Ireland's leading Oto-Ophthalmologic (ear and eye) surgeon and was knighted in 1864 for his services to medicine. William also wrote books on archaeology and folklore. He was a renowned philanthropist, and his dispensary for the care of the city's poor, in Lincoln Place at the rear of Trinity College, Dublin, was the forerunner of the Dublin Eye and Ear Hospital, now located at Adelaide Road.

In June 1855, the family moved to 1 Merrion Square in a fashionable residential area, where Wilde's sister, Isola, was born in 1856. Here, Lady Wilde held a regular Saturday afternoon salon with guests including Sheridan le Fanu, Charles Lever, George Petrie, Isaac Butt and Samuel Ferguson. Wilde was educated at home up to the age of nine.

He attended Portora Royal School in Enniskillen, Fermanagh from the ages of nine to sixteen, spending the summer months with his family in rural Waterford, Wexford and at Sir William's family home in Mayo. Here the Wilde brothers played with the older George Moore. After leaving Portora, Wilde studied classics at Trinity College, Dublin, from 1871 to 1874, sharing rooms with his older brother Willie Wilde for two years. His tutor, John Pentland Mahaffy the leading Greek scholar at Trinity awakened his interest in greek literature. He was an outstanding student, and won the Berkeley Gold Medal, the highest award available to classics students at Trinity. He was awarded a scholarship to Magdalen College, Oxford, where he continued his studies from 1874 to 1878 and where he became a part of the Aesthetic movement, one of its tenets being to make an art of life.

Wilde had a less than happy relationship with the prestigious Oxford Union. On matriculating in the autumn of 1874, Wilde applied to join the Union, but failed to be elected. When the Union's librarian requested a presentation copy of *Poems* (1881), Wilde complied. After a debate called by Oliver Elton, the gift was condemned for supposed plagiarism and returned.

While at Magdalen, he won the 1878 Newdigate Prize for his poem *Ravenna,* which he read out at Encaenia; he failed, though, to win the Chancellor's English Essay Prize for an essay that would be published posthumously as *The Rise of Historical Criticism* (1909). In November 1878, he graduated with a double first in classical moderations and *Literae Humaniores*, or 'Greats'.

AESTHETICISM AND PHILOSOPHY

While at Magdalen College, Wilde became particularly

well known for his role in the aesthetic and decadent movements. He began wearing his hair long and openly scorning so-called "manly" sports, and began decorating his rooms with peacock feathers, lilies, sunflowers, blue china and other *objets d'art*.

Legends persist that his behaviour cost him a dunking in the River Cherwell in addition to having his rooms (which still survive as student accommodation at his old college) trashed, but the cult spread among certain segments of society to such an extent that languishing attitudes, "too-too" costumes and aestheticism generally became a recognised pose. Publications such as the *Springfield Republican* commented on Wilde's behaviour during his visit to Boston in order to give lectures on aestheticism, suggesting that Wilde's conduct was more of a bid for notoriety rather than a devotion to beauty and the aesthetic.

Wilde's mode of dress also came under attack by critics such as Higginson, who wrote in his paper *Unmanly Manhood,* of his general concern that Wilde's effeminacy would influence the behaviour of men and women, arguing that his poetry "eclipses masculine ideals [..that..] under such influence men would become effeminate dandies". He also scrutinised the links between Oscar Wilde's writing, personal image and homosexuality, calling his work and lifestyle 'Immoral'.

Wilde was deeply impressed by the English writers John Ruskin and Walter Pater, who argued for the central importance of art in life, an argument laced with a strongly philhellenic and homoerotic subtext. Wilde later commented ironically on Pater's suppressed emotions: on being informed of the man's death, he replied, "Was he ever alive?" Reflecting on Pater's view of art, he wrote, in *The Picture of Dorian Gray,* "All art is quite useless".

The statement was meant to be read literally, as it was in keeping with the doctrine of Art for art's sake, coined by the philosopher Victor Cousin, promoted by Theophile Gautier and brought into prominence by James McNeill Whistler. In 1879 Wilde started to teach Aesthetic values in London.

The aesthetic movement, represented by the school of

William Morris and Dante Gabriel Rossetti, had a permanent influence on English decorative art. As the leading aesthete in Britain, Wilde became one of the most prominent personalities of his day. Though he was sometimes ridiculed for them, his paradoxes and witty sayings were quoted on all sides.

Aestheticism in general was caricatured in Gilbert and Sullivan's operetta *Patience* (1881). While *Patience* was a success in New York it was not known how much the aesthetic movement had penetrated the rest of America.

So Richard D'Oyly Carte invited Wilde for a lecture tour of North America. D'Oyly Carte felt this tour would "prime the pump" for the tour of *Patience,* making sure that the ticket-buying public was aware of one of the movement's charming personalities. This was duly arranged, Wilde arriving on 3 January 1882, aboard the *SS Arizona.* Wilde is reputed to have told a customs officer "I have nothing to declare except my genius", although there is no contemporary evidence for the remark.

During his tour of the United States and Canada, Wilde was torn apart by no small number of critics—*The Wasp,* a San Francisco newspaper, published a cartoon ridiculing Wilde and Aestheticism—but he was also surprisingly well received in such rough-and-tumble settings as the mining town of Leadville, Colorado. On his return to the United Kingdom, he worked as a reviewer for the *Pall Mall Gazette* in the years 1887-1889. Afterwards he became the editor of *The Woman's World.*

POLITICS

Wilde, for much of his life, advocated socialism, which he argued "will be of value simply because it will lead to individualism." He also had a strong libertarian streak as shown in his poem "Sonnet to Liberty" and, subsequently to reading the works of Peter Kropotkin—whom he described as "a man with a soul of that beautiful white Christ which seems coming out of Russia"—he declared himself an anarchist.

Other political influences on Wilde may have been William Morris and John Ruskin. Wilde was also a pacifist and quipped that "When liberty comes with hands dabbled in blood it is hard to shake hands with her".

In addition to his primary political text, the essay "The Soul of Man under Socialism", Wilde wrote several letters to the *Daily Chronicle* advocating prison reform and was the sole signatory of George Bernard Shaw's petition for a pardon of the anarchists arrested (and later executed) after the Haymarket massacre in Chicago in 1886.

In Lady Florence Dixie's 1890 novel *Gloriana, or the Revolution of 1900,* women win the right to vote after the protagonist, Gloriana, poses as a man to get elected to the House of Commons. The male character she impersonates is clearly based on that of Wilde. Dixie was an aunt of Lord Alfred Douglas.

MARRIAGE AND FAMILY

After graduating from Oxford, Wilde returned to Dublin, where he met and courted Florence Balcombe. She, however, became engaged to the writer Bram Stoker. On hearing of her engagement, Wilde wrote to her stating his intention to leave Ireland permanently.

He left in 1878, and returned to his native country only twice, for brief visits. He spent the next six years in London and Paris, and in the United States, where he traveled to deliver lectures. Wilde's address in the 1881 British Census is given as 1 Tite Street, London. The head of the household is listed as Frank Miles with whom Wilde shared rooms at this address.

In London, he met Constance Lloyd, daughter of wealthy Queen's Counsel Horace Lloyd. She was visiting Dublin in 1884, when Wilde was in the city to give lectures at the Gaiety Theatre. He proposed to her, and they married on 29 May 1884 in Paddington, London. Constance's allowance of £250 allowed the Wildes to live in relative luxury. The couple had two sons, Cyril (1885) and Vyvyan (1886).

After Wilde's downfall, Constance took the surname Holland for herself and the boys. She died in 1898 following spinal surgery and was buried in Monumental Cemetery of

Staglieno in Genoa, Italy. Cyril was killed in France in World War I. Vyvyan also served in the war and later became an author and translator. He published his memoirs in 1954. Vyvyan's son, Merlin Holland, has edited and published several works about his grandfather. Wilde's niece, Dolly Wilde, had a lengthy lesbian relationship with writer Natalie Clifford Barney.

SEXUALITY

Though Wilde's sexual orientation has variously been considered bisexual and homosexual, Wilde himself felt he belonged to a culture of male love inspired by the Greek paederastic tradition. In describing his own sexual identity, Wilde used the term *Socratic*. He may have had significant sexual relationships with (in chronological order) Frank Miles, Constance Lloyd (his wife), Robert Baldwin Ross, and Lord Alfred Douglas ("Bosie"). Wilde also had numerous sexual encounters with working-class male youths, who were often rent boys.

Biographers generally believe Wilde was made fully aware of his own and others' homosexuality in 1885 (the year after his wedding) by the 17-year-old Robert Baldwin Ross. Neil McKenna's biography *The Secret Life of Oscar Wilde* (2003) theorises that Wilde was aware of his homosexuality much earlier, from the moment of his first kiss with another boy at the age of 16. According to McKenna, after arriving at Oxford in 1874, Wilde tentatively explored his sexuality, discovering that he could feel passionate romantic love for "fair, slim" choirboys, but was more sexually drawn towards the swarthy young rough trade.

By the late 1870s, Wilde was already preoccupied with the philosophy of same-sex love, and had befriended a group of Uranian (pederastic) poets and homosexual law reformers, becoming acquainted with the work of gay-rights pioneer Karl-Heinrich Ulrichs. Wilde also met Walt Whitman in America in 1882, writing to a friend that there was "no doubt" about the great American poet's sexual orientation—"I have the kiss of Walt Whitman still on my lips", he boasted. He even lived with the society painter Frank Miles, who was a few years his senior and may have been his lover. However, writes McKenna, he was at one time unhappy with the direction of his sexual and romantic desires, and, hoping that marriage would 'cure' him, he married Constance Lloyd in 1884. McKenna's account has been criticised by some reviewers who find it too speculative, although not necessarily implausible.

Whether or not Wilde was still naïve when he first met Ross, the latter did play an important role in the development of Wilde's understanding of his own sexuality. Ross was aware of Wilde's poems before they met, and indeed had been beaten for reading them. He was also unmoved by the Victorian prohibition against homosexuality. By Richard Ellmann's account, Ross, "...so young and yet so knowing, was determined to seduce Wilde."

Later, Ross boasted to Lord Alfred Douglas that he was "the first boy Oscar ever had" and there seems to have been much jealousy between them. Soon, Wilde entered a world of regular sex with youths such as servants and newsboys, in their mid to late teens, whom he would meet in homosexual bars or brothels.

In Wilde's words, the relations were akin to "feasting with panthers", and he revelled in the risk: "the danger was half the excitement." In his public writings, Wilde's first celebration of romantic love between men and boys can be found in *The Portrait of Mr. W. H.* (1889), in which he propounds a theory that Shakespeare's sonnets were written out of the poet's love of Elizabethan boy actor "Willie Hughes".

In the early summer of 1891 he was introduced by the poet Lionel Johnson to the twenty-two-year-old Lord Alfred Douglas, an undergraduate at Oxford at the time. An intimate friendship immediately sprang up between the two, but it was not initially sexual, nor did the sexual activity progress far when it did eventually take place.

According to Douglas, speaking in his old age, for the first six months their relations remained on a purely intellectual and emotional level. Despite the fact that "from the second time he saw me, when he gave me a copy of *Dorian Gray* which

I took with me to Oxford, he made overtures to me. It was not till I had known him for at least six months and after I had seen him over and over again and he had twice stayed with me in Oxford, that I gave in to him.

I did with him and allowed him to do just what was done among boys at Winchester and Oxford... Sodomy never took place between us, nor was it attempted or dreamed of. Wilde treated me as an older one does a younger one at school." After Wilde realised that Douglas only consented in order to please him, as his instincts drew him not to men but to younger boys, Wilde permanently ceased his physical attentions.

For a few years they lived together more or less openly in a number of locations. Wilde and some within his upper-class social group also began to speak about homosexual law reform, and their commitment to "The Cause" was formalised by the founding of a highly secretive organisation called the Order of Chaeronea, of which Wilde was a member.

A homosexual novel, *Teleny or The Reverse of the Medal*, written at about the same time and clandestinely published in 1893, has been attributed to Oscar Wilde, but was probably, in fact, a combined effort by a number of Wilde's friends, which Wilde edited. Wilde also periodically contributed to the Uranian literary journal *The Chameleon*.

Lord Alfred's first mentor had been his cosmopolitan grandfather Alfred Montgomery. His older brother Francis Douglas, Viscount Drumlanrig possibly had an intimate association with the Prime Minister Archibald Philip Primrose, 5th Earl of Rosebery, which ended on Francis' death in an unexplained shooting accident.

Lord Alfred's father John Sholto Douglas, 9th Marquess of Queensberry came to believe his sons had been corrupted by older homosexuals, or as he phrased it in a letter, "Snob Queers like Rosebery". As he had attempted to do with Rosebery, Queensberry confronted Wilde and Lord Alfred on several occasions, but each time Wilde was able to mollify him.

Divorced and spending wildly, Queensberry was known for his outspoken views and the boxing roughs who often accompanied him. He abhorred his younger son and plagued the boy with threats to cut him off if he did not stop idling his life away. Queensberry was determined to end the friendship with Wilde.

Wilde was in full flow of rehearsal when Bosie returned from a diplomatic posting to Cairo, around the time Queensberry visited Wilde at his Tite Street home. He angrily pushed past Wilde's servant and entered the ground floor study, shouting obscenities and asking Wilde about his divorce.

Wilde became incensed, but it is said he calmly told his manservant that Queensberry was the most infamous brute in London, and that he was not to be shown into the house ever again. It is said that, despite the presence of a bodyguard, Wilde forced Queensberry to leave in no uncertain terms.

On the opening night of *The Importance of Being Earnest* Queensberry further planned to insult and socially embarrass Wilde by throwing a bouquet of turnips. Wilde was tipped off, and Queensberry was barred from entering the theatre.

Wilde took legal advice against him, and wished to prosecute, but his friends refused to give evidence against the Marquess and hence the case was dropped. Wilde and Bosie left London for a holiday in Monte Carlo. While they were there, on 18 February 1895, the Marquess left his calling card at Wilde's Club, with a scrawled inscription accusing Wilde of being a "posing somdomite [sic]".

TRIAL, IMPRISONMENT, AND TRANSFER TO READING GAOL

Wilde made a complaint of criminal libel against the Marquess of Queensberry based on the calling card incident, and the Marquess was arrested but later freed on bail. The libel trial became a *cause célèbre* as salacious details of Wilde's private life with Alfred Taylor and Lord Alfred Douglas began to appear in the press. A team of detectives, with the help of the actor Charles Brookfield, had directed Queensberry's lawyers (led by Edward Carson QC) to the world of the Victorian underground. Here Wilde's association with blackmailers and male prostitutes, crossdressers and homosexual brothels was recorded, and various persons involved were interviewed, some being coerced to appear as witnesses.

The trial opened on 3 April 1895 amongst scenes of near hysteria both in the press and the public galleries. After a shaky start, Wilde regained some ground when defending his art from attacks of perversion. *The Picture of Dorian Gray* came under fierce moral criticism, but Wilde fended it off with his usual charm and confidence on artistic matters. Some of his personal letters to Lord Alfred were examined, their wording challenged as inappropriate and evidence of immoral relations.

Queensberry's legal team proposed that the libel was published for the public good, but it was only when the prosecution moved on to sexual matters that Wilde balked. He was challenged on the reason given for not kissing a young servant; Wilde had replied, "He was a particularly plain boy—unfortunately ugly—I pitied him for it." Counsel for the defence, scenting blood, pressed him on the point. Wilde hesitated, complaining of Carson's insults and attempts to unnerve him.

The prosecution eventually dropped the case, after the defence threatened to bring boy prostitutes to the stand to testify to Wilde's corruption and influence over Queensberry's son, effectively crippling the case. After Wilde left the court, a warrant for his arrest was applied for and (after a delay that would have permitted Wilde, had he wished, to escape to the continent) later served on him at the Cadogan Hotel, Knightsbridge.

That moment was immortalised by Sir John Betjeman's poem. He was arrested for "gross indecency" under Section 11 of the Criminal Law Amendment Act 1885. In British legislation of the time, this term implied homosexual acts not amounting to buggery, which was an offence under a separate statute. After his arrest Wilde sent Robert Ross to his home in Tite Street with orders to remove certain items and Ross broke into the bedroom to rescue some of Wilde's belongings. Wilde was then imprisoned on remand at Holloway where he received daily visits from Lord Alfred Douglas.

Events moved quickly and his prosecution opened on 26 April 1895. Wilde had already begged Douglas to leave London for Paris, but Douglas complained bitterly, even wanting to take the stand; however, he was pressed to go and soon fled to the Hotel du Monde. Ross and many others also left the United Kingdom during this time. Under cross examination Wilde presented an eloquent defence of pederasty:

CHARLES GILL (PROS.)

Wilde: "The love that dares not speak its name" in this century is such a great affection of an elder for a younger man as there was between David and Jonathan, such as Plato made the very basis of his philosophy, and such as you find in the sonnets of Michelangelo and Shakespeare. It is that deep spiritual affection that is as pure as it is perfect. It dictates and pervades great works of art, like those of Shakespeare and Michelangelo, and those two letters of mine, such as they are.

It is in this century misunderstood, so much misunderstood that it may be described as "the love that dares not speak its name", and on that account of it I am placed where I am now. It is beautiful, it is fine, it is the noblest form of affection. There is nothing unnatural about it. It is intellectual, and it repeatedly exists between an older and a younger man, when the older man has intellect, and the younger man has all the joy, hope and glamour of life before him. That it should be so, the world does not understand. The world mocks at it, and sometimes puts one in the pillory for it."

The trial ended with the jury unable to reach a verdict and Wilde's counsel, Sir Edward Clark, was finally able to agree bail. Wilde was freed from Holloway and went into hiding at the house of Ernest and Ada Leverson, two of Wilde's firm friends.

The Reverend Stewart Headlam put up most of the £5,000 bail, having disagreed with Wilde's heinous treatment by the press and the courts. Edward Carson, it was said, asked for the service to let up on Wilde. His request was denied. If the

Crown was seen to give up at that point, it would have appeared that there was one rule for some and not others, and outrage could have followed. The final trial was presided over by Justice Sir Alfred Wills. On 25 May 1895 Wilde was convicted of gross indecency and sentenced to two years' hard labour. The judge himself described the sentence as 'totally inadequate for a case such as this', although it was the maximum sentence allowed for the charge under the Criminal Law Amendment Act of 1885. His conviction angered some observers, one of whom demanded, in a published letter, "Why does not the Crown prosecute every boy at a public or private school or half the men in the universities?" in reference to the presumed pederastic proclivities of British upper class men.

Wilde was imprisoned first in Pentonville and then in Wandsworth prison in London, and finally transferred in November to Reading Prison, some 30 miles west of London. Wilde knew the town of Reading from happier times when boating on the Thames and also from visits to the Palmer family, including a tour of the famous Huntley & Palmers biscuit factory which was quite close to the prison. Now known as prisoner C. 3.3, (which described the fact that he was in block C, floor three, cell three) he was not, at first, even allowed paper and pen, but a later governor was more amenable. Wilde was championed by the Liberal MP and reformer Richard B. Haldane who had helped transfer him and afforded him the literary catharsis he needed. During his time in prison, Wilde wrote a 50,000 word letter to Douglas, which he was not allowed to send while still a prisoner, but which he was allowed to take with him at the end of his sentence. On his release, he gave the manuscript to Ross, who may or may not have carried out Wilde's instructions to send a copy to Douglas (who later denied having received it).

Ross published a much expurgated version of the letter (about a third of it) in 1905 (four years after Wilde's death) with the title *De Profundis*, expanding it slightly for an edition of Wilde's collected works in 1908, and then donated it to the British Museum on the understanding that it would not be made public until 1960. In 1949, Wilde's son Vyvyan Holland published it again, including parts formerly omitted, but relying on a faulty typescript bequeathed to him by Ross. Its complete and correct publication first occurred in 1962, in *The Letters of Oscar Wilde.*

Release and Death

Prison was unkind to Wilde's health and after he was released on 19 May 1897, he spent his last three years penniless, in self-imposed exile from society and artistic circles. He went under the assumed name of Sebastian Melmoth, after the famously "penetrated" Saint Sebastian and the devilish central character of Wilde's great-uncle Charles Robert Maturin's gothic novel *Melmoth the Wanderer*. Nevertheless, Wilde lost no time in returning to his previous pleasures. According to Douglas, Ross "dragged [him] back to homosexual practices" during the summer of 1897, which they spent together in Berneval. After his release, he also wrote the famous poem *The Ballad of Reading Gaol*. Wilde spent his last years in the Hôtel d'Alsace, now known as L'Hôtel, in Paris, where it is said he was notorious and uninhibited about enjoying the pleasures he had been denied in Britain.

Again, according to Douglas, "he was hand in glove with all the little boys on the Boulevard. He never attempted to conceal it." In a letter to Ross, Wilde laments, "Today I bade good-bye, with tears and one kiss, to the beautiful Greek boy... he is the nicest boy you ever introduced to me." Just a month before his death he is quoted as saying, "My wallpaper and I are fighting a duel to the death. One or other of us has got to go." His moods fluctuated; Max Beerbohm relates how, a few days before Wilde's death, their mutual friend Reginald 'Reggie' Turner had found Wilde very depressed after a nightmare. "I dreamt that I had died, and was supping with the dead!". "I am sure", Turner replied, "that you must have been the life and soul of the party." Reggie Turner was one of the very few of the old circle who remained with Wilde right to the end, and was at his bedside when he died.

Wilde died of cerebral meningitis on 30 November 1900. Different opinions are given as to the cause of the meningitis;

Richard Ellmann claimed it was syphilitic; Merlin Holland, Wilde's grandson, thought this to be a misconception, noting that Wilde's meningitis followed a surgical intervention, perhaps a mastoidectomy; Wilde's physicians, Dr. Paul Cleiss and A'Court Tucker, reported that the condition stemmed from an old suppuration of the right ear (*une ancienne suppuration de l'oreille droite d'ailleurs en traitement depuis plusieurs années*) and did not allude to syphilis. Most modern scholars and doctors agree that syphilis was unlikely to have been the cause of his death.

On his deathbed Wilde was received into the Roman Catholic church and Robert Ross, in his letter to More Adey (dated 14 December 1900), states "He was conscious that people were in the room, and raised his hand when I asked him whether he understood. He pressed our hands. I then sent in search of a priest, and after great difficulty found Father Cuthbert Dunne... who came with me at once and administered Baptism and Extreme Unction. - Oscar could not take the Eucharist". Wilde was buried in the Cimetière de Bagneux outside Paris but was later moved to Père Lachaise Cemetery in Paris. His tomb in Père Lachaise was designed by sculptor Sir Jacob Epstein, at the request of Robert Ross, who also asked for a small compartment to be made for his own ashes. Ross's ashes were transferred to the tomb in 1950. The epitaph is a verse from The Ballad of Reading Gaol:

And alien tears will fill for him
Pity's long-broken urn,
For his mourners will be outcast men,
And outcasts always mourn.

The numerous spots on the tombstone are lipstick traces from admirers. The modernist angel depicted as a relief on the tomb was originally complete with male genitals which were broken off and kept as a paperweight by a succession of cemetery keepers; their current whereabouts are unknown.

In the summer of 2000, intermedia artist Leon Johnson performed a forty minute ceremony entitled *Re-membering Wilde* in which a commissioned silver prosthesis was installed to replace the vandalised genitals.

Chapter 2

Oscar and the Scarlet Woman

Oscar Wilde once commented, I look on all the different religions as colleges in a great university. Roman Catholicism is the greatest and most romantic of them." It was undoubtedly the it romance" of Catholicism which crept continually into his life and writings that held a life-long attraction for Wilde. The sensuous beauty of richly ornate vestments, the fragrance of incense, and the various rituals of the Church all figure prominently in Wilde's poems and fiction.

He liked to speak of the "perfume of belief" and wore an oval amethyst on his third finger, vaguely resembling a bishop's ring. "We spend our days looking for the secret of life. Well, the secret of life is art,"3 he proclaimed on his American tour. Decidedly the attraction of Catholicism was artistic and, it would seem, part of the aesthetic pose.

Shortly after his release from prison, Wilde remarked to Reginald Turner, "The Catholic Church is for saints and sinners alone. For respectable people the Anglican Church will do." Again, the flippant tone suggests the *poseur* and yet, beneath all that, there lies another facet of Wilde's attraction to Catholicism: its essential isolation from the mainstream of English society. Again, the exotic, Italianate beauties of Catholicism, still a somewhat suspect minority religion in England, could not help but appeal to the socially alienated, decadent sensibility.

Another of Wilde's pronouncements on Catholicism is better understood when placed in its context. When, to the horror of the papal Chamberlain of Honour, Hartwell de la Garde Grissell, he was publicly blessed by the Pope, Wilde vented his anger at the disapproval of "the withered eunuch of the Vatican Latrines" as follows: "It is a curious, and therefore natural thing, but I cannot stand Christians because they are never Catholics, and I cannot stand Catholics because they are never Christians. Otherwise I am ht one with the Indivisible Church.

It is often difficult to know how seriously to take this conversationalist who regaled his audience with every verbal extravagance; yet, from the frequency and length of time over which references to Catholicism were made, it is certain that he was deeply moved by the "awful fascination" and "extreme beauty and sentiment" of the Roman Catholic Church.

According to his latest biographer, Oscar Wilde was received twice into the Church. The first baptism, a private affair arranged by his mother, took place when Wilde was four or five years of age; the second was the dramatic death-bed scene of 29 November 1900. In fact, Wilde disregarded the first baptism, since he spent much of his time at Oxford deliberating upon possible conversion to Rome.

As to his deathbed baptism ("Catholicism is the only religion to die in," he insisted), no one will ever know for certain if he were actually conscious when the sacrament wa- , administered and if, had he lived, he would have continued to be a devout Catholic. The fact remains, nevertheless, that Wilde was drawn to Catholicism from his early years at Oxford to his last wasted days in France and Italy.

The effect of all this in his writings is considerable. Wilde borrowed freely from Catholic ritual to portray, in picturesquely aesthetic imagery, the themes of victim, sacrifice, and individualism. An understanding of his concept of the Incarnation is necessary to appreciate fully the themes of the short stories, *De Profundis,* and *The Soul of Man Under Socialism.* While these views are scarcely orthodox, they do shed light on his personality and artistic theories.

The Roman Church also provided him with the means to express the personal and aesthetic tensions between Hellenism and Hebraism and his own artistic fusion of the two. In order to provide a balanced assessment, this examination of the role of Catholicism in the life and works of Oscar Wilde will be placed in the context of the lives and works of such other Catholic converts of the English decadence as Ernest Dowson, Lionel Johnson, Aubrey Beardsley, John Gray, and Frederick Rolfe.

Oxford in the 1870s offered the undergraduate diverse currents of thought, and Oscar Wilde fell under the spell of most of them. The embers of the Oxford Movement were still glowing: memories of Newman's apostasy were reinforced with his return to Oxford after an absence of thirty-two years to receive an honorary fellowship.

Wilde went eagerly to hear Cardinal Manning preach in July 1876 and his personal reaction was that "I feel an imposter and traitor to myself on these occasions and must do something decided." His friend, David Hunter Blair, himself a notable Catholic convert, prodded Wilde constantly in these years, but was unable to do more than to lead him to an abyss of indecision. In March 1877, Wilde could write enthusiastically to William Ward:

> *I now breakfast with Father Parkinson, go to St. Aloysius, talk sentimental religion to Dunlop and altogether am caught... in the wiles of the Scarlet Woman - I may go over in the vac. I have dreams of a visit to Newman, of the holy sacrament in a new church, and of a quiet and peace afterwards in my soul. I need not say, though, that I shift with every breath of thought and am weaker and more self deceiving than ever.*

In fact, these remarks are immediately preceded by a statement that he has become "rather keen on Masonry lately." (He had been received into the Apollo Lodge in February 1875.) One of the attractions of Masonry for Wilde was the costume with its knee breeches and black hose, which he would later take to America as part of his aesthetic attire. Could it be that Wilde wanted to enjoy the exotic richness of the priestly vestment (one thinks of the dazzling description in *The Picture of Dorian Gray*, partially quoted below) without having to make the necessary religious commitment? Ten years later, Lionel Johnson was to make a similar shift from Buddhism to Browning and to Newman for sources of inspiration. As well, both Johnson and Wilde came under the spell of Walter Pater, but in markedly different ways. Pater's book, *Studies in the History of the Renaissance,* was published in 1873 and grasped Wilde's attention almost immediately.

Burning with a "hard, gemlike flame" became his life-long concern, and much of Pater's interest in ritual and the pictorial quality of Catholicism was eagerly assimilated by his discipline. Wilde, characteristically, seems not to have concerned himself with that aspect of Pater's religiosity that held meaning for Johnson and later for Aubrey Beardsley in both life and art - *acesis.*

A test of Wilde's commitment to Catholicism came in 1877 when he went to Greece with his tutor, Rev. John Pentland Mahaffy, who was anxious to stifle Wilde's Romish leanings. The trip included a visit to Rome on the way and Wilde rhapsodized in anticipation to Reginald Harding:

> *This is an era in my life, a crisis. I wish I could look into the seeds of time and see what is coming. I shall not forget you in Rome, and will burn a candle for you at the Shrine of Our Lady.*

This was followed by a postcard dated 2 April 1877, ivhich opens with the stark exclamation, "I never went to Rome at all!" Persuaded by Mahaffy to continue on to Greece immediately, Wilde, nevertheless, made good his promise to visit Rome on the way home - a visit which included, under the management of Hunter Blair, an audience with Pope Pius IX.

On the more practical side, Wilde's principal reason for not converting to Catholicism during his Oxford years was his father's threat to cut him off financially. The episode became bitterly ironical when Sir William Wilde died leaving his family a disastrously disappointing legacy. To William Ward he wrote, "If I *could hope* that the Church would wake in me some earnestness and purity I would go over as a *luxury,* if for no better reasons. But I can hardly hope it would, and to go over to Rome would be to sacrifice and give up my two great gods 'Money and Ambition'."

There were two occasions on which Wilde did show an aggressive interest in becoming Catholic. The first was in 1878, when he applied to Rev. Sebastien Bowden for a private interview. It would seem that his motivation at this time was based on fear and shame, since he had just previously contracted syphilis.

Although Father Bowden encouraged him to join the Church, Wilde again refused, sending instead a large bouquet of lilies to Brompton Oratory. The second application followed his release from prison. The scene was poignantly remembered by Ada Leverson:

> *He talked on lightly for some time, then wrote a letter, and sent it in a cab to a Roman Catholic Retreat, asking if he might retire there for six months.... The man returned with the letter. We all looked away while Oscar read it. They replied that they could not accept him in the Retreat at his impulse of the moment. It must be thought over for at least a year. In fact they refused him.*
>
> *Then he broke down and sobbed bitterly.*

This snub, coming at a time when Wilde was vulnerable, both physically and mentally, might well account for the mood of cynicism which pervades many of his remarks about Catholicism in the final years. Whether or not he would have been accepted had he made a personal application is a matter of speculation.

Wilde's situation was similar in some ways to that of Frederick Rolfe ("Baron Corvo") a few years previously. Rolfe, who, unlike Wilde, had been received into the Church in 1886 "at 24 hours' notice," was later discharged from St. Mary's College, Oscott, where he had been previously accepted as a student for the priesthood. He was also expelled from the seminary of Scots College in Rome in 1890, a little more than six months after his arrival there. These two deeply felt blows, accounting for Rolfe's disenchantment with mankind in general and clerics in particular, correspond closely with Wilde's later moments of cynicism and flippancy.

The years of exile, 1897-1900, saw Wilde hovering between the cloister and the café more often, it seems, toward the café. Upon arrival in France, however, he did become friendly with the *curé* at the local church in Berneval and he recorded his visits to Mass and Benediction to his Catholic friends with the utmost relish. A letter to Robert Ross written injune 1897 reveals quite candidly the state of Wilde's mind and his attitude toward Catholicism at the time:

> *I visited M. le Cure today... he showed me over the church: tomorrow I sit in the choir by his special invitation. He showed me all his vestments: tomorrow he really will be charming in his red.*

The closest that Wilde came to conversion at this stage was undoubtedly around 13 June 1897, but still, for reasons he assigned to his unworthiness, the final step was never taken. As he wrote to Ross, "Have just seen a *premiére communion,* very sweet, and flowerlike with children. The curé's hopes are at their highest. *Sed non cum dignus.*"

Wilde went to Rome in Passion Week of 1900. There he was more than ever before impressed by the outward splendour of the. Easter celebrations. Particularly, he was struck by the figure of the Pope whom he thought was wonderful "as he was carried past me on his throne, not of flesh and blood, but a white soul robed in white, and an artist as well as a saint -" It would seem that Wilde's attraction to the Papacy was a form of hero-worship, the same kind of admiration that he felt toward royalty.

Having been delighted with Alfred Douglas's claim to the aristocracy, or any person who could claim aristocratic connexions (including himself, as he persistently maintained), Wilde, in being drawn toward the ancient institution of the Church, with all its pageantry and tradition, was quite naturally impressed by the successor of St. Peter and Vicar of

Christ. At this time, Wilde liked to assume the pose of a not-altogether penitent Tannhäuser making his pilgrimage to Rome. Made voguish in Aubrey Beardsley's *Under the Hill*, the Tannhiiuser figure had become a persistent image of the decadent-turned penitent. There are comical references to Wilde-as-Tannhiiuser in two letters to Robert Ross written during Easter 1900:

> *I... hope to be in Rome in about ten days.*
> *It will be delightful to be together again,*
> *and this time I really must become a Catholic,*
> *though I fear that if I went before the Holy*
> *Father with a blossoming rod it would turn at*
> *once into an umbrella or something dreadful of*
> *that kind. It is absurd to say that the age of*
> *miracles is past. It has not yet begun.*31

In the Vatican, while expressing his enthusiasm for the Easter Papal blessings, Wilde admitted that his "walking-stick. showed signs of budding; would have budded indeed, only at the door of the chapel it was taken from me by the Knave of Spades. This strange prohibition is, of course, in honour of Tannhäuser."

Of Wilde's death-bed conversion, much has been written and little needs to be said. The priest who administered the sacrament, Father Dunne, stated, "Indeed I was fully satisfied that he understood me when told that I was about to receive him into the Catholic Church and give him the Last Sacraments."

Lord Alfred Douglas, who was not present at Wilde's death, was naturally infuriated "by the R. Catholic tomfoolery" and loathed "the whole idea of his 'being received' on his death-bed à la Aubrey Beardsley. It was so utterly unlike him." (Only eleven years later, Douglas himself would be converted to Rome.) Perhaps Richard Ellman best sums up Wilde's situation: "The application of sacred oils to his hands and feet may have been a ritualized pardon for his omissions or commissions, or may have been like putting a green carnation in his buttonhole."

Oscar Wilde's study of Catholic dogma was certainly no

match for the rigorous and intellectual researches undertaken by Lionel Johnson; rather, like John Gray, his friend André Raffalovich and, to a certain extent, Ernest Dowson, Wilde's appreciation of Catholicism was aesthetic and emotional.

There are, nevertheless, certain aspects of religion, such as the Immaculate Conception and the Incarnation, about which he did have definite opinions and which had their influence upon his writings.

Wilde's interest in the Blessed Virgin can be seen in the number of sonnets addressed to her written in the 1870s. Like Lord Alfred Douglas who, when he became Catholic, had little difficulty believing in miracles, Wilde could easily accept the dogma of the Immaculate Conception. Writing to William Ward in 1876, he stated his position:

> *I never knew how near the English Church was to joining with Rome. Before the promulgation of the Immaculate Conception Pusey and Liddon and others were working hard for an Eironicon and union with Rome but now they look to the Greek Church. But I think it is a mere dream, and very strange that they should be so anxious to believe the Blessed Virgin conceived in sin.*

From the early days at Oxford, Wilde was fascinated by the figure of Christ.

Under the influence of Browning, perhaps, in such poems as "Saul" - like Lionel Johnson a decade later in his Winchester Letters - Wilde stressed the need for belief in the Incarnation. He wrote to William Ward:

> *I wonder you don't see the beauty and necessity for the incarnation of God into man to help us to grasp at the skirts of the Infinite. The atonement is I admit hard to grasp. But I think since Christ the dead word has woke up from sleep. Since him we have lived. I think the greatest proof of the Incarnation aspect of Christianity is its whole career of noble men and thoughts and not*

the mere narration of unauthenticated
histories.

The image of Christ became a source of fascination for Wilde, especially as he pictured himself as a kind of Christ-figure, enduring the hostility of society and - before 1895, at least - not suffering the supreme penalty. He is like the young man discovered by Joseph of Arimathea in one of Wilde's parables, "The Master," who says that he too has wrought miracles, has changed water into wine, healed the sick and raised the dead, yet he has not been crucified.

In the *De Profundis* letter, Christ becomes linked to the personality of the artist: Christ, he said, "realised in the entire sphere of human relations that imaginative sympathy which in the sphere of Art is the sole secret of creation." And: "Christ's place indeed is with the poets... There is still something to me almost incredible in the idea of a young Galilean peasant imagining that he could bear on his own shoulders the burden of the entire world."

In addition to Christ's being the greatest human artist, Wilde, in *De Profundis* and *The Soul of Man Under Socialism,* cast Him as the supreme Individualist. Wilde felt that Christ's interest in the individual's soul stemmed from His desire that each person should achieve his potential as a human being. One only realizes one's soul, says Wilde, "by getting rid of all alien passions, all acquired culture, and all external possessions be they good or evil."

Finally, Christ for Wilde was the quintessential Lover. "He saw that' love was that lost secret of the world for which the wise men had been looking, and that it was only through love that one could approach either the heart of the leper or the feet of God."" Christianity, Wilde felt, was a religion of love and it has managed to link love with the outward acts of religion: "Love is a sacrament that should be taken kneeling, and *Domine non sum dignus* sh'd be on the lips and in the hearts of those who receive it."

It can easily be seen that Wilde's Catholicism was both romantic and aesthetic. It lacked the firm intellectual bite of Lionel Johnson's faith; moreover, it did not appear to be a means of rising above sin through renunciation and repentance, a quality that characterized Johnson's wrestling with the Dark Angel or Aubrey Beardsley's agonies and repeated references to attending mass and confession in the *Last Letters*. For Wilde, the Catholic Church was not so much an avenue to salvation through triumph over sin as another means of incorporating sensuous beauty and romance into life and art.

Wilde's Catholic poetry was written for the most part between the year 1876 and 1879 and was collected for the first time in *Poems*, 1881. The poetry is addressed or refers primarily to Christ, the Blessed Virgin, or the Pope. More appropriate to Wilde's temperament, also, is the conscious attempt to fuse the pagan and Christian traditions in a recognition of the beauties of the former and a dutiful attraction to the latter.

In "E Tenebris," I Wilde prays in characteristically lush aesthetic diction that Christ will make good his salvation. In the closing lines, he promises the crucifix that he shall behold "The feet of brass, the robe more white than flame,/The wounded hands, the weary human face". Here, Wilde's fascination with Christ stems from His humanity and the treatment warrants comparison with John Gray's poem, "A Crucifix."

While Christ in "E Tenebris" is seen as a Saviour with both human and divine qualities, He is insolently chided for being merely a man, and a dead man at that, in the sonnet, "On the Massacre of the Christians in Bulgaria": "Come down, 0 son of Man! and show thy might,/Lest Mahomet be crowned instead of Thee!".

A typically aesthetic approach to the terrors of the Second Coming is clear in the sonnet, "On Hearing the Dies Irae Sung in the Sistine Chapel." Trying to obliterate all traces of the horror to come, suggested by the *Dies Irae*, Wilde hopes for a calmer, more beautiful coming of Christ, which has been suggested to him by the natural beauty of "sad olive groves," "the silver-breasted dove" (1. 2), "the empurpled vines", and a bird at evening flying to its nest".

The poems addressed to Mary are mainly of a

conventional nature; the familiar epithets of the Litany of the Blessed Virgin Mary and variations upon them are worked and reworked. In "San Miniato," for example, Mary is addressed as "Mother of Christ; 0 mystic wife!;; (1. 10) and "O crowned by God with love and flame;/O crowned by Christ the Holy One!" (11. 13 -14).

She is praised for an outward beauty especially in "Madonna Mia" and her features are analysed in a studied, literary manner that clearly resembles the word-paintings of the Pre-Raphaelites: "A lily-girl, not made for this world's pain,/With brown, soft hair close braided by her ears,/And longing eyes half veiled by slumberous tears... " (11. 1-3). The pictorial aspects of the poem conclude, not surprisingly, with the image of Dante and Beatrice seeing "The Seventh Crystal, and the Stair of Gold".

Wilde's early poetry also develops several aspects of the papacy. In the " Sonnet on Approaching Italy," for example, the "imprisonment of the Vatican" is bemoaned as follows: "But when I knew that far away at Rome/In evil bonds a second Peter lay,/l wept to see the land so very fair" (11. 12-14). One of the most repeated images of Wilde's poetry about the papacy is that of the Pope being carried through the streets on his chair.

More than any other aspect of the liturgy of the Vatican, this seemed to have appealed to him especially. Perhaps, like Frederick Rolfe, he saw himself as the gorgeously clad Pope, revered by the cheering multitude, and carried aloft on the sturdy shoulders of the Swiss Guard. In "Rome Unvisited," he describes this scene as follows:

When, bright with purple and with gold,
Come priest and holy Cardinal,
And bome above the heads of all
The gentle Shepherd of the Fold (II. 33-36).53

One of the most persistent themes in Wilde's early poetry is the juxtaposition, by comparison and contrast, of paganism and Christianity. This is abundantly apparent in the sonnet, "Written in Holy Week at Genoa." Wilde describes the luxuriant orchards of oranges, the "startled bird" (1. 4), and "the curved waves that streaked the sapphire bay" (1. 7). The poet is awakened from his reverie by the "young boy-priest" (1. 9), urging those passing by to strew flowers upon the grave of Christ. The "dear Hellenic hours" (1. 12) have almost overwhelmed the poet's thoughts of the slain Christ. The purely sensuous delight in Nature is much more immediate than "The Cross, the Grown, the Soldiers and the Spear" (1. 14): these, he says, are merely a memory (1. 13).

Wilde often combined pagan and Christian images in poems of a strong Hellenic bias. In "The Garden of Eros," for example, he speaks of "fox-gloves with their nodding chalices" (I. 57) and, more specifically, "Time's palsied fingers count in vain his rosary of suns" (1. 252).

In "The New Helen," Wilde uses the following invocation, partly drawn from the Litany of the Blessed Virgin, to describe Helen of Troy: "Lily of love, pure and inviolate:/ Tower of ivory: red rose of fire:/Thou hast come down our darkness to illumine" (11. 91-93).

In "Santa Decca," Wilde goes so far as to hope for a return of the ancient gods, even though "no longer do we bring/To greyeyed Pallas crowns of olive leaves" (11. 1-2). Perhaps, he muses "in this sea-tranced isle" (1. 9), there might yet be some longforgotten deity, "hidden in the asphodel" (1. 11).

Imagery of paganism and Christianity have so often been fused, from Dante and Milton to Keats and Swinburne, but here, in a manner that owes much to the latter, Wilde attempts successfully to "paganise" Christianity, to distil all the beauty out of it, leaving a residue of Hebraism in the Arnoldian sense forever buried. Unlike the Swinburne of *Dolores* or the Beardsley of *Under the Hill,* Wilde does not set out to pervert Christianity; rather, his treatment is primarily aesthetic: he truly wants to find the Beauty of Catholicism.

In A *House of Pomegranates,* Wilde incorporates aspects of Catholic ritual into several stories with exotic effects. The young fisherman who gave up his soul for the love of a mermaid in "The Fisherman and His Soul," is cursed by the priest: "The love of the body is vile... and vile and evil are the pagan things God suffers to wander through His world." Yet, after the fisherman and the mermaid have died, the priest who has continually railed against earthly love undergoes a strange experience as he offers benediction: "And when the third year was over... the Priest went up to the chapel, that he might show to the people the wounds of the Lord, and speak to them about the wrath of God." He discovers strange flowers on the altar and is troubled by their presence: "And he speaks not of the wrath of God, but of the God whose name is Love. And why he so spake, he knew not." Love and beauty have triumphed. The priest, leading a procession of monks and musicians, candle bearers and swingers of censers, goes to the sea and blesses "all the wild things that are in it." Wilde converts the conscience-ridden priest to an appreciation of a sensuousmystical love and the discovery of beauty.

The Christ-figure is also prominent in these stories. In "The Young King," the hero is converted, after surrendering himself to the workship of beauty, to a life of love for his fellow men and a desire to live like the poor. The peasantry, misunderstanding his motivation, wishes the king to be as they feel a king should be wealthy and powerful. "Surely we will slay him," they declare, "for he is unworthy to.rule over us."

At this point, the young King undergoes a transfiguration in which he becomes divine, Christ-like and still human: "And lo! through the painted windows came the sunlight streaming upon him, and the sunbeams wove round him a tissued robe that was fairer than the robe that had been fashioned for his pleasure. The dead staff blossomed, and bare lilies that were whiter than pearls.... He stood there in a king's raiment, and the Glory of God filled the place, and the saints in their carven niches seemed to move."

The function of the trappings of Catholicism in this story is to link the Christ-like man with Christ himself. It was a step further that Wilde took in *The Soul of Man Under Socialism* to suggest that Christ was the quintessential artist.

Wilde's jewelled and decadent prose describes the sensuous attraction to Catholicism in *The Picture of Dorian Gray*. After a lengthy and detailed account of Dorian's collection of vestments, an imitation of Des Esseintes in Huysmans' *A*

Rebours, the following, rather cryptic, statement'is made: "In the mystic offices to which such things were put, there was something that quickened his imaginatign." *In The Picture of Dorian Gray*, the Catholic Church acts only as a means of stimulating beauty and exotic sensations in true Paterian fashion.

Written first in French and translated into English by Lord Alfred Douglas, Wilde's *Saloné*, like *The Picture of Dorian Gray*, was also inspired by Huysmans. Des Esseintes' ruminations on the two works by Gustave Moreau - one a picture of Salomé, the other a water-colour called "The Apparition" depicting the scene after the murder of John the Bapti' t - are reflected in Wilde's stylized speeches.

The continually recurring image of the moon, at first clouded, then naked and seeking covering, becomes symbolic of the guilty soul once the pose has been abandoned and the mask torn away. In the confrontation of pagan and Christian, we have no attempt at reconciliation as in the sonnet, "Written in Holy Week at Genoa," but rather, a struggle ending in the destruction of both. The religious distortion of *Salomé* is-mingled with sexual perversion after the manner of the French decadence; Barbey D'Aurevilly's *Diaboliques* come to mind.

Catholicism in Wilde's life and writings may best be described as "aesthetic" in the 1870s and 1880s and "decadent" in the 1890s. The sensuous appreciation of beauty evoked in the early poems gives way to the self-conscious and stylized art of *The Picture of Dorian Gray* and *Salomé*.

The tensions of body and soul, Hebraism and Hellenism, renunciation and indulgence, however, were never quite reconciled and it is characteristic of Oscar Wilde that, while he was wallowing in debauchery in the years following his release from prison, he could produce his most moral, most Christian and, indeed, his best poem, *The Ballad of Reading Gaol*.

Chapter 3

Paterian Self-Development versus Gothic Degeneration

"Culture and corruption," murmured Dorian, "I have known something of both."

-Oscar Wilde, The Picture of Dorian Gray

I hold that no work of art can be tried otherwise than by laws deduced from itself: whether or not it be consistent with itself is the question.

-Thomas Wainewright, quoted by Wilde in "Pen, Pencil, and Poison"

Recent genre theory reminds us of just how often our disagreements about the meaning or interpretation of a text are actually debates about how the text should be read, or, more precisely, what kind of text it should be read as. If we are persuaded that a text is indeed an urban eclogue, a Bildungsroman, a Horatian ode, a parody of pastoral, or an example of postmodern female Gothic, we are more likely also to be persuaded of the critic's interpretation of that text's meaning.

Thus a critic who interprets Who's Afraid of Virginia Woolf? as a modern secular morality play is not so much claiming to have found the meaning of the text as he or she is trying to persuade us to read the text as a particular kind of play. What a text means is inseparable from how it is read, and since we must always read a text as something, genre often asserts itself as a set of instructions, implicit or explicit, on how to read a text. The debate over the genre, and thereby the meaning, of Oscar Wilde's novel The Picture of Dorian Gray exemplifies this protocol of reading. Dorian Gray has always provoked contradictory interpretations, but underlying the disagreements about the work's meaning there has persisted a more fundamental debate about what kind of novel it should be read as. This debate is discernible in the early reviews, though somewhat obscured by the hysteria over the novel's alleged immorality.

Reading the novel as an English imitation of a decadent French text, for example, the reviewer for the Daily Chronicle denounced it as "a tale spawned from the leprous literature of the French Decadents, a poisonous book, the atmosphere of which is heavy with mephitic odours of moral and spiritual putrefaction".

The St. James Gazette repeated this attack: "The writer airs his cheap research among the garbage of the French Decadentslike any drivelling pedant" (NCE 333). But while the popular secular press was denouncing Wilde's novel for its "spiritual putrefaction," Christian publications, such as the Christian Leader, the Christian World, and Light, which interpreted it as an ethical parable or moral fable, praised it as "a work of high moral import" (qtd. in Pearce 169).

In America, Julian Hawthorne (son of Nathaniel Hawthorne) was undecided whether Dorian Gray was "a novel or romance (it partakes of both)." But he finally settled on "parable" and pronounced the novel "a salutary departure from the ordinary English novel" (NCE 348-349). Clearly, the judgment of early reviewers depended, at least to some extent, on the genre in which they placed the novel.

Modern critics are as divided about the novel's meaning as the original reviewers were obsessed with its morality. But what has not changed is the role the perceived genre of the novel plays in interpretation. While some critics read the novel as belonging to a single genre and assume that the conventions of that genre provide the key to unlock the text's meaning, others see it as a kind of heteroglossia combining two or more genres. In "The Picture of Dorian Gray: Wilde's Parable of the Fall," for example, Joyce Carol Oates finds the novel to be "a curious hybrid. Certainly it possesses a 'supernatural' dimension, and its central image is Gothic; yet in other respects it is Restoration comedy". For her, the novel's generic anomalies make its message at once transparently clear and enigmatically opaque:

While in one sense The Picture of Dorian Gray is as transparent as a medieval allegory, and its structure as workman-like as Marlowe's Dr. Faustus, to which it bears an obvious family resemblance, in another sense it remains a puzzle: knotted, convoluted, brilliantly enigmatic. (Oates 422-23)

But, as her title indicates, Oates ultimately sees the primary, governing genre as parable. Even those critics who find multiple genres in Dorian Gray tend to privilege one. The two most favoured candidates for the novel's controlling genre have remained fable and parable. Joseph Pearce has recently joined this chorus: "The plot of the novel," he says, "unfurls like a parable, illuminating the grave spiritual dangers involved in a life of immoral action and experiment", language that echoes that of the Christian reviewers in 1890. In a dissenting voice, Shelton Waldrep argues for Dorian Gray as a realist novel: "Wilde had to work within the confines of some specific variation on the theme of realism".

Kerry Powell has uncovered Wilde's indebtedness to a popular, late-Victorian sub-genre that he designates as "'magic' picture fiction". In "Fiction and Allegory," Edouard Roditi classifies Dorian Gray as an "Erziehungsroman of dandyism" (NCE 371) in the tradition of Robert Plumer Ward's Tremaine (1825), Disraeli's Vivian Gray (1826), and Bulwer Lytton's Pelham (1828). Confronted with the novel's generic diversity, Rachel Bowlby concludes that "Donan Gray does not in fact fall straightforwardly into any generic category" and finds it to be an amalgam of "innumerable different forms and styles... alternating and overlapping in no particular order and with no... appearance of either a conventional linear narrative in the mode of realism, or a consistent symbolic line in the mode of allegory". As if parodically anticipating later critics, Wilde, in a letter to the editor of the Daily Chronicle, called Dorian Gray "an essay on decorative art" (qtd. in

Ellmann 321). Mindful of Jerusha McCormack's warning that "it is hard to say anything original about The Picture of Dorian Gray, largely because there is so little that is original in it", I have no desire to referee this debate or to offer my own candidate for the true genre of Dorian Gray. Nevertheless, I hope to shed some new light on the conflicting readings of the novel's generic affiliations, as well as on its meaning and artistic success, by arguing that The Picture of Dorian Gray is neither governed by a single unifying genre nor dispersed intertextually (and unoriginally) among multiple heterogeneous ones, but rather is disjunctively situated between two conflicting genres, each of which is related to one of the two antithetical literary and cultural discourses that the novel engages but cannot successfully integrate: namely, self-development (including what we would today call "sexual liberation") and Gothic degeneration.

The degeneration theme links the novel generically to such other fin-de-siecle Gothic stories as Robert Louis Stevenson's Strange Case of Dr. Jekyll and Mr. Hyde (1886) and Arthur Machen's The Great God Pan (1894), while the self-development theme relates it to the novel of self-development, of which Walter Pater's Manus the Epicurian (1885) and the unfinished Gaston de Latour (1888) are perhaps the most obvious generic models, given Pater's acknowledged influence on Wilde.

The novel's indebtedness to Pater's Marius the Epicurian and to the Gothic tradition is well established. In her introduction to the Oxford English Novels edition of Dorian Gray (1974), Isobel Murray argues that Wilde is "combining two fairly well known traditions, the 'Gothick' one of, for example, Maturin's Melmoth the Wanderer and Poe's 'The Oval Portrait', and the 'decadent' one of Gautier's Mademoiselle de Maupin, Huysmans' A Rebours and Pater's Marius the Epicurian". I agree that the intertexts Murray identifies are present in Dorian Gray, but, in my view, the Gothic texts most relevant to Wilde's novel are not the earlier ones of Maturin (to whom Wilde was distantly related) and Poe, but the contemporary fin-de-siecle Gothic tales of

Stevenson, Machen, Wells, and Stoker, among which David Punter places it in his study The Literature of Terror (1980). "One thing can be said at the outset which underlies the meaning of decadence in connexion with these texts," says Punter about the Gothic revival, "and that is that they are all concerned in one way or another with the problem of degeneration".

Decadence and degeneration in Dorian Gray are thus related primarily to fin-de-siecle Gothic rather than to the Paterian novel of self-development. As I hope to show, however, the Gothic plot of Dorian Gray is ultimately inconsistent with the Paterian plot of self-development, for the twin themes of self-development and degeneration are antithetical, if not contradictory, suggesting as they do positive and negative movements, respectively.

These double genres-the literary and the popular-create generic dissonances as the Gothic plot of degeneration takes over and eventually supersedes the incompatible Paterian plot of self-development and individual liberation. The "Gothic" Wilde thus finds himself committed to the implications of a narrative of degeneration that undercuts the Paterian ideal of self-development posited by Lord Henry in the early chapters.

In particular, the goal of (homo)sexual liberation promised by the self-development plot is subverted by the necessity, within the conventions of the fin-de-siecle Gothic tale of degeneration, of seeing Dorian's emerging homosexuality, along with his other crimes and sins, as further evidence of his degeneration. Jeremy Reed, in his introduction to a recent edition of Dorian Gray, places the novel in a tradition of subversive fiction: "One could justifiably argue for Oscar Wilde's The Picture of Dorian Gray comprising a blueprint for the subversive genre of fiction which in the 20th century has counted amongst its numbers the works of Jean Genet, William Burroughs, and J. G. Ballard". But much as I would like to see Wilde as fathering such a tradition-and there can be little doubt that Dorian Gray is a subversive work-I believe that the potentially subversive homosexual plot of the novel is itself seriously, even fatally, subverted by the association between homosexuality and degeneration required by the Gothic plot. The early chapters of Dorian Gray are dominated by the Paterian self-development plot, so much so that Isobel Murray classifies the novel as the story of "the growth, education and development of an exceptional youth, who through personalities, a book, a picture, is moulded or moulds himself, discovering himself what he believes in" (viii).

The first half of the novel is certainly indebted to the Bildungsroman. Wilde's preoccupation with the idea of self-development is clearly evident from the works he published as he wrote and then revised Dorian Gray. Four months before the novel appeared in Lippincott's Monthly Magazine, Wilde reviewed a translation of the writings of the Chinese philosopher Chuang Tsu. In "A Chinese Sage" (published in The Speaker, February 8, 1890), Wilde wrote,

It may be true that the ideal of self-culture and self-development, which is the aim of his scheme of life, and the basis of his scheme of philosophy, is an ideal somewhat needed by an age like ours, in which most people are so anxious to educate their neighbours that they have actually no time left in which to educate themselves. (Soul of Man 294-95)

But it is in "The Soul of Man Under Socialism," his most important and ambitious essay on culture and politics, that Wilde most fully explores the issue of self-development, or what he calls "Individualism." In that essay, which appeared in The Fortnightly Review in February 1891 while he was revising Dorian Gray, Wilde explores the political conditions of self-development.

As Jonathan Dollimore points out, individualism for Wilde "is both desire for a radical personal freedom and a desire for society itself to be radically different, the first being inseparable from the second". Sounding like a socialist Lord Henry, Wilde expresses his regret "that society should be constructed on such a basis that man has been forced into a groove in which he cannot freely develop what is wonderful, and fascinating, and delightful in him-in which, in fact, he misses the true pleasure and joy of living" (Soul of Man 255).

In keeping with Wilde's project of self-development, the

opening chapters of Dorian Gray focus on the innocent Dorian's awakening, under the twin influences of Basil's homoerotic painting and Lord Henry's subversive philosophy, into "the true pleasure and joy of living":

He [Dorian] was dimly conscious that entirely fresh impulses were at work within him, and they seemed to him to have come really from himself. The few words that Basil's friend had said to him-words spoken by chance, no doubt, and with willful paradox in them-had yet touched some secret chord, that had never been touched before, but that he felt was now vibrating and throbbing to curious pulses. (DG 90:186)

Moreover, as words such as "vibrating," "throbbing," "secret chord," "curious pulses" (the last phrase changed to influences in DG 91) all suggest that, as recent critics have argued, a central element of that development is Dorian's discovery of his own homosexuality. "By projecting the revelation, growth, and demise of Dorian's 'personality' onto an aesthetic consideration of artistic creation," says Ed Cohen, "Wilde demonstrates how the psychosexual development of an individual gives rise to the 'double consciousness' of a marginalized group" (166-67). It was precisely the explicitness of the homosexual theme, we must not forget, that outraged many early reviewers.

Just how explicitly homoerotic the 1890 version is became readily evident in 1988, when the Norton Critical Edition printed both the 1890 Lippincott Aversion and the revised (expanded and expurgated) 1891 edition. It is clear, for example, that the reason Hallward does not want to exhibit Dorian's painting is that it discloses Hallward's obvious homosexual attraction to Dorian (just as Wilde's novel revealed the sexual inclination of its author). Basil's final declaration of his true feelings for Dorian is unmistakably homoerotic:

"It is quite true that I have worshipped you with far more romance of feeling than a man usually gives to a friend. Somehow, I had never loved a woman.... Well, from the moment I met you, your personality had the most extraordinary influence over me. I quite admit that I adored you madly, extravagantly, absurdly. I was jealous of every one to whom you spoke. I wanted to have you all to myself. I was only happy when I was with you. When I was away from you, you were still present in my art. It was all wrong and foolish. It is all wrong and foolish still. Of course I never let you know anything about this. It would have been impossible. You would not have understood it; I did not understand it myself." (DG 90: 232-33)

In contrast to Hallward's repression of his sexual attraction to Dorian (sublimated through art), Lord Henry's philosophy of unfettered self-development can be read as an implicit recommendation to homosexuals to realise their true being, despite the misguided restraints of society and religion. "The aim of life is self-development," he tells Dorian:

"To realise one's nature perfectly,-that is what each of us is here for. People are afraid of themselves nowadays. They have forgotten the highest of all duties, the duty that one owes to one's self.... The terror of society, which is the basis of morals, the terror of God, which is the secret of religion-these are the two things that govern us." (DG 90: 185)

Furthermore, Lord Henry explicitly links the quest for self-development, "the duty that one owes to one's self," to an attack on restrictive laws; and, in the homosexual context of the scene, it would be hard not to see his words-especially "monstrous laws"-as alluding to the Labouchere Amendment to The Criminal Law Amendment Act (1885), which criminalized private consensual sexual acts between adult males:

"I believe that if one man were to live his life out fully and completely, were to give form to every feeling, expression to every thought, reality to every dream,-I believe that the world would gain such a fresh impulse of joy that we would forget all the maladies of mediasvalism, and return to the Hellenic ideal,-to something finer, richer, than the Hellenic ideal, it may be. But the bravest man among us is afraid of himself. The mutilation of the savage has its tragic survival in the self-denial that mars our lives.

We are punished for our refusals. Every impulse that we strive to strangle broods in the mind, and poisons us.... The only way to get rid of a temptation is to yield to it. Resist it, and your soul grows sick with longing for the things it has forbidden to itself, with desire for what its monstrous laws have made monstrous and unlawful." (DG 90: 185-6)

It is hard to imagine that a sophisticated homosexual man reading Lord Henry's subversive words in 1890 would not see their immediate and obvious relevance to his own life, regardless of what other meanings could legitimately be attributed to them. Society's "monstrous laws" have made male-to-male sex "monstrous and unlawful," and the "self-denial that mars our lives" includes the denial of those sexual impulses that are not monstrous in themselves, but made monstrous only by monstrous laws.

Moreover, Lord Henry's opposition between mediævalism and "the Hellenic ideal" echoes the terms in which contemporary apologies for homosexuality were argued. Even more importantly, Lord Henry articulates here an early theory of the evils of repression. For it is the repression of same-sex sexuality, and not the sexual acts themselves, that poisons and mutilates the mind and the soul.

Consequently, liberation from that repression is seen as necessary for the full development of the individual personality. John Addington Symonds expressed a similar view in A Problem in Modern Ethics, his apologia for homosexuality published in 1891: "It is this forcible suppression of an instinct so deeply rooted in our nature," he argued, "which first originates the morbid symptoms, that may often be observed in Urnings [sexual inverts]".

Lord Henry's liberationist project, when applied to Dorian's sexual development, however, encounters a major obstacle: in Victorian society, especially after the Labouchere Amendment, it could be carried out only in secrecy. As Symonds points out,

[T]he comrades [in a homosexual relationship] are continually forced to hide their liaison; their anxiety on this point is incessant; anything like an excessive intimacy, which could arouse suspicion (especially when they are not of the same age, or do not belong to the same class in society), has to be concealed from the external world. In this way, the very commencement of the relation sets a whole chain of exciting incidents in motion; and the dread lest the secret should be betrayed or divined, prevents the unfortunate lover[s] from ever arriving at a simple happiness. (Problem 72)

Now the self-development novel does not generically require that its protagonist lead a double life: Pater's heroes-Marius and Gaston-do not. But the homosexual theme of Wilde's novel does require that Dorian live a double life. The theme of the double had, of course, long been associated with the Gothic novel, and just four years before Dorian Gray was published there appeared the classic novel of the double life, Robert Louis Stevenson's Strange Case of Dr. Jekyll and Mr. Hyde (1886). Early reviewers of Dorian Gray noted the obvious parallels with Jekyll and Hyde, and later critics have pointed to Stevenson's Gothic "shilling shocker" as a likely source. Stevenson's sensational tale of the double self would certainly have resonated particularly strongly with Wilde and other members of the homosexual subculture that was emerging in London at the end of the nineteenth century.

Lord Alfred Douglas's infatuation with the novel-he read it, on different estimates, nine or fourteen times before he met Wilde-certainly attests to its immediate appeal to homosexuals (D. Murray 32). By the 1880s, as such scholars as Jeffrey Weeks, Richard Dellamora, and Elaine Showalter have documented, the Victorian homosexual world had evolved into a secret but active subculture, with its own language, styles, practices, and meeting places.

For most middle-class inhabitants of this world, homosexuality represented a double life, in which a respectable daytime world often involving marriage and family, existed alongside a night world of homoeroticism. (Showalter 10)

Dr. Jekyll's account of his youth, in particular, is described in a way that must have struck a responsive chord in contemporary homosexual readers struggling against what conventional morality-and more recently the law-regarded as "irregularities" and "degradation," and who were forced, as a result of their dual nature, to "conceal" their "pleasures":

And indeed the worst of my faults was a certain impatient gaiety of disposition, such as... I found it hard to reconcile with my imperious desire to carry my head high, and wear a more than commonly grave countenance before the public. Hence it came about that I concealed my pleasures; and that when I reached years of reflection... I stood already committed to a profound duplicity of life.

He goes on to refer to "such irregularities as [he] was guilty of," adding that he regarded and hid them with an

almost morbid sense of shame.... I was driven to reflect deeply and inveterately on that hard law of life, which lies at the root of religion and is one of the most plentiful springs of distress. Though so profound a double-dealer, I was in no sense a hypocrite; both sides of me were in dead earnest; I was no more myself when I laid aside the restraint and plunged in shame, than when I laboured, in the eye of day, at the furtherance of knowledge or the relief of sorrow and suffering. (Stevenson 75-76)

Jekyll's language here-"concealed my pleasures," "profound duplicity of life," "so profound a double-dealer," "laid aside the restraint and plunged in shame"-would certainly not be out of place in Dorian Gray, and a "profound duplicity of life" combined with a "morbid sense of shame" perfectly describes the lives of many gay men at the time. Later in his "statement of the case," Jekyll describes the feeling of liberation that accompanies his transformation:

Men have before hired bravos to transact their crimes, while their own person and reputation sat under shelter. I was the first that ever did so for his pleasures. I was the first that could plod in the public eye with a load of genial respectability, and in a moment, like a schoolboy, strip off these lendings, and spring headlong into the sea of liberty. (80-81)

What Jekyll has accomplished through science is what many contemporary homosexual men desired: the ability to safely lead a double life. They, too, longed to "plod in the public eye with a load of genial respectability" and then be able to "strip off" their conventional respectability and "spring headlong into the sea of liberty." Indeed, that is precisely what Wilde and Lord Alfred Douglas did-with ever increasing recklessness.

As Elaine Showalter has pointed out, the homosexual nature of Hyde's pleasures is even more strongly hinted at in the manuscript of the novel:

In his original draft of the manuscript, Stevenson was more explicit about the sexual practices that had driven Jekyll to a double life. Jekyll has become "from an early age... the slave of certain appetites," vices which are "at once criminal in the sight of the law and abhorrent in themselves. They cut me off from the sympathy of those whom I otherwise respected."

Whatever Stevenson's own sexuality, Showalter is surely right when she says "Stevenson was the fin-de-siecle laureate of the double life". The description of Jekyll's appetites as "criminal in the sight of the law" is especially revealing when we realise that the novel was published in the same month as The Criminal Law Amendment Act went into effect. Many homosexual readers of the novel in early 1886 must have linked it to the public debate on criminalizing private male-to-male sexual acts and to their own double lives.

Even if a modern "gay" sexual identity was still embryonic, it is hard to believe that members of this subculture could have read Jekyll and Hydewithout seeing the relevance of Jekyll's double life to their own lives. So when Wilde came to write Dorian Gray-the story of a man who "felt keenly the terrible pleasure of a double life" (DG 91: 135)-he would have found in Jekyll and Hyde a recent model for using Gothic fiction to explore the double lives of closeted homosexuals in late-Victorian England.

In addition to the obvious Gothic theme of the double, Wilde adapts-and modifies-several other conventions of earlier Gothic fiction. In Art of Darkness: A Poetics of Gothic, Anne Williams identifies several conventions "familiar in gothic narratives from Walpole to the present: a vulnerable and curious heroine; a wealthy, arbitrary, and enigmatic hero/ villain; and a grand, mysterious dwelling concealing the violent, implicitly sexual secrets of this homme fatal". Wilde transforms the innocent heroine into the (initially) innocent Dorian; the wealthy and enigmatic hero/villain into the wealthy, aesthetic, and epigrammatic Lord Henry (who, Satan-like, tempts Dorian in Basil's garden); and the mysterious dwelling concealing violent, implicitly sexual secrets into Dorian's townhouse with the locked attic that hides his not so implicitly sexual secret.

(The word secret occurs 37 times in the novel.) Wilde also appropriates a convention common to Frankenstein, Jekyll and Hyde, and The Great God Pan: the scientific experiment with unexpectedly horrific consequences. In Jekyll and Hyde an experiment transforms Jekyll's personality. Wilde's novel is also the story of an experiment: Dorian's development is explicitly characterized as the result of an experiment that Lord Henry, the Gothic scientist in the role of decadent aesthete, performs on the young Dorian.

Lord Henry had always been enthralled by the methods of science, but the ordinary subject-matter of science had seemed to him trivial and of no import. And so he had begun by vivisecting himself, as he had ended by vivisecting others. Human life,-that appeared to him the one thing worth investigating.

And so Dorian becomes the subject of his unusual experiment:

To a large extent the lad was his [Wotton's] own creation. He had made him premature. That was something....Yes, the lad was premature. He was gathering harvest while it was yet spring. The pulse and passion of youth were in him, but he was becoming self-conscious. It was delightful to watch him. (DG 90: 204)

The last line in particular suggests the empirical pose of the disinterested scientist. A few lines later, the narrator adds, "It was clear to him [Lord Henry] that the experimental method was the only method by which one could arrive at any scientific analysis of the passions; and certainly Dorian Gray was a subject made to hand, and seemed to promise rich and fruitful results" (DG 90: 205; italics added). Later Lord

Henry says that "[Dorian] would be a wonderful study" (DG 90: 207).

Lord Henry's effort "to project [his] soul into" Dorian's "gracious form" is described (in the 1891 edition) through a metaphor of chemical infusion: "to convey one's temperament into another as though it were a subtle fluid" (DG 91: 33)-just like the draught that changes Jekyll into Hyde. In Jekyll and Hyde, of course, the experimenter and the subject of the experiment are the same person; Wilde separates them into two characters.

He also changes the mode of the transformation from science to art, and the location from the laboratory to the artist's studio. Art replaces science, hence the dominant role that works of art and books play in Wilde's novel, especially the "poisonous" book that acts like Jekyll's mysterious chemical agent.

Even more important than either these borrowings or the theme of the double is yet another convention of Gothic fiction that Wilde would have found particularly suitable to his project in Dorian Gray: the perennial Gothic theme of transgression. Since Lord Henry's theory of liberation from repression leading to self-realization requires transgression of existing social, moral, religious, and especially legal codes, Wilde needed a plot that could combine self-development with transgression, the later being a necessary precondition of the former.

Since its beginnings in Walpole, Gothic fiction has always been a transgressive genre; as Kelly Hurley reminds us, "Gothic provided a space wherein to explore phenomena at the borders of human identity and culture-insanity, criminality, barbarity, sexual perversion". This transgressiveness coincides with Wilde's own anti-authoritarian ideas expressed in his essays at this time. "Disobedience, in the eyes of anyone who has read history," he says in "The Soul of Man Under Socialism," "is man's original virtue. It is through disobedience that progress has been made, through disobedience and through rebellion" (Soul of Man 231).

In "The Critic as Artist," the first part of which appeared in The Nineteenth Century in the same month that Dorian Gray appeared in Lippincott's, Gilbert, Wilde's spokesman, says, What is termed Sin is an essential element of progress. Without it the world would stagnate, or grow old, or become colourless. By its curiosity Sin increases the experience of the race. Through its intensified assertion of individualism it saves us from monotony of type.

In its rejection of the current notions about morality, it is one with the higher ethics.... Self-denial is simply a method by which man arrests his progress, and self-sacrifice a survival of the mutilation of the savage, part of that old worship of pain which is so terrible a factor in the history of the world.

The first half of this passage could easily be Lord Henry's project for Dorian's self-realization, and the last lines actually echo Lord Henry's own words: "The mutilation of the savage has its tragic survival in the self-denial that mars our lives" (DG 90: 186). In Wilde's view, says Richard Ellmann, "Sin is more useful to society than martyrdom, since it is self-expressive not self-repressive.

The goal is the liberation of the personality". "One can fancy an intense personality being created out of sin," Wilde wrote in "Pen, Pencil, and Poison" (Soul of Man 103). Since "Wilde's notion of individualism," as Jonathan Dollimore explains, "is inseparable from transgressive desire and a transgressive aesthetic", and since the Gothic portrays sin as self-expressive, not self-repressive, it is hardly surprising that Wilde would have found the Gothic aesthetically appealing.

The problem is that fin-de-siecle Gothic texts like Jekyll and Hyde and The Great God Pan include not just the traditional Gothic theme of transgression but also the fin-de-siecle theme of degeneration, and the discourse of degeneration on which these texts draw is, quite simply, incompatible with the Paterian goal of self-development.

"Degenerationism," says Kelly Hurley in The Gothic Body: Sexuality, Materialism, and Degeneration at the Fin de Siecle, "is a 'gothic' discourse, and as such is a crucial imaginative and narrative source for the fin-de-siecle Gothic".

When viewed from the perspective of such fin-de-siecle Gothic texts as Jekyll and Hyde and Arthur Machen's The Great God Pan, the corruption mirrored in Dorian's picture is not so much "a visible symbol of the degradation of sin" (DG 90: 220) as it is a sign of his degeneration.

The Great God Pan was published as a novella in 1894 by John Lane, who also published Wilde's Salome, but an extract from it had appeared in December 1890 in a short-lived magazine called Whirlwind. In Machen's Gothic tale of degeneration, a doctor performs an experiment designed to open a young girl's "inner eye" to the continuing presence of the Great God Pan.

Although the girl dies, the exp^riment succeeds and she gives birth to a child, Helen, the result of her mother's coupling with the primordial Pan. Helen, who then becomes the focus of the story, reveals to a series of admiring men the horror that lies beneath the surface of their conventional lives, driving them to madness and death. When Helen dies, she degenerates, passing through all the stages of evolution as she reverts to the primordial slime.

"The paradox of The Great God Pan," says Punter, "is that the visitation which liberates the human being from the repression of false assumptions also destroys the barriers which retain human individuation: the liberation of desire returns man to his primal associations with the beast and destroys the soul".

A similar paradox of sexual liberation leading to destruction and degeneration takes place in Dorian Gray. Like Dorian, Helen-that both have Greek names cannot be accidental-seduces her male victims and then reveals to them something so horrible that they go mad and commit suicide. (Helen Vaughan's victims commit suicide when they learn her unspeakable secret; Dr. Lanyon dies of shock when he learns Dr. Jekyll's secret; and Alan Campbell commits suicide after he disposes of Basil Hallward's body by decomposing it in acid.) Dorian exercises a fatal sexual power over young men, especially young aristocrats. In his final, fatal confrontation with Dorian, Hallward asks,

"Why is your friendship so fateful to young men? There was that wretched boy in the Guards who committed suicide. You were his great friend. There was Sir Henry Ashton, who had to leave England, with a tarnished name. You and he were inseparable.

What about Adrian Singleton, and his dreadful end? What about Lord Kent's only son, and his career?... What about the young Duke of Perth? What sort of life has he got now? What gentleman would associate with him? Dorian, Dorian, your reputation is infamous.... They say that you corrupt everyone whom you become intimate with." (DG 90: 257-58)

Although Helen's power is unspecified in the text, it is, like Dorian's, obviously sexual. "I knew I had looked into the eyes of a lost soul," says a witness to Helen's power; "the man's outward form remained, but all hell was within it. Furious lust, and hate that was like fire, and the loss of all hope and horror that seemed to shriek aloud in the night, though his teeth were shut; and the utter blackness of despair" (Machen 97). Dorian's "outward form" (his youthful beauty) also remains, but his "lost soul," mirrored in the picture, shrieks its black despair to Hallward, who recoils in horror:

An exclamation of horror broke from Hallward's lips as he saw in the dim light the hideous thing on the canvas leering at him. There was something in its expression that filled him with disgust and loathing. Good heavens! It was Dorian Gray's own face that he was looking at! The horror, whatever it was, had not yet entirely marred that marvellous beauty. (DG 90: 261)

The paradox of beauty and repulsiveness in Dorian is also present in Helen Vaughan: "Every one who saw her at the police court said she was at once the most beautiful woman and the most repulsive they had ever set eyes on. I have spoken to a man who saw her, and I assure you he positively shuddered as he tried to describe the woman, but he couldn't tell why" (Machen 64; italics added).

The Gothic plot in Dorian Gray, then, is the typical plot of fin-de-siecle Gothic-degeneration from a higher to a lower state, from the well-formed, respectable, upper-class Dr. Jekyll to the bestial, murderous, lower-class Hyde. As Stephen Arata has observed, "Jekyll and Hyde articulates in Gothic fiction's exaggerated tones late-Victorian anxieties concerning degeneration, devolution, and 'criminal man'".

When Dr. Jekyll metamorphoses into Mr. Hyde, he degenerates to a lower, more primitive form of existence, a degeneration signaled in the novel by the repeated comparisons of him to an ape. Dorian similarly degenerates to a lower, bestial level of existence. He hides the portrait in the attic, where "the face painted on the canvas could grow bestial, sodden, and unclean" (DG 90: 238; italics added). Dorian's descent into the Victorian underworld of criminality, drugs, and sexual depravity is portrayed in language similar to that describing Hyde's parallel excursions into the same nether regions:

He [Dorian] remembered wandering through dimly-lit streets with gaunt black-shadowed archways and evil-looking houses. Women with hoarse voices and harsh laughter had called after him. Drunkards had reeled by cursing, and chattering to themselves like monstrous apes. He had seen grotesque children huddled upon doorsteps, and had heard shrieks and oaths from gloomy courts. (DG 90: 215; italics added)

The lower classes are described as ape-like, and by his increasing association with them, Dorian becomes bestial and ape-like, too. (Not insignificantly, the word monstrous occurs over twenty times in the novel.) As Joseph Bristow has perceptively remarked, Dorian's personality, like that of Jekyll/Hyde, is divided between upper and lower classes as much as between good and evil: "Dorian wears a fine aristocratic face but possesses what may be referred to as a working-class (debased, gross, indecent) body, as he moves across and between different echelons of society". (Wilde's own sexual encounters, it is worth recalling, were primarily with lower-class youths.)

In addition to its affinities with the degenerationist themes of contemporary Gothic fiction, Dorian Gray also shows unmistakable traces of contemporary non-fictional degenerationist writings, especially Richard von Krafft-Ebing's theory of the etiology of sexual perversion, specifically homosexuality.

Krafft-Ebing's Psychopathia Sexualis, with Especial Reference to Contrary Sexual Instinct: A Clinical Forensic Study, first published in German in 1886 and translated into English in 1892, offered an exhaustive catalogue-238 cases by the twelfth edition-of sexual variations. It established the new discipline of Sexualwissenschaft and created the paradigm, namely the case study, for sexological research for the rest of the century. As Sam Binkley points out, Krafft-Ebing's theory of sexual deviancy was part of the larger cultural discourse of degeneration:

Krafft-Ebing's thesis on degeneracy attributed the nebulous causes of [cultural] decline to the sexual behavior and condition of a morbid type, an invert, whose moral character was depleted by the same corrosive social forces and technological changes that had eroded and shaken the moral authority of the West.

Krafft-Ebing believed that most homosexuals-a term he popularized-had a mental disease caused by hereditary degeneration, although environmental factors could influence this inborn neuropathic disposition, or "taint" as he repeatedly called it:

Since, in nearly all such cases, the individual tainted with antipathic sexual instinct displays a neuropathic predisposition in several directions, and the neuropathic predisposition may be related to hereditary degenerate conditions, this anomaly of psychosexual feeling may be clinically called a functional sign of degeneration. This inverted sexuality appears spontaneously, without external cause, with the development of sexual life as an individual manifestation of an abnormal form of sexual life, and has the force of a congenital phenomenon; or it develops upon a sexuality which in the beginning was normal, as a result of definite injurious influences, and thus appears as an acquired anomaly. Upon what conditions this enigmatic phenomenon of acquired homosexual instinct depends still remains unexplained, and is a mere hypothetical matter. Careful examination of the so-called acquired cases make it probable that predisposition-also present here-consists of a latent homosexuality, or, at least, bisexuality, which, for it to become manifest, requires the influence of accidental stimulating causes to rouse it from its dormant state. (Krafft-Ebing 239).

This model of a hereditary degenerative predisposition combined with "injurious influences" is certainly consistent with Wilde's representation of Dorian and his degeneration, which appears to be the result both of malign influence (Lord Henry's theories, the "poisonous book") and of "tainted" heredity. Read in the context of Krafft-Ebing's theories of a congenital neuropatic predisposition to degeneracy, Dorian's speculation that "his very flesh was tainted with the monstrous maladies of the dead" (DG 90: 253; italics added) is not only a fin-de-siecle version of what Richard Davenport-Hines calls "[G]othic's obsession with family secrets and hereditary doom" but also evidence of the extent to which degenerationist discourse has penetrated Wilde's text.

Significantly, the words "taint" and "tainted" are Krafft-Ebing's favourite ones for attributing hereditary causes to all types of sexual deviancy: "heavily tainted by heredity"; "hereditary taint"; "mother deeply tainted"; "heavily tainted by heredity"; "tainted by heredity"; "from a tainted family"; "probably from a tainted family"; "from a badly tainted family"; "hereditarily tainted".

In The Pathology of Mind (1895), Henry Maudsley claimed that "beneath every face are the latent faces of ancestors, beneath every character their characters". When viewed from these perspectives, Dorian's speculations about his ancestors' influences on him are further evidence of degenerationist discourse in the novel:

He loved to... look at the various portraits of those whose blood flowed in his veins. Here was Philip Herbert, described by Francis Osborne, in his "Memoires of the Reigns of Queen Elizabeth and King James," as one who was "caressed by the court for his handsome face, which kept him not long company." Was it young Herbert's life that he sometimes led?

Had some strange poisonous germ crept from body to body till it had reached his own? (DG 90: 253; italics added)

(Osborne's original text, revealingly, reads "caressed by KING JAMES for his handsome face" [I. Murray 246], clearly an allusion to James's homosexuality.) Of his ancestor Sir Anthony Sherard, Dorian wonders, "What had this man's legacy been? Had the lover of Giovanna of Naples bequeathed him some inheritance of sin and shame?

Were his [Dorian's] own actions merely the dreams that the dead man had not dared to realise?" (DG90: 253). And what of Lady Elizabeth Devereux? "He knew her life, and the strange stories that were told about her lovers. Had he something of her temperament in him?" (DG 90: 253). In particular, the use of poisonous here, paralleling Dorian's later application of it to the book Lord Henry gives him, implies that his degeneration is both intrinsic and acquired.

But it was not just degenerationists who attributed sexual deviation to hereditary "taint" or predisposition. Even John Addington Symonds, who in A Problem in Modern Ethics explicitly challenged Krafft-Ebing's theories, held that some forms of sexual inversion are inheritable:

That sexual inversion may be and actually is transmitted, like any other quality, appears to be proved by the history of well-known families both in England and in Germany. That it is not unfrequently exhibited by persons who have a bad ancestral record, may be taken for demonstrated.

Clearly, this degenerationist discourse has seeped into Dorian Gray. The problem with representing Dorian's career through the language of contemporary degenerationist discourse is that doing so undermines the liberationist programme articulated by Lord Henry early in the novel. Lord Henry sees degeneration as the consequence of repressing our desires: "The pulse of joy that beats in us at twenty," he tells Dorian, "becomes sluggish.

Our limbs fail, our senses rot. We degenerate into hideous puppets, haunted by the memory of the passions of which we were too much afraid, and the exquisite temptations we did not dare to yield to" (DG90:189; italics added). For Lord Henry, the price of not rebelling against repression is degeneration, and so he recommends the Paterian ideal of self-realization. As his other writings show, Wilde certainly believed in this ideal. But he also believed that transgression and disobedience are necessary to achieve it.

Wilde's theory of self-development (individualism) requires the transgressiveness of crime: "Like Jean Genet after him," says Richard Ellmann, "[Wilde] proposed an analogy between the criminal and the artist.... Rebelliousness and extravagance are needed if society's moulds are to be broken, as broken they must be.

Art is by nature dissident". "It is well for our vanity that we slay the criminal," Wilde writes in "The Critic as Artist," "for if we suffered him to live he might show us what we had gained by his crime" (Soul of Man 126). But the plot in which Wilde finds it necessary to embody that rebellion, a plot common to the novels of the recent Gothic revival, is one that could represent Hyde-like degeneration as the only alternative to a Jekyll-like life of conformity and repression.

And so all forms of transgression, including homosexuality, become, within the conventions of that plot, signs of degeneration. "In the loosening of moral, aesthetic and sexual codes associated with fin de siecle decadence," writes Fred Botting, "the spectre of homosexuality as narcissistic, sensually indulgent and unnaturally perverse, constituted a form of deviance that signalled the irruption of regressive patterns of behaviour".

Transgression, what Wilde calls sin and disobedience, is first posited as necessary for self-development to take place, but is then, in compliance with the Gothic plot, shown to lead inevitably to degeneration.

And while the Paterian plot of Dorian Gray condemns the laws that criminalize transgressive sexual acts, the Gothic degenerationist plot requires that homosexual acts be a sin and a crime from which nothing can be gained. Thus Dorian Gray, like most fin-desiecle Gothic fictions, is pessimistic that crime can lead to gain.

According to Punter, the "underlying pessimism" of Jekyll

and Hyde "resulls from Stevenson's difficulty in seeing any alternative structure for the psyche: once the beast is loose, it can resolve itself only in death". Similarly, in Dorian Gray Wilde cannot imagine any alternative to repression other than degeneration-and finally death. "Gothic," pronounces Richard Davenport-Hines, "is nothing if not hostile to progressive hopes". The Gothic plot in Dorian Gray is ultimately hostile to the progressive hopes held out by the Paterian plot of self-actualization.

"Any attempt to extend the subject matter of art," wrote Wilde in "The Soul of Man Under Socialism," "is extremely distasteful to the public, and yet the vitality and progress of art depend in large measure on the continual extension of subject matter" (Soul of Man 249). The Picture of Dorian Gray is, a provocative and important work, and in it Wilde indisputably extended the subject matter of the English novel.

After June 20, 1890, the date the July issue of Lippincotl's Monthly Magazine appeared, "Victorian literature had a different look" (Ellmann 314). But Dorian Gray is also a flawed work, riven by generic dissonances. The incompatibility of the novel's double genre undermines Wilde's attempt to tell a subsversive story of dissidence and transgression leading to self-development and liberation.

Chapter 4

The Rhetoric of Agency

DeProfundis occupies a precarious place in Oscar Wilde's canon and for several reasons is often skirted by wary interpreters: it does not fit neatly into any single genre; it does not resemble any of the other works that made Wilde famous; it is full of irritating inconsistencies and contradictions; and it seems ambiguously aimed at a wider audience than its inscription to Alfred Douglas suggests. After all, there are the enduring plays, the fascinating novel, the engaging dialogues; why struggle with a reader-resistant text framed as a personal letter?

Its handling in the recent Cambridge Companion to Oscar Wilde (1997) illustrates this critical uneasiness. De Profundis is almost completely ignored in this collection of essays. In her chapter, for example, Regenia Gagnier (a sympathetic interpreter of De Profundis in an earlier study) devotes one sentence to it, calling it "perhaps his greatest work of art"-but does not elaborate. Nowhere in this volume is there a sustained effort to assess the place of De Profundis in Wilde's canon or to set it within the context of his life.

Many readers disparage or dismiss De Profundis. It has been condemned as a "venomous dossier" and "obsessive piece of writing" (Julian 352), and it has been dismissed as the complaint of a very unhappy prisoner who "thereafter lost interest in" the work (Croft-Cooke 231). Even good-faith interpretive efforts run aground: Avrom Fleishman speaks of being "unpreparedeven after several readings, in my own case-to believe my eyes" at its shifts of tone and attitude (285-86). There are some sympathetic interpretations, however. One is biographer Richard Ellmann's judgment that De Profundis is "one of the greatest love letters ever written," but that it suffers from a "disjointed structure". Another is Gagnier's own earlier interpretation of the work as a response to the degradation of prison life; shifting between "realism and romance," "Wilde kept a positive past and created a possible future" as "romance" (Idylls 192).

"He reconstructed the world," says Gagnier, "in order to show that he is above it" (Idylls 190). Both interpretations are insightful. Certainly De Profundis is a record of Wilde's deeply divided feelings for Douglas. And it is also at times a romance through which Wilde imagines a future for them both, in which he recovers aesthetic and moral superiority over Douglas.

But there are significant aspects of De Profundis that are not considered in the interpretations by Ellmann or Gagnier. Neither asks why its structure appears disjointed or what might account for its subversive energies-its disconcerting shifts in tone, its abrupt swings in self-positioning, or its figurative intensity. Though Wilde creates a vision of his post-prison future, this vision entails at least as much irony as romance, because much of the time Wilde seems to be writing against himself, constructing self-representations that seem to hide as much as they reveal.

Throughout much of the text Wilde seems up to something but unwilling to declare what that might be. I want to look again at the elements of De Profundis that make it unreadable for some and to propose that it has a significant place in Wilde's work. From my perspective, the disjunctions arise from irresolvable tensions lurking in Wilde's rhetorical goals as he sought both to hide and to reveal his own agency within the events of his life.

These tensions are not idiosyncratic but are inherent in the sociocultural space Wilde occupied as an active homosexual. He took it as obligatory that he must displace and disguise his motives and actions even as he explained them.

The tonal inconsistencies of De Profundis thus need to be read as manifestations of the tectonic pressures embedded in his life-pressures until 1895 kept more or less under control. In DeProfundis Wilde was trying to demonstrate not so much that he was above the world, but that he had been-and still could be-an agent in a world that required duplicity and disguise for survival.

When he went to jail in 1895, Wilde resisted his ruin; he did not accept that his work as a writer was finished, though the public thought so. What he viewed as the first step in his project of self-rehabilitation was the letter to Douglas that became De Profundis. In a letter to his friend Robert Ross he declared its purpose: "I want you, and others who still stand by me and have affection for me, to know exactly in what mood and manner I hope to face the world" after prison (Letters 512).

He was defending not only his conduct with Douglas but also his stature as an artist, since The Picture ofDorian Gray and other writings had been used as corroborating evidence of moral impropriety in the trials. Thus in DeProfundis Wilde hoped to rebuild his earlier stature as an artist and to articulate the terms on which he might be judged by posterity.

De Profundis is thus the best evidence we have of Wilde's efforts to rescue himself for history; it is made more poignant by contrast with the self-destructive conduct of his final years. Because DeProfundis is so deeply embedded in his life and work, it must be read in the context of the earlier work and his life in the crisis years.

In De Profundis Wilde writes to Alfred Douglas, " [y] ou knew what my art was to me, the great primal note by which I revealed, first myself to myself, then myself to the world".' It is this basic purpose that Wilde describes for Ross:

"[y]ou must be in possession of the only document that really gives any explanation of my extraordinary behavior with regard to Queensberry and Alfred Douglas.... Some day the truth will have to be known: not necessarily in my lifetime or in Douglas's: but I am not prepared to sit in the grotesque pillory they put me into, for all time. I don't defend my conduct. I explain it. (Letters 512)

Though De Profundis is addressed to Douglas, Wilde wanted it read by any reader interested in "the truth" as he would tell it. For these readers he wanted to show his "mental development in prison, and the inevitable evolution of character and intellectual attitude towards life that has taken place" (Letters 512). Because he knew Wilde wanted it to be read, Ross eventually overcame his reluctance, gave the text a title, and published a sanitized version of it after Wilde's death (Letters 423).

De Profundis reproduces that fundamental conflict between power and victimization underlying the social identity Wilde had come to inhabit as an active homosexual. In the text he casts himself alternately as a tragic protagonist undone by hubris and a victim overwhelmed by repressive social forces.

It is the tension between these roles that destabilizes the tone of DeProfundis and creates abrupt shifts of mood. Wilde uses a variety of rhetorical strategies to disguise the erotic implications of his relationship with Douglas and to displace what was culturally inscribed as a moral issue into the realm of aesthetic fulfillment. Some of these strategies draw upon his earlier revisions of Dorian Gray for book publication in 1891.

His wariness of the impact of covertly homoerotic language upon readers at that time had been reawakened during the trials, in the course of acerbic exchanges with the prosecutor over the "immorality" of his writings. De Profundis reveals Wilde's calculated efforts to disguise and deflect homoerotic elements of his relationship with Douglas.

The perspective of subjectivity theory offers a useful starting point for discussing Wilde's intentions in DeProfundis. In defining individuality within this perspective, Paul Smith points out that "a person is not simply determined and dominated by the pressures of any overarching discourse or ideology" but "is the agent of a certain discernment" capable of "reading [these discourses] in order to insert himself/herself into them-or not" (emphasis Smith; xxxiv-xxxv). This "discernment" is "agency," the power of the individual to identify, confront, and resist dominant cultural forces. For Wilde language itself is the primary arena within which agency is asserted. Talk is more important than action, says Gilbert in The Critic as Artist, because words determine thoughts and actions: "language... is the parent, and not the child, of thought... Men are the slaves of words" (7576).

Wilde's resistance to dominant mores of his time was articulated, made public, and critiqued in his textual identities. His agency thus declares itself in his texts, which become the sites of his resistance to the proscriptions against what the Criminal Law Amendment Act of 1885 called "acts of gross indecency with another male person."

As recent interpreters have demonstrated, Wilde encodes homoerotic desire as an aesthetic construct throughout his plays and prose writings: "sexual subject matter was at the core of his aesthetics," says Patricia Flanagan Behrendt, who labels the transgressive identity Wilde constructs in his writings a "homosexual Eros."

In dialogues like The Decay of Lying (1891) Wilde developed wordplay that implied erotic interest. In the plays that established his artistic pre-eminence in the first half of the 1890's, continues Behrendt, "homosexual Eros rather than heterosexual pandering informs the meaning of all four plays". Behrendt identifies the theatrical figure of the posturing dandy as the dramatic vehicle by means of which in his plays Wilde critiques "a society that repudiated homosexuality in its laws yet refused to acknowledge the reality of its many manifestations" in the arts.

It is in Wilde's earlier prose writings that explanatory grounding is begun for the erotic aesthetic later inscribed in DeProfundis. In The Soul of Man Under Socialism (1891) Wilde rejects the idea that art is dependent upon the psychic consistency of an essential self. Instead, he says, art is anti-essentialist because it requires the freedom to reinvent one's identity against the grain: "art is Individualism and Individualism is a disturbing and disintegrating force, for what it seeks to disturb is monotony of type, slavery of custom, tyranny of habit" (Soul ofMan 249). True individuality resists the "immoral ideal of uniformity of type and conformity to rule"; only within the framework of a self-expressive freedom-to-be will "man develop Individualism out of himself". Precisely because no one "type" or character represents a real or essential self, all identities must be masks. Thus the artist must use masks: he "is least himself when he talks in his own person.

Give him a mask, and he will tell you the truth," says Gilbert in The Critic as Artist. Masks, then, provide essential space within which "Individualism" can be asserted against cultural pressures; posing is an essential act of self-definition. But posing requires interpretation in response: the beholder must attempt to read the pose-and Wilde often used this interpretive space for evasion and disguise.

Indeed, since the beginning of his public career Wilde had cultivated a reputation as a poser: "the first duty in life is to assume a pose; what the second duty is no one yet has found out" (Ellmann 311). The strategies of disguise and displacement embedded in De Profundis had been years in preparation and use.

The controversy over Dorian Gray exacerbated what by 1890 had already become a rich intertext of posing: the early stories, newspaper and magazine articles and photos, Punch caricatures, and word of mouth, all contributed to the complex public persona. The homoerotic overtones of Wilde's posing blended both assertion and evasion, deflecting direct attacks from those who were suspicious of what lay beneath the pose. It was the cumulative impact of Wilde's "homoerotic signifying," suggests Moe Meyer that drove Alfred Douglas's father Lord Queensberry to call Wilde a "posing Sodo [m] ite in the insult that triggered the trials of 1895:

> Wilde's experiments to produce an embodied homoeroticism had yielded... signifying practices that included dress, speech, gesture, and even a mode of text production. This was his contribution to the State's establishment of the homosexual social identity [during his trials]. (qtd. in Meyers 97)

The accumulated force of Wilde's provocative texts and public utterances, as well as his behavior with Alfred, finally goaded Queensberry into action with the energetic outrage he assumed was shared by all decent Englishmen. His attorneys planned to use The Picture of Dorian Gray, says Meyer, as "primary evidence for the defence [against Wilde's libel charge]". In particular, The Picture of Dorian Gray remained a source of scandalized discussion even as his reputation as a playwright grew.

In Dorian Gray Wilde fully articulates the theme of aestheticized sensuality that later informs his self-representation in De Profundis. The parallels between Dorian Gray's characters and Wilde's own life in the early 1890s are emphasized by biographer Richard Ellmann, who interprets Dorian Gray as a covert dramatization of Wilde's homosexuality.

"Wilde put into the book a negative version of what he had been brooding about for fourteen years and, under a veil, what he had been doing sexually for four," says Ellmann, creating "one of the first attempts to bring homosexuality into the English novel". Indeed, during the period of Dorian Gray's composition the pressure of Wilde's sexual activity surged against the boundaries of his life: "in the early 1890's Oscar's cult of Youth became increasingly populous," says Gary Schmidgall.

Caricatures in such publications as Punch increased as Wilde's reputation grew more bipolar: while his popularity as a playwright intensified, whispers and hints of his domestic and private behavior also gained currency. In the years of increasing success following the publication of Dorian Gray in 1890, Wilde was obliged to maneuver between his role as an active but covert homosexual and his other roles as apostle of aestheticism, popular playwright, husband, and father.

Wilde knew that he could not publicly confront his own notoriety without cost to himself, indeed, notoriety enhanced his commercial appeal as a playwright and writer in the 1890's. Thus the homoerotic implications embedded the novel's main relationships-carefully downplayed in its revision from magazine to book form-recapitulate the generalized transgressiveness already associated with Wilde the public figure. Early in Dorian Gray Wilde encodes erotic pleasure as spiritual fulfillment in Lord Henry Wotton's doctrine of self-enrichment:

I believe that if one man were to live out his life fully and completely, were to give form to every feeling, expression to every thought, reality to every dream-I believe the world would gain such a fresh impulse of joy that we would... return to the Hellenic ideal.... We are punished for our refusals. Every impulse that we strive to strangle broods in the mind, and poisons us. The body sins once, and has done with its sin, for action is a mode of purification.

Wilde thus defines erotic agency as its own redemption: once enacted, desire purifies itself. It is this formulation of unlicensed desire played out in the scenes of Dorian Gray that hastened the darkening of Wilde's reputation in the early 1890's. Many came to perceive the texts of life and novel inseparable: the flamboyant dresser and public posturer looked like and drew life from the characters in his novel.

Wilde's earlier efforts to disguise the homoerotic implications of his language as he revised Dorian Gray point toward his later use of the same strategies in DeProfundis. In revising Dorian Gray Wilde altered the depiction of Basil Hallward's fascination with Dorian to muffle the erotic implications of their relationship.

Donald Lawler points out that even though "the theme of Platonic, homosexual romance... still haunts the final version of the novel," this theme "had been so radically suppressed by Wilde even in the first edition that he may well have wondered why his novel was called immoral". Wilde's ongoing efforts to tone down the implication that Basil is sexually fascinated by Dorian are evident in the changes Wilde made between the Lippincott's Magazine version and the book version.

Early in the Lippincott's version, for example, Basil asserts that "I couldn't be happy if I didn't see him every day. Of course it is sometimes only for a few minutes. But a few minutes with somebody one worships mean a great deal". The revised version replaces the notion of "worship" with the more pragmatic ground of aesthetic necessity: "I couldn't be happy if I didn't see him every day. He is absolutely necessary to me.... He is all my art to me now".

In addition, wary of the implications of the term "romance" for one man's feelings about another, Wilde repeatedly deletes the words "romance" and "passion" from Basil's descriptions of his own feelings and from Lord Henry's characterizations of him. Wilde's strategy was to replace the motif of romance with that of the less erotically charged motif of aesthetic idealism.

Early in the Lippincott's version Lord Henry asks Basil why he will not exhibit his painting of Dorian: "Because," says Basil, "I have put into it all the extraordinary romance of which, of course, I have never dared to speak to him". In the book version of the passage Basil says "Because, without intending it, I have put into it some expression of all this curious artistic idolatry, of which, of course, I have never cared to speak to him".

Changing "dare" to "care," Wilde transforms a lover's anxious hesitancy into an artist's self-reserve, changing Basil's motives into the deliberate agency of aesthetic judgment. This same strategy-downplaying the homoeroticism embedded in domination and sexual fascination-appears again in De Profundis as Wilde seeks to frame his corrupting relationship with Alfred Douglas in ways that disguise his own agency in their lives together.

Also relevant to DeProfundis is a significant thematic element developed early in both The Critic as Artist and Dorian Gray: the concept of "insincerity." Sincerity itself, says Gilbert wickedly in The Critic as Artist, limits individualism and the freedom-to-be: "a little sincerity is a dangerous thing, and a great deal of it absolutely fatal."

Instead, the true critic/artist "will realise himself in many forms, and by a thousand different ways, and will ever be curious of new sensations and fresh points ofview". The doctrine of insincerity is most fully elaborated in Dorian Gray. Dorian's covert exploration of alternate identities forbidden by "the canons of good society" foregrounds "insincerity" as a shaping principle:

Is insincerity such a terrible thing? I think not. It is merely a method by which we can multiply our personalities.

Such, at any rate, was Dorian Gray's opinion. He used to wonder at the shallow psychology of those who conceive the Ego in man as a thing simple, permanent, reliable, and of one essence.

Thus the power of free agency appears to Dorian in the novel as a continuous series of choices that can be enjoyed only through active pursuit: "To [Dorian], man was a being with myriad lives and myriad sensations, a complex multiform creature that bore within itself strange legacies of thought and passion".

Wilde intends this doctrine as a subversion of publicly inscribed morality, argues Jonathan Dollimore: "deviant desire reacts against, disrupts and displaces from within," creating a transgressive aesthetic of "insincerity, inauthenticity and unnaturalness". Sincerity limits full selfhood; insincerity is the process by which the self pursues its freedom-to-be. Lord Henry's drawled aphorism encapsulates the mandate of self-fulfillment: "We are punished for our refusals.... The only way to get rid of a temptation is to yield to it".

While Lord Henry outlines his desires in lengthy monologues, Dorian pursues active sensual fulfillment. Lord Henry describes his longing to dominate Dorian in phrases similar to those used by Wilde later in letters to Douglas.4 For example, Lord Henry imagines his power to gain a "grace," the "white purity of boyhood, and beauty such as old Greek marbles kept for us" (33-34), by mastering Dorian. Yes, concludes Lord Henry, "[h]e would seek to dominate him-had already, indeed, half done so.

He would make that wonderful spirit his own. There was something fascinating in this son of love and death". Lord Henry's words signal the exciting risk of such desire: "you, Mr. Gray, you yourself, with your rose-red youth... have passions that have made you afraid, thoughts that have filled you with terror.... to which Dorian cries "[s]top!... stop! you bewilder me". The desires implicit in Lord Henry's words shape themselves in Dorian's thoughts and then in his actions:

Then, suddenly, some night he would creep out of the house, go down to dreadful places near Blue Gate Fields, and stay there, day after day, until he was driven away. On his return he would sit in front of the picture, sometimes loathing it and himself, but filled, at other times, with that pride of individualism which is half the fascination of sin.

So Dorian actualizes Lord Henry's metaphors in the pursuit of sensual satiety. He prowls "the foulest dens of London" even as Hallward tells him that "the most dreadful things are being said against you". But self-denial would, of course, limit the freedom to transgress, and Dorian is unwilling to set limits on his drive for satiety.

He makes a final effort to free himself from the persistent demands of "conscience," but he only succeeds in canceling the magic transformation that had freed him to pursue his appetites. Through his actions Dorian destroys himself. In De Profundis, self-destruction emerges again as a fundamental theme: "the appalling results of my friendship with you," writes Wilde, were "destructive to my work as an artist". As he began his letter to Douglas, seven years after publishing Dorian Gray and after a year in prison, he realized he had to return to the themes of pursuit, domination, and self-degradation.

While in prison, Wilde was allowed limited writing materials. Before he could begin the task of reconstructing his life on his own terms, he had to win more writing privileges by gaining the sympathy of prison officials. He realized that in order to strike the correct attitude of penitence he had to characterize his deeds within the framework of the authoritative medical discourse of the day.

Thus he wrote a self-abasing letter to the Home Secretary confessing that he had committed "monstrous sexual perversion" and was still capable of "loathesome modes of erotomania," but also saying that he feared "the terror of madness" if he were not given more freedom (Letters 403). Of course, once his petition had gained him more writing materials, he wished it to be clear, as he had written to Ross, that official contrition was only a "grotesque pillory," not the "mood and manner" in which he hoped "to face the world." For that task "the truth" was needed. At the same time, writing "the truth" about behavior officially judged criminal in a manuscript that would have to be handed over to prison officials for safekeeping required strategy rather than confessional directness.

Thus Wilde decided to frame his self-reconstruction as a letter to Douglas in which he could create his own version of his motives and behavior. Within this rhetorical context he sought to maneuver between his need to position himself as the dominant agent of his own successes and the need to portray himself as a victim of Douglas's shallowness and inconstancy.

The first part of De Profundis offers a selective narrative marked by disconcerting shifts of position and tone and driven by the dual purposes of assertion and disguise. Accusatory passages describe Douglas's shallowness and willfulness: "[yl our interests were merely in your meals and moods. Your desires were simply for amusements, for ordinary or less ordinary pleasures. They were what your temperament needed". These accusations are often followed by self-recriminations: "I blame myself" for "having allowed you to bring me to utter and discreditable financial ruin", and "for the entire ethical degradation I allowed you to bring on me".

Wilde's pained indictments of Douglas's flaws in DeProfundis replay the motif of destructive domination found in Dorian Gray—but with a deeply altered tone. In the novel Wilde portrays Basil Hallward obsessed with Dorian's beauty. But in DeProfundis Wilde revises the novel's celebratory rhetoric of sensual beauty; he has no intention of eliciting parallels between himself and Basil, or between his own motives and Basil's covert homoerotic desires. Unlike Basil Hallward and Dorian, Wilde in DeProfundis does not try to capture what fascinated him about Douglas; instead, he catalogs his own weaknesses that led him to the young Oxford student.

Thus DeProfundis opens with a wounded, recriminating lament depicting Wilde's attachment to Douglas as the fatal yielding of the superior to the lesser being who "couldn't know, couldn't understand, couldn't appreciate", but whose "life of reckless profusion" was indulged by a fond lover's tolerance.

Of himself Wilde says, "I blame myself for allowing an unintellectual friendship... to entirely dominate my life. From the very first there was too wide a gap between us.... [Y] ou could not understand the conditions necessary for the production of artistic work". Wilde often phrases his actions as passive submission: "My will-power completely failed me.... Blindly I staggered as an ox into the shambles".

But just as he did in revising The Picture of Dorian Gray, Wilde also calibrates his language to disguise and displace the homoerotic agency implicit in the story De Profundis tells. While in many passages he denies his own will-power, in other places he takes pains to claim a covert agency for himself.

Even in what he describes as his most submissive moments, Wilde implies volition: I "admit the folly of throwing away all this money on you, and letting you squander my fortune. Wilde "allows" Douglas to behave badly, "throws away" money on him, "lets" him waste his income. Even his most abject yieldings are represented as acts of commission:

I had always thought... that when a great moment arrived I could reassert my will-power in its natural superiority. It was not so.... My habit... of giving up to you in everything had become insensibly a real part of my nature.... it had stereotyped my temperament to one permanent and fatal mood.

Wilde asserts a superior "will-power" that is given up as a "habit"-that is, unreflective behavior that dulls the awareness of consequences. Even as he subtly affirms his own responsibility for enabling and furthering relations with Douglas, he also displaces the reader's attention away from his own complicity towards the insatiable shallowness of Douglas's demands:

You must see now that your incapacity of being alone: your nature so exigent in its persistent claim on the time of others: your lack of any power of sustained intellectual concentration... were as destructive to your own progress in culture as they were to my work as an artist? Commenting on this continuous cycle of accusation and self assertion, James Winchell suggests that Wilde was evidently "strangely puzzled by the continuing riddle" of blame and responsibility in his own narrative. But the polarity of Wilde's rhetorical strategy here is intentional. Portraying himself as a fond companion to a foolish and willful boy, he can displace fault onto Douglas even as he retains the stature of a temporarily yielded superiority.

Such a strategy allows him to construct the impression of self-analytic honesty uncompromising enough to validate the accompanying, damning judgments of Douglas. He portrays himself as an indulgent collaboratora fond lover who just could not say no. By this means he hopes to sustain the implication of his own agency within the framework of a systematic plan to discredit Douglas.

It is not hard to see why Wilde adopts a strategy of displacement. His own letters suggest that he was not only an enabler, but often in fact the dominator in the relationship with Douglas. He reveled in the life he led with Douglas between 1893 and 1895, often encouraging and approving Douglas's impulses: "Dearest Boy," he wrote during rehearsals of A Woman of No Importance in 1893, "We have only just finished Act 2!! Don't wait. Order, of course, what you want. Lunch 1.30 tomorrow: at Albemarle.... Ever Yours Oscar" (Letters 337).

The reason he refused to break with Douglas even as the trial loomed was not passive submission to Douglas but Wilde's own eager pleasure in their activities. Moreover (as Ellmann recounts it and as the trial testimony repeatedly establishes), Wilde enjoyed dominating the boys who circled around the two of them in their Savoy Hotel rooms in London, and he actively planned and funded travels to Europe and North Africa with Douglas for new sexual encounters. When friends remonstrated with him about his increasing absence from his family in the period 1893-1895, Wilde would not listen. Indeed, he would retail to others his own sarcastic versions of such remonstrances when they were offered by wellmeaning friends. In his strategy of displacement, Wilde glosses his own appetites as Douglas's callow whims. He describes an episode "in September `93" when, Douglas having left Wilde to go to France for a few days, Wilde went over to bring him back: "I then, of course, had to go over to Calais to fetch you back. For one of my nature and position it was a position at once grotesque and tragic". Of course, nobody forced Wilde to embark for Calais; he wanted Douglas back, the turbulence and risk of their relationship suiting him more than continuing absence from Douglas.

Again, in early 1895, even as rehearsals of The Importance of Being Earnest were beginning, Wilde and Douglas traveled to Algiers for three weeks for new sexual adventures. In a letter to his friend Ada Leverson Wilde wrote, "I fly to Algiers with Bosie tomorrow. I begged him to let me stay to rehearse, but so beautiful is his nature that he declined at once" (Letters 381). The graceful absurdity of Wilde's irony in these lines-a sort of wink between friends- seems a tacit admission of his own complicity in events.

Indeed, given Douglas's irresponsibility and alienation from parental support, Wilde undoubtedly planned and probably paid for most of this trip. Wilde was evidently willing to risk even the success of his newest play in order to devote energy and money to continuing activity with Douglas.

Perhaps the clearest example of Wilde's efforts to encode his own willful risk-taking as misplaced loyalty to Douglas can be found in his narrative of events just prior to the first trial of April, 1895. Wilde details his time spent with Douglas:

At a time when I should have been in London taking wise counsel... you insisted on my taking you to Monte Carlo, of all revolting places on God's earth, that all day, and all night as well, you might gamble as long as the Casino was open. As for me... I was left alone outside to myself.

Going to Monaco was the worst thing he could have done. Foregged on by Douglas-he had decided to sue Queensberry for libel, the trial was about to begin, and his attorneys were anxious for his help in building his case against Queensberry (Ellmann 439). Wilde's senseless decision required profound volition. In part no doubt he wanted to escape the pressure of the looming unpleasantness and found it convenient to flee London once more with Douglas, returning just in time to consult his own counsel before the trial began (Ellmann 442). Devious as it is, the narrative framing of this episode may be read as a sensible rhetorical strategy, given Wilde's goal of disguising his own agency while invoking sympathy for his misery.

But Wilde, sensing that it ran counter to his larger rehabilitative purpose to deny responsibility or invoke pathos consistently, moves gradually towards a more self-affirming perspective. With the skill born of his mastery of classical forms, he introduces the motif of tragedy by invoking the notion of divine punishment to explain a period in 1894 when Wilde and Douglas were separated and then reunited: "[t] he gods are strange. It is not of our vices only they make instruments to scourge us.

They bring us to ruin through what in us is good, gentle, humane, loving". His overindulgence of Douglas's whims is transmuted into hamartia: "[b]ut for my pity and affection for you and yours, I would not now be weeping in this terrible place". He describes the crisis events of 1895 in terms of peripeteia: "I found it to be a revolting and repellent tragedy, and that the sinister occasion of the great catastrophe... was yourself, stripped of that mask of joy and pleasure by which [I] had been deceived and led astray".

He becomes a protagonist taking on a tragic burden: "I cannot allow you to go through life bearing in your heart the burden of having ruined a man like me.... I must take the burden from you and put it on my own shoulders".

Wilde reads his fall as a tragedy in which a great nature is pulled down by "smaller natures and meaner minds." In so doing, he recognizes that to cast himself as a tragic protagonist he must acknowledge some transgression on his part:

Tired of being on the heights I deliberately went to the depths in the search for new sensations. What the paradox was to me in the sphere of thought, perversity became to me in the sphere of passion. Desire, at the end, was a malady, or a madness, or both. Wilde describes his "passion," which passes finally into "madness," emphasizing both the intensity of his desires and the difficulty in making sense of them. The ambiguities of"paradox" and "perversity" create an interpretive latitude within which Wilde can both affirm and explain his actions: he goes "to the depths" by the force of will, whose very intensity must be evaluated not morally, but in the context of disease or madness.

Some readers have found this strategy self-defeating. In his study of the signifiers at play in interpreting Wilde's life, Schmidgall mocks Wilde's persistent applications of the tragic motif to himself: "Oscar... fancied himself wearing the mask of the tragic pessimist in the ancient Greek fashion: the hero doomed by his own hubris" and foreshadowed by an "amazing minutiae of ironic coincidences and strange anticipations that the ever-witty Fates arranged".

Of course, given the self-aggrandizing intentions of Wilde's rhetoric, such befittling may seem fair enough. But insofar as it interprets the tragic motif in DeProfundis simply as one more convenient pretense for the master of disguise, it misses the constitutive force of such a textual mask. The motif of tragedy allows Wilde to portray his downfall as the inevitable fate of individual desire within an oppressive world.

In the context of a tragic perspective, Wilde begins to portray himself as a sorrowing aesthete spiritualized by suffering. He had achieved "almost everything," he says, until he brought about his own fall: "I made art a philosophy, and philosophy an art.... I treated Art as the supreme reality, and life as a mere mode of fiction: I awoke the imagination of my century". He even recognizes the necessity of embracing his own suffering:

[I must] absorb into my nature all that has been done to me, to make it part of me, to accept it without complaint... The plank-bed, the loathsome food, the hard ropes shredded into oakum till one's fingertips grow dull with pain... the dreadful dress that makes sorrow grotesque to look at-each and all of these things I have to transform into a spiritual experience.

But organized religion "does not help me" in this

transformation, continues Wilde, because it is abstract and alienating: instead "I give to what one can touch, and look at". Wilde's world is transformed by the "supreme emotion" of "sorrow": "I now see that sorrow, being the supreme emotion of which man is capable, is at once the type and test of all great Art".

Wilde reconstructs Christ as the supreme aesthete, the quintessence of the artistic consummation Wilde has already claimed for himself. This strategy opens the field for Wilde to aestheticize his own suffering and simultaneously link it with Christ's. "The artistic life is simple self-development," says Wilde, not in the passive, spectating sense represented by Pater's Marius the Epicurean, but in an active union of being and action whose truest type is "Christ himself". Wilde's Christ attains apotheosis through his imaginative reach. He connected with the world's suffering, says Wilde, by "imagining that he could bear on his own shoulders the burden of the entire world".

He possessed a fullness of being that made him a true "artist" who "realised in the entire sphere of human relations that imaginative sympathy which in the sphere of Art is the sole secret of creation". Indeed Wilde had already claimed, in The Soul of Man Under Socialism, that unselfishness is Christlike because it "recognizes infinite variety of type as a delightful thing, accepts it, acquiesces in it, enjoys it".

Building on this earlier formulation, Wilde at this point begins to develop a more direct parallel between himself and Christ. As he develops this parallel, Wilde reaffirms the values of potentiality and "sincerity" articulated earlier in The Picture of Dorian Gray. To be sure, Wilde is careful to distinguish Christand thus himself-from Dorian Gray. While Dorian pursued "strange legacies of thought and passion" into the dens of London, Wilde's Christ embraces humankind only through imagination. Because Christ valued plenitude-"variety of type"- he participated imaginatively in every human situation: "he understood the leprosy of the leper, the darkness of the blind, the fierce misery of those who live for pleasure, the strange poverty of the rich".

In this sense Christ, "the palpitating centre of romance," is the fullest incarnation of the aesthete whose commitment to "Art" has "made us myriad-minded". Just here is the "romance" to which Gagnier refers Wilde's effort to transform suffering into aesthetic fulfillment. And if Wilde had contented himself with representing Christ as an embodiment of spiritualized aestheticism, DeProfundis would remain well within the modality of romance.

But Wilde's motives are deeply implicated with irony, as he continues to build the parallels between himself and Christ by describing the Christ-story in the unmistakable terms of an aestheticized sensual satiety. The imagery is suffused with homoerotic overtones: "The little supper with his companions... the anguish in the quiet moonlit olive-garden: the false friend coming close to him so as to betray him with a kiss... ".

This erotic imagery shows Wilde's strategy of displacement at its most aggressive, as Christ is rendered in something like homoerotic pastoral. Christ's story "is really an idyll," continues Wilde, for "one always thinks of him as a young bridegroom with his companions... or as a shepherd straying through a valley with his sheep in search of green meadow or cool stream... or as a lover for whose love the whole world was too small".

Yet Wilde does not devise his figure of Christ merely as a signifier of sensual fulfillment. Christ becomes a betrayed aesthete whose power of sympathetic imagination enables him to sustain suffering-just like Wilde. Wilde's Christ purifies contradictions through the intensity of his renunciation: "one realizes one's soul by getting rid of all alien passions, all acquired culture, and all external possessions be they good or evil".

Teaching us how to live for ourselves, Christ makes it possible for us to become agents of our own fulfillment. In this fashion, having already portrayed himself as a man of sorrow and suffering, Wilde completes the bond of identification by saying of Christ what he had written of himself elsewhere in De Profundis. "Christ... had the power not merely of saying beautiful things himself, but of making other people say beautiful things to him".

Irritated by the bold effrontery of this presentation, some interpreters have lost sight of Wilde's rhetorical intentions in this section of the text. Fleishman argues that "Wilde's appropriation of religious language for his secular concerns cannot fail to seem bathetic.... Such appropriation... must seem another Wildean mask, another exercise in style". John Allen Quintus notes disapprovingly Wilde's "self-serving" interest in the Christ motif and points out that he "defends his own 'sins' on the grounds that they brought him suffering and individuality and Christ's acceptance".

But of course the mask is deliberate. Wilde intends to transmute his eros into an aesthetic that could be identified with Christ. He brings Christ into his text when the rhetorical need arises to hedge his transgressive persona within a moral framework of regenerative suffering.

To emphasize his intentions, Wilde concludes this section with a confident assertion of Christ's artistic vision of human life: "that which is the very keynote of romantic art was to him the proper basis of actual life". As Christ fulfills the power of imaginative sympathy, so Wilde implies that "each man" may similarly be transformed by identifying himself with Christ:

Christ... is just like a work of art himself. He does not really teach one anything, but by being brought into his presence one becomes something... Once at least in his life each man walks with Christ to Emmaus.

With this renewed feeling of possibility Wilde begins to write himself a new future: "I hope to live long enough, and to produce work of such a character, that I shall be able at the end of my days to say, 'Yes: this is just where the artistic life leads a man". He recognizes "a new spirit working in this prison through men and things" so that his refrain "What an appalling ending!" has become "What a wonderful beginning" (618-19). He is now able to think beyond prison walls: "much is waiting for me outside that is very delightful," he says, and his readiness for new joy comes about because he has "become a deeperman" and acquired the "privilege of those who have suffered".

Having fully imagined an aesthetic transformation, Wilde projects himself into the forms of material agency by which his future life will be managed. He outlines how he will handle money, meetings, and travel after his release. In these pages the pathos of victimization vanishes before the optimistic good humour of the active, knowing agent of change. He surveys the debts that remain to him to pay upon his release, reminds Douglas of his responsibility in helping Wilde incur them, and hints that Douglas ought to help pay them.

To anchor his reconstructed identity in the familiar discourse of sensuous aestheticism, he invokes the persona of the aesthete and bon vivant. Recounting the "Savoy dinners" and "the suppers at Willis's" he and Douglas had enjoyed, he lingers on the details of "the clear turtle soup, the luscious ortolans wrapped in their crinkled Sicilian vine-leaves... [and] the amber-scented champagne". Wilde furthers his new sense of empowerment by planning his travel after release from prison.

"I have to speak with you," he says to Douglas, "with regard to the conditions, circumstances and place of our meeting," perhaps "in some quiet foreign town like Bruges, whose grey houses and green canals and cool still ways had a charm for me". To reinforce his sense of control, Wilde admonishes Douglas that there is now both a "wide chasm... of achieved Art and acquired culture" between them, as well as a "still wider chasm... of Sorrow".

Wilde clearly wants renewed life with Douglas, cast in terms of the mentoring role he believes had always existed between them: "You came to me to learn the pleasure of Life and the Pleasure ofArt. I am chosen to teach you something much more wonderful, the meaning of Sorrow, and its beauty". In this fashion Wilde completes his effort to write a new life for himself out of elements of the old.

Wilde could not sustain the demands of the future he had imagined in De Profundis. His plays had disappeared from the theaters, his reputation was ruined, and his suffering wife died. He depended on financial support from a variety of friends who pitied him. Gradually as he moved from place to place in France he fell back into a relationship with Douglas, who spent Wilde's money and came and went as he wished. The idyll of fulfilled desire so elegantly reconstructed in the last pages of DeProfundis was emptied by the ironies of Douglas's inconstancy and Wilde's increasing despair and illness. Images of the costs of transgression drawn from his texts appeared in the stories he told about himself to those who visited him.

During these often chance encounters with friends, Wilde represented himself variably as a victim of the gods and as a Dorian Gray come face-to-face with his own self-destruction. Ellmann recounts one "fable" told by Wilde to a visiting friend, in which Wilde dreams of confronting a faceless "being" who turns out to be "the face of [my] soul, and it is horrible".

The same polarities of victimization and self-destruction underlie many of the posthumous evaluations of Wilde by those who knew him. The same textual images Wilde used in De Profundis reappear in these assessments.

Frank Harris, prominent journalist and editor who was a friend and admirer of Wilde, found the motif of Christ-like suffering and tragedy equally compelling in his representation of Wilde's life. Echoing Wilde's emphasis on Christ's embodiment of "self-realization," Harris sees redemptive power in Wilde's access to the mystery of Christ:

"In the beautiful pages about Jesus which form the greater part of De Profundis, Oscar... divined the very secret of Jesus," for "in these pages Oscar Wilde really came close to the divine Master," as "by bitter suffering he had been brought to see that the moment of repentance is the moment of absolution and self-realization" (233-44). Harris sees Wilde as a tragic victim of a harsh society, punished like a Greek protagonist at the peak of preeminence: he was punished for his popularity and pre-eminence, for the superiority of his mind and wit... a tragic figure of imperishable renown".

Even Douglas's own representation of Wilde refers to "the frightful tragedy of Oscar Wilde's terrible pilgrimage."

Douglas depicts Wilde as a victim of the "frightful penalties" of repressive laws and public censure, asserting that the worst aspect of Wilde's "cruel fate" was the loss of a great writer who could have entertained the world with "a dozen plays as good as The Importance of Being Earnest".

George Bernard Shaw, on the other hand, will have none of the tragic or the Christ-like in his view of Wilde. For Shaw, Wilde appeared always as a knowing, acutely self-aware agent of his own appetites, able to cast himself in redemptive terms only because of gullible readers like Harris: "Oscar," wrote Shaw to Harris, "was not sobre, not honest, not industrious," yet by persecuting him, society made "a hero of him... for it is in the nature of people to worship those who have been made to suffer horribly" (qtd. in Harris 341).

But Wilde "could not write about his own individual share in that suffering with any conviction or sympathy," and while he "does not appear a selfish or base-minded man," in the end he became "an unproductive drunkard and swindler" (qtd. in Harris 341-42).

These divergent readings of Wilde's last textualization of his life suggest how challenging it was for his friends-as for interpreters now-to read Wilde's complex life through his art. That the final years of his life were far more painful than the future envisioned in De Profundis is testimony to the truth of Wilde's comment there that "the final mystery is oneself".

Chapter 5

A Reading of Oscar Wilde's Salome

Oscar Wilde began to write Salome still enjoying, but being frustrated by, the critical attention given to his novel The Picture of Dorian Gray. The summer of 1890 had been exhausting for Wilde: Dorian Gray had been published in shorter form, and Wilde had written many letters to disgruntled reviewers defending the work, reluctantly pointing out the moral qualities in an art form he had previously claimed was incompatible with moralistic purposes.

The newspapers' focus on whether Wilde lauded or deplored Dorian's actions directed public attention away from the novel's critique of image and desire. Dorian Gray actually is highly skeptical about the aestheticism Wilde represented in the eighties, treating it, as Richard Ellmann put it, as "not a creed but a problem".

Specifically, Wilde's problem with aestheticism is that, following Pater, the self cultivates and expresses itself through both physical and intellectual experiences, and that gives rise to the danger that either the physical or intellectual experience will be valued at the expense of the other.

Aestheticism allows individuals to transcend the Philistinism within their own culture, but it also narrows the cultural experiences open to them. In particular, aestheticism runs the risk of robbing sexual desire of its power by attempting to transform all walks of experience into contemplative acts.

Salome in fact extends this critique of aestheticism. Like Dorian, Salome is trapped in her persona-an aestheticized image of herself that she projects to the public-as an object of desire. Because Salome, like Dorian, can only function as an object of desire, she is afforded no psychic space to develop subjective desire.

As Freud notes, the repressed endeavors to break through the pressure of the ego and either forces its way into consciousness or reveals itself through action. The resulting action invariably throws out of balance the ego's role of stabilizing the individual; in other words, the individual's desire becomes perverted.

In Salome, Wilde gives us direct access to the princess's perverted desire. (And this intimate view of Salome paradoxically makes her less attractive than Dorian Gray but slightly more sympathetic.) In the double play of worshiping and fearing Salome's image, Herod's court fails to take into account what she represses in order to project her image. The result is a Salome using the power gotten from her persona to destroy the very system that imbued her with this power.

Although Oscar Wilde began writing Salome in 1891, he had toyed with the idea of contributing to the vast body of nineteenth-century literature on the Biblical figure for some time. Wilde was familiar with the iconography that had sprung up around Salome in the decades prior to his drama, from Flaubert's "Herodias" to Mallarme's unfinished poem "Herodiade" to the Moreau paintings of Salome immortalized by J.K. Huysmans in A Rebours, to name a few.

From the beginning, however, Wilde planned to distinguish his portrayal of Salome from those of the writers and painters before him. He found, for example, previous depictions of the princess by artists such as Leonardo and Durer unsatisfactory (Ellmann 342). The Salome of Wilde's drama differs also from her previous literary incarnations.

In Flaubert's story, for instance, Herodias is the instigator of both Salome's dance and request for John the Baptist's head. Salome is merely a pawn in Herodias's struggle for power with Herod in Flaubert's story. Wilde, by giving Salome her own motive for dancing before Herod, gives back to the princess a measure of subjectivity that had been denied her since the Bible omitted her name from its tale of John the Baptist's beheading.

Of all the previous depictions of Salome, the paintings by Gustave Moreau, and especially Huysmans's description of them, influenced Wilde the most in his conception of the princess. According to Richard Ellmann, Wilde liked to recite the passages in A Rebours about the Moreau paintings. From the beginning, then, Wilde conceived of Salome in aesthetic terms.

Wilde saw Salome as the representation of all the unspoken impulses and desires in Donan Gray. Yet Wilde takes his character of Salome further than he does Dorian. Not only does his Salome articulate the motivations that are kept concealed in Donan Gray, but Wilde gives her a justification for her actions that he deliberately keeps ambiguous with Dorian.

Indeed, Wilde's conception of Salome attributes to her a great deal more subjectivity than Dorian. Originally, Wilde intended to call his drama The Decapitation of Salome and planned to have Salome become a saint at the play's end (Ellmann 344). Although he abandoned that idea in favour of exploiting the legacy of Salome as a femme fatale, vestiges of the more hagiographic version remain in the play.

Wilde's Salome is an attempt to combine her iconic reputation with a more psychologically-based portrait. It is sometimes an uneasy mix in the play; the aesthetic discourse and intoning language of the play diverts from Salome's character and encourages looking at her only as an image rather than as a motivated character.

Jean Paul Riquelme, representing the views of several critics, argues, "Any interpretation that understands Salome's language as realistic, that is, as a transparent vehicle for rendering the thoughts of a psychologically believable character, presents a distorted view of the play". Such a view overlooks the point Wilde is making in the play about the dangers involved in treating Salome exclusively as an image.

While Riquelme is right in cautioning against looking at

Salome as realistic discourse, he dismisses the possibility that Wilde is juxtaposing psychological realism with aesthetic discourse in order to argue that, by privileging the effects of the language over its content, the audience commits the same errors against Salome that the other characters in the play do, appreciating her image at the expense of her subjectivity.

Thus, in examining the consequences of such a view, Wilde includes the audience as being complicit in the fundamental problem of the play, overlooking the anger and destructiveness inherent in Salome's persona.

For Salome in effect extends and complicates the argument Wilde puts forth in Dorian Gray, namely that when control over persona is taken away from the individual behind it, the individual's desires and will threaten to pervert his or her persona.

Moreover, Salome shows, as Dorian Gray did previously, that through the misreading of persona, an individual can assume a sort of power that threatens the established order of things. Salome in fact blatantly expresses the will, desire, and quest for power that Dorian Gray leaves ambiguous. As Christopher Nassaar notes, "Salome sheds Dorian's inhibitions and emerges as an unrestrained sexual murderess".

The character of Salome suggests that persona has a greater importance for the female performer. As a dancer and an icon of beauty, Salome is, as several scholars have noted, particularly susceptible to the male gaze. Furthermore, her status as a woman who can perform implies that her persona is vulnerable to chameleon-like change. After having written Salome, Wilde had hoped that Sarah Bernhardt would perform the role.

As Riquelme points out, casting the middle-aged Bernhardt as Salome would have prohibited the audience from interpreting the play literally. Bernhardt, herself an example of a powerful and influential persona, would also have underscored his argument that Salome's persona is what is under siege in the play.

Presumably, as the audience looks at Salome, they would see not only Wilde's character, but the Salomes of past writers and artists, as well as Bernhardt's persona. Wilde's Salome therefore is trapped within her own persona as the epitome of the modern femme fatale, and his play, rather than being a literal retelling of the Biblical story, becomes an exploration of the limits of persona and of its symbolic value.

In Salome, the moon serves as a metaphor for the empty canvas and for Salome herself. Like Dorian Gray, the moon assumes whatever significance the viewer attributes to it. In the play, the moon is a "dead woman" according to Herodias's Page, a "princess" according to the Syrian Narraboth, a "mad woman" according to Herod, and "money" and a "virgin" according to Salome herself.

These descriptions of the moon reveal the various watchers' desires for Salome up to a point. More specifically, however, the descriptions point to the way their desires construct their respective states of mind. For instance, the "dead woman" of the Page's vision can be attributed partially to a moment of prescience on his part (about either Salome's or Narraboth's imminent demise) and partially to his jealousy of Narraboth's fascination with Salome.

Herod's image of the moon as a "mad woman" is based upon his uncontrollable desire for Salome. Indeed, his lust for her will eventually cause him to make the mad gesture of offering her whatever she wants provided she satisfies his desire. In light of Herod's perspective, Salome's view of the moon as both "money" and a "virgin" points to her awareness that her body, at least as far as Herod is concerned, has an exchangeable value.

Interestingly, the only figure who sees nothing in the moon but its own image is Herodias, who snipes at Herod that "the moon is like the moon". In her refusal to interpret the moon, Herodias displays her unwillingness to acknowledge her daughter's importance to these men and underscores her recalcitrance with admonitions to Herod that he "look[s] at her too much". (It is worth noting that the Page is also upset when his loved one, Narraboth, "looks too much" upon Salome.) Salome poses a distinct threat to Herodias; as Herod has a history of taking the women he likes to look upon, the possibility exists for Salome to unseat her mother's throne. For Herodias, then, Salome possesses a power through her desirability that has the potential to usurp Herodias's position. Salome's connection to the moon, then, threatens to destabilize the power held by the other woman in the court. Because of this threat, she is isolated from her mother.

Thus Salome is set up from the beginning as being a woman whose persona is a figure of iconic beauty and an object of sexual desire, and not much else. The danger in this, according to Wilde, is that Salome indeed has a will and desires of her own, but because of her position in the play has no outlet to express them. Hanna B. Lewis notes that "Salome is presented as a 'fait accompli'", and the reason for this is that the characters in the play have conspired to keep Salome from expressing her subjectivity.

As an object of the gaze, Salome is kept inanimate and stagnant. But Salome's status as an object is misleading. Since she cannot exert her own power in creating her own persona, her frustration and resentment cause her to seek other avenues for power.

A persona, cautions Wilde, is neither static nor inanimate; it generates its own energies that, if not used to develop itself, may emerge in dangerous and destructive ways. Salome's actions turn destructive because her limited ability to exert her will causes her power to be perverted.

Because of the emphasis Wilde places upon the act of looking, the play in large part attempts to negotiate between the dangers of looking too much and the dangers of not looking enough. As Brad Bucknell notes, "There is almost no one in the play who is not involved in some kind of projection, some kind of complex interplay between the eye and the object of vision".

Because this interplay takes the form of a narcissistic relationship with the self (in that the object of vision, Salome, invariably takes the form of the viewer's desires), an excess of looking leads to destruction, as evidenced by both Narraboth's suicide and Herod's unwitting murder of Jokanaan. Looking at Salome for any length of time leads to the consumption of the self by its own desire. Salome, for instance, compels Narraboth to do her bidding with the promise of a future look, and Narraboth commits suicide because of his inability to cope with Salome looking at someone else. Looking at Salome is an attempt to own Salome, to turn her into the Salome each one who looks at her wants her to be.

Salome's persona is therefore malleable; the image she projects shifts according to the desires of those who encounter her. But Salome's relationship to her own persona is refracted through the perceptions of the other characters. Since she is seen as an object of desire, the only actions she knows how to perform are those that stem from desire.

Of course, the only character who steadfastly refuses to look at Salome is Jokanaan. Jokanaan is often read as an oral rather than a visual character, but, while this is true to a great extent, Jokanaan is actually more image-sensitive than he is usually given credit for being. Jokanaan speaks in images; his prophecies of the coming of Christ are evocative word-paintings.

"The son of man hath come," he intones. "The centaurs have hidden themselves in the rivers, and the sirens have left the rivers, and are lying beneath the leaves of the forest". More importantly, as Jokanaan is forced to engage with Herod's court, his language becomes even more descriptive. He cries about Herodias,

Where is she who gave herself unto the Captains of Assyria, who have baldricks on their loins, and tiaras of divers colours on their heads? Where is she who hath given herself to the young men of Egypt, who are clothed in fine linen and purple, whose shields are of gold, whose helmets are of silver, whose bodies are mighty?

Jokanaan's aesthetic prose ties him to the men of Herod's court, particularly Herod himself and, to a lesser degree, the Page. He speaks about Herodias in terms of commodities, categorizing her and by extension Salome as the sum of her material goods. This is where Jokanaan errs with respect to Salome and where precisely he makes the same mistake as Herod: by being unable to see Salome as anything other than a materialistic creature, he dismisses the passion and the rage underlying Salome's actions and therefore underestimates her reaction to him.

For the one thing that characterizes Salome above all else is her resentment about being limited by her visuality, particularly when this visuality fragments her into fetishized parts. Herod, for instance, is fixated upon her mouth. To him, it is a symbol of sexual orality, and Herod heightens his desire of Salome by both infantilizing her and linking her mouth directly to intoxicating wine and fertile fruit.

About the wine, Herod says, "Dip into it thy little red lips, that I may drain the cup", and, when he asks her to eat some fruit, he asserts, "I love to see in a fruit the mark of thy little teeth.

Bite but a little of this fruit and then I will eat what is left". With these requests, Herod makes clear that Salome is an object of desire that he, as king, has the power to consume sexually, by literally consuming the fruit and wine bearing the mark of Salome's fetishized mouth.

When Salome resists Herod's advance by maintaining that she is neither thirsty nor hungry, Herod petulantly turns on her mother and then offers Salome Herodias's throne to sit on. His implication is that if Salome allows her beauty to be exploited, then she can achieve the power of a queen. The power that Herod offers Salome is qualified, however, since she can only flourish by being bounded by the parameters of his desire for her.

Moreover, Herod makes it plain that his desire, by focusing exclusively on her sexualized parts, dismisses Salome as a subjective entity. By treating Salome as an object, Herod neglects the fact that Salome too can see, can desire, and can use the power she possesses as princess of the court to her own ends.

When Salome focuses her desire on Jokanaan, she pointedly appropriates Herod's seductive discourse, as if by doing so she gets to appropriate his power. Like Herod's fixation on her mouth and teeth, Salome's desire for Jokanaan takes the form of ever-increasing synecdoche, first concentrating on his body, then his hair, then his mouth. Salome also speaks in the aesthetic discourse used by the men in the play: "Thy hair is like the cedars of Lebanon... that give their shade to the lions and to the robbers who would hide themselves by day".

Salome purposefully ignores what Jokanaan is saying in order that she may look at him. Like Herod, Salome overlooks Jokanaan's subjectivity in favour of an appreciation of his body, an aggressive move that she is clearly not that comfortable with, since she appears to be unsure of which tack she should take in her attempt at seduction.

Jokanaan's body, to Salome, is "white like the lilies of the field", then it is "like a leper" and "like a whitened sepulchre full of loathsome things", moving from an image of fertility to an image of decay. His hair is first "like clusters of grapes", but Salome changes this description to "a crown of thorns which they have placed on thy forehead" and "a knot of black serpents writhing around thy neck".

In her attempted seduction, Salome draws her imagery from Jokanaan's Biblical story. The leper is obviously Lazarus, raised by Christ from the dead. The "whitened sepulchre" is a reference to Christ's criticism of the Jewish practice of painting tombs white in order to purify them; Christ chastises the Jews for this practice because the coat of paint provides a superficial veneer of cleanliness.

He rebukes the Jewish elders by claiming that they "are like whitewashed tombs which on the outside appear beautiful, but inside they are full of dead men's bones and all uncleanness" (Matthew 23:27). With this allusion, Salome turns the words of Christ back onto Jokanaan, focusing not only on his surface qualities but implicitly accusing him of believing that her surface beauty necessarily conceals a degenerated interior.

Salome's description of Jokanaan's hair contains, besides the clear reference to Christ's crown of thorns worn at the Crucifixion, another allusion to the Biblical story of John the Baptist. In the gospel according to St. Matthew, John is preaching in the wilderness of Judea, clad, as the First Soldier in Salome reiterates, in "camel's hair, and round his loins he had a leathern belt". The "knot of vipers" refers to the epithet "brood of vipers" hurled by John at the Pharisees and Sadducees, who insincerely request to be baptized (Matthew 3:7).

In Salome's description, however, the vipers are crawling around Jokanaan's neck, threatening to strangle him. Salome mocks Jokanaan's intolerance; the infidels that he sought to bar from God's grace literally return to kill him.

When Salome shifts her gaze to Jokanaan's mouth, the instrument for both his prophecies and his censures, she has no need to draw a Biblical analogy. Salome's images of Jokanaan's mouth are a mix of sensuality-she compares his mouth to pomegranates and precious stones-and, when she compares his mouth to the blast of military trumpets and the feet of a hunter, violence.

As an object of sexual desire in Herod's court, Salome is well aware that passion is fraught with danger, and Wilde also uses the combination to point out that every passion contains within it its own potential for destruction.

It is in these successive attempts of Salome's to seduce Jokanaan that Wilde insert his most blatant autobiographical allusion. Constantly quarreling with Alfred Douglas and still well aware of the stigma attached to his relationship with Douglas, Wilde gives Salome the knowledge that passion is both unstable and dangerous.

More importantly, though, as Eibhar Walshe notes, "Salome offends against a traditional system of male desire by articulating her own, independent desire for the body of the Prophet". As Salome becomes more passionate, she also becomes more subversive, and her power over her own image (as the subject rather than the object of desire) palpably grows until Herod quashes it with his gaze.

When Salome uses Biblical analogies to describe Jokanaan's physical attributes, she throws Jokanaan's perception of her back in his face because, as Martine Thomas points out, Salome and Jokanaan "are unable to hear the meaning of their mutual words, since they only feel the resistance their words imply". Salome uses Jokanaan's reputation in order to construct her perception of him.

Whereas Jokanaan reviles Salome based on his preconceptions of her as her mother's daughter, Salome uses established preconceptions of Jokanaan to fuel her attraction towards him. But while Jokanaan limits his view of Salome to her persona, Salome refuses to dismiss him on account of his image as an infidel-hating ascetic.

Salome sees in her fixation on Jokanaan's image a way to attain the power denied her as a perpetual object. She too can manipulate perceptions in order to get the object of her desire, and, significantly, she can do so with a man outside of Herod's court hierarchy. Salome's attempted seduction of Jokanaan is an endeavor to find power outside of the court and particularly to find a form of subjective power, one in which her power is not dependent on the gazes of others.

Salome and Jokanaan thus relate to each other from their own isolated perceptions. Elliott L. Gilbert notes that the play is "a veritable taxonomy of solipsism". Just as Salome is trapped within her visualization of Jokanaan, Jokanaan is likewise circumscribed by how he sees the princess.

When he looks at Salome, he only sees Herodias. When Salome introduces herself to him, Jokanaan responds by crying out, "Back! Daughter of Babylon!" and continues, "Thy mother hath filled the earth with the wine of her iniquities, and the cry of her sins hath come up to the ears of God". Jokanaan refuses to look at Salome because he has already seen her before. Salome's persona, as far as Jokanaan is concerned, is not even her own-she is merely a reflection of Herodias. Jokanaan denies Salome the right to even have a persona that is identifiably hers, something Herod and his court at least grant her. His vision of her is one based on preconception. In other words, when he encounters Salome, his image of Herodias replaces any actual perception he might have of her. As Austin E. Quigley notes, Jokanaan's "unwillingness to look at a woman as beautiful as Salome can suggest diminished ability somewhere, weakness as well as strength". Jokanaan, trapped in his dark cistern, is correspondingly blinded by his idealism. By refusing to look beyond Salome's persona, he shows himself to be complicit in the patriarchal structure of the court that has defined Salome by her image.

Salome's request for Jokanaan's head is thus predicated upon two things: her resentment of Herod's incestuous desire for her and a more generalized resentment of the fact that she is constantly objectified, even and especially by Jokanaan. Herod, in order to cajole Salome into performing an erotically-coded dance for him, actually gives Salome the freedom to exert her will in whatever fashion she desires. Herod's offer is in a sense a sign of defeat for Salome; unable to exert her will onto Jokanaan, Herod's offer makes it clear that the only power Salome can have access to is through her position as an object of desire. Thus her request for Jokanaan's head is a double attack against Jokanaan, for refusing to see her as an individual and not just as a type of royal harlot, and against Herod, for perpetuating her objectification in order to satisfy his own sexual desire for her.

To Salome, both refusals to take her subjectivity into account have contributed to her request. As she says in her morbid address to the beheaded Jokanaan, "Well, thou hast seen thy God, Jokanaan, but me, me, thou didst never see. If thou hadst seen me thou wouldst have loved me". Salome's death, noted tersely in the play as a stage direction, ultimately points to the ambivalent light in which Wilde depicts her.

Wilde portrays Salome as uncontrollable desire while also giving her motivation for such desire. In light of this ambivalence, Salome's death appears to be less a punishment for her actions than the inevitable consequence of them. Salome dies because, like Dorian Gray, a persona left unchecked cannot be sustained. And, as Dorian's final hypocritical gesture towards Hetty seals his corrupt behavior, Salome's final monologue brings the expression of her desire to completion. Yet, like Dorian, Salome realizes that unbounded desire literally means that it will never be satisfied. She concedes, "Neither the floods nor the great waters can quench my passion". Salome's desire, breaking free from the limits her persona imposed on it, ends up consuming her as well.

Chapter 6

Wilde, Society, and Society Drama

On February 14—St. Valentine's Day—1895, London was choked with a major snow storm. But this could not prevent the opening night of *The Importance of Being Earnest*, at the St. James's Theatre, from being a major social event.

This was in part due to the stunning popularity of Oscar Wilde in the theatre: *The Importance of Being Earnest* was Wilde's fourth popular West End play in only three years, and *An Ideal Husband* had only opened a month before and was still playing to packed house at the Haymarket Theatre a few blocks away. Fashionable London was out in force, in their most elegant clothes.

As a tribute to Wilde's dandified aestheticism, women wore sprays of lilies as corsages; and many young men wore lilies of the valley in the buttonholes of lapels of their tailcoats. Wilde spent most of the performance backstage, but he was nevertheless dressed in what one biography called "the depth of fashion": "his coat had a black velvet collar; he carried white gloves; a green scarab ring adorned one of his fingers; a large bunch of seals on a black moir ribbon watch chain hung from his white waistcoat; and, like the young men in the stalls, he wore lilies of the valley in his buttonhole."

Audiences came dressed in evening formal to opening nights then; in fact, you *had* to wear evening formal dress *any* night if you wanted to sit in the stalls (what we call the orchestra) or the dress circle (the first balcony). And this was true not only at the St. James's Theatre but throughout "Theatreland," the entertainment district in the West End of metropolitan London.

For theatregoing was more than an entertainment medium or an art form: it was major leisure activity for people of all social classes, part of a network of urban activities that included private clubs, restaurants, pubs, cafes, hotels, and casinos.

In the 1890s, there were over fifty theatres in greater London, most of the them in the West End, a half dozen alone along Shaftesbury Avenue, which had been completed in 1886 as part of an urban renewal plan off of Picadilly Circus. The theatres drew their patrons from the greater metropolitan area, who came to the theatre by carriage, omnibus, streetcar, and underground railway.

Each theatre was exclusively leased by a manager, often an "Actor-Manager," who established a reputation for his theatre (the actor-managers were most often men) through the style of his acting, the physical splendor of the production, and the type of dramatic entertainment offered.

Of the older and larger theatres, Covent Garden had become the home of grand opera, and Drury lane was famous for its spectacular autumn melodramas and elaborates Christmas Pantomimes.

The most famous "classical" actor of the time, Henry Irving, had managed the Lyceum Theatre for over twenty years, producing a series of major Shakespeare revivals for himself and his stage partner, Ellen Terry. (When *The Importance of Being Earnest* opened, Irving and Terry could be seen at the Lyceum in J.

Comyns Carr's *King Arthur*, a top-of-the-line costume epic with armor designed by the pre-Raphaelite artist Sir Edward Burne-Jones and incidental music by Sir Arthur Sullivan; Irving would join their ranks when he received a knighthood—the first actor to be thus honored—later that year).

You could see melodrama at the Adelphi Theatre, operetta at the Savoy (where the Gilbert and Sullivan collaborations had received their premieres), and musical comedies at the Gaiety (*An Artist's Model*, one of a series of musicals with working-class heroines, had just opened there in February, 1895). Variety entertainment of all sorts could be seen in the

Music Halls, either in smoke-filled taverns in working class neighborhoods, in chic cosmopolitan halls tucked away in the West End, or in glittering theatres like the Empire on Leicester Square, which offered picturesque ballet-extravaganzas.

Several actor-managers—Charles Wyndham at the Criterion on Picadilly Circus, John Hare at the Garrick on Charing Cross Road, and George Alexander at the St. James's—specialized in "Society Drama," plays of modern life set in the rarefied world of the upper classes.

These plays could be witty and frivolous light comedies; or they could be ponderous dramatic treatises on difficult social issues, most often the sexual "double standard" and the "problem" of the "fallen woman." One such play, *The Second Mrs Tanqueray* by Arthur Wing Pinero, had been presented by George Alexander at the St. James's Theatre two years earlier, with the fiery and exotic actress Mrs.

Patrick Campbell becoming an instant star as the former kept-woman trying to fit into the respectable world of her upper-class husband. We hear a parodic echo of plays like *The Second Mrs Tanqueray* when Jack Worthing (played by Alexander), in the final act of *The Importance of Being Earnest*, says of Miss Prism (who he mistakenly believes to be his long-lost and unmarried mother), "who has the right to cast a stone against one who has suffered?

Cannot repentance wipe out an act of folly? Why should there be one law for men, and another for women?" But for all of their epigramatic wit and paradoxical attitudes towards life, Oscar Wilde's other 1890s society comedies (*Lady Windermere's Fan, A Woman of No Importance,* and *An Ideal Husband*) are all serious "problem" dramas about the intractability of sexual double-standards and the personal costs of respectability, precisely those issues that Wilde appears (at least) to be satirizing in *The Importance of Being Earnest.*

At the beginning of Pinero's *The Second Mrs Tanqueray,* Aubrey Tanqueray (played by Alexander) rebukes his friend Cayley Drummle (a man-about-town modelled in part on Oscar Wilde) for sharing in the values of "The Way of World" and condemning all women of doubtful moral reputation.

Drummle responds, "My dear Aubrey, I *live* in the world." Aubrey ruefully defines what Drummle means by "the world": "The name we give our little parish of St. James's."

For an upper-class bachelor in the 1890s, the little parish of St. James's *was* the world. Exclusive gentleman's clubs line Pall Mall. Along Jermyn Street are the custom shirtmakers and bootmakers. A few blocks away are hotels, shops, and galleries of Picadilly, and the "bespoke" tailors of Saville Row.

Within a short walk or a carriage ride, a young man could leave his bachelor apartment in the Albany (where Jack Worthing resides, under the name "Ernest," in *The Importance of Being Earnest*), shop, pay an "at-home" call in Mayfair or Belgravia, dine at his club, take in a play at one of a dozen theatres, or see a ballet at the Empire.

And at the St. James's Theatre (now demolished), right at the centre of "our little parish of St. James's," a young man could take a seat in the stalls for *Lady Windermere's Fan* or *The Importance of Being Earnest.*

The Importance of Being Earnest at the St. James's Theatre was a Society Comedy about life in St. James's for audiences who lived or shopped or dined in St. James's.

And Society Drama as a whole was a mirror in which fashionable audiences could see fashionable images of their own fashionable world of at-homes, dinner parties, and country-house weekends; a world in which gentlemen with hyphenated surnames, dressed in carefully-creased trousers and elegant cravats, made small talk with titled ladies dressed *a la mode,* and flirted, for a moment only, with the dreaded possibilities of adultery and interclass marriage; a world in which one could pause for a moment to consider what to do with the women of doubtful reputation in one's midst, but where one would not hesitate to banish these "fallen" women back to their *declasse* world of Parisian boarding houses and second-rate continental resort towns.

With regard to clothing, Society Drama at the fashionable theatres was a mirror literally as well as figuratively. Actors employed by George Alexander at the St. James's were contractually required to dress appropriately "off-stage as well as -on," and could be fired if spotted walking in Picadilly during the day in anything less than a well-tailored morning coat.

New Society Dramas would often premier at the beginning of the London "season," and women would wait until they saw the fashions worn by the female characters in the play before they ordered their new gowns and hats. And would-be high-fashion couturiers with assumed French names would design theatrical costumes for Society Dramas and then, their reputations established, became high-society dress designers in the "real" world instead.

But if theatre is a mirror, it is a flattering mirror that lets the viewer see only what he or she wants to see. And the mirror-image relationship between the audience and the play in late-Victorian Society Drama is more notable for what the theatre chose to leave out than what it mirrored. For the world of high society and high fashion was more porous than anyone in society cared to admit; and the theatre, as it often does, embodied by its very theatrical nature the instability of the English class system.

This was certainly true of the theatre auditorium. Audiences in even the most fashionable theatres included members of every class, from aristocrats and financiers, to businessmen and professionals, to shopkeepers, clerks, and artisans, to servants and laborers. The lower classes had their own seating areas, with their own entrances, lobbies, bars, and bathrooms in the theatre.

But, in the more expensive parts of the house, the auditorium was by no means as segregated as members of "society" might wish. After all, not everyone could be admitted to a fashionable drawing-room; but anyone who could afford the higher-priced ticket and had the right clothing could sit in the stalls or the dress circle.

The actors on stage embodied these social ambiguities. Towards the end of the century, as the theatrical profession became more respectable, acting was no longer the exclusive province of theatrical families, social outcasts, and women of loose morals—the class of people that centuries before had been legally classified as "rogues and vagabonds"; and respectable, educated people from the middle classes could now enter the profession without too much social stigma. But even then, actors were certainly not, in their social origins, the aristocrats and ladies and gentlemen they successfully pretended to be on stage in Society Drama.

George Alexander was typical of his generation of actors: his father was in dry goods, and he dropped out of school when he was fifteen to be a clerk in a London office, joined a part-time amateur dramatic society, and then went into acting professionally.

No wonder Alexander insisted that his actors dress well on-stage and -off: only by their ability to wear perfectly-tailored clothes and a perfectly-chosen buttonhole could actors convince audiences that they were, in manners, the gentlemen they pretended to play. One of Alexander's most popular roles—in a dramatization of the popular novel, *The Prisoner of Zenda*—is emblematic of the actor's theatrical status as a gentleman. In it, Alexander played a middle-class English tourist with an uncanny resemblance to the embattled King of Ruritania; just put the middle-class Englishman in the right clothes, and he can play the part of a King to perfection.

The social ambiguities present on the stage andd in the auditorium of the St. James's Theatre were present in the entertainment industry as a whole. Not all of the pleasures to be found for money in "our little parish of St. James's" were dignified, or even legal.

Then, as now, the theatre was only one of the trades that offered the spectacle of bodies for public scrutiny and sale: the West end offered patrons not only theatres, restaurants and bars, but streetwalkers and brothels. The worlds of the late-Victorian theatre and the flesh trade overlapped directly, particularly at the Empire Theatre in Leicester Square.

There, in the infamous "promenade"—a wide horseshoe-shaped bar and lobby space behind the first tier of gallery seats, with an open view of the auditorium and the stage—high-priced prostitutes and elegantly-dressed gentlemen would make their assignations. Even after a well-publicized series of public hearings, the scandalous practice continued openly. And a compromise arrangement that had been reached—to let the open solicitations continue, but to screen off the promenade from the auditorium with a low barrier—did not last long: on the first night after the barrier was installed, it was torn down in protest by a gang of young, fashionable, gentlemen-about-town, led by the young Winston Churchill.

If anyone knew about the theatricality of late-Victorian High Society, it was Oscar Wilde. He was, after all, a perpetual outsider in the world of elegant fashion and society he frequented.

An Irishman of middle-class origins among the English, he gained access to the upper-class worlds of Oxford and London through his sheer intellectual and artistic brilliance. An espouser of the "truth of masks," he constantly wore the mask of the dandy and the aesthete. And he wrote plays about the impenetrability of the very "society" that he had, in fact, successfully penetrated. All of these dualities are reflected in the fun-house mirror of *The Importance of Being Earnest*. We can see why Jack Worthing, a respectable provincial justice of the peace, would need to invent a ne'er-do-well younger brother to justify his frequent trips to his bachelor rooms up in London. We can easily picture how he spends his time in London when he is not paying at-home calls to the Hon. Gwendolyn Fairfax. We can guess why Jack (under his assumed name) and his friend Algernon Montcrieff go to the Empire.

And we can only imagine where Algernon goes on his "Bunburying" expeditions once he's gotten out of his dinner engagement with his Aunt, Lady Bracknell. We can certainly see why Lady Bracknell is so concerned about her daughter's prospective fiance's qualifications for marrying into the family, and whether Worthing's father was born in the "purple of commerce," or whether he rose "from the ranks of the aristocracy." And we can see why Worthing's "contempt for the ordinary decencies of family life" reminds Lady Bracknell "of the worst excesses of the French Revolution... and I presume you know what that unfortunate movement led to?"

The Importance of Being Earnest depicts a world in which

the best kept secrets are the ones that everyone knows; a world in which everyone knows very well that their world is not as stable, as exclusive, or as moral as it pretends to be; and a world in which everyone appreciates the vital importance of maintaining at all cost what they know to be the fictions of everyday life.

Which brinngs us back to the opening night of *The Importance of Being Earnest* at the St. James's Theatre on Valentine's Day, 1895, and the lily of the valley in Oscar Wilde's lapel. Two years before, at the opening of *Lady Windermere's Fan* at the same theatre, Wilde, along with one of the characters in the play, had worn a green carnation, an open acknowledgement of the homosexual sub-culture to which Wilde and many of his friends belonged.

In 1895, while *The Importance of Being Earnest* was in rehearsal, Wilde was in the middle of his troubled but long-term relationship with Lord Alfred Douglas, and was being pursued by Douglas's father, the pugnacious and homophobic Marquis of Queensbury (author of "Queensbury rules" of boxing).

Queensbury had bought a ticket to the opening night of *The Importance of Being Ernest*, planning to disrupt the play with a demonstration. A policemen met Queensbury at the door and prevented his admission. Two weeks later, Queensbury left a calling card in Wilde's mailbox at the Albemarle club, with a note written on it: "To Oscar Wilde, posing as a Somdomite." The spelling error (he no doubt meant "sodomite") and the cautious reference to Wilde's "pose" notwithstanding, Wilde decided to take legal action and sued Queensbury for libel. Wilde lost the case; he was arrested for sodomy immediately after, tried, convicted, and sentenced to two years hard labour.

During the height of the controversy, Alexander withdrew *The Importance of Being Earnest* from performance. He revived it in 1902, without the disgraced author's name on the programme. Only in a revival in 1909 did Alexander return Wilde's name to the bill, and the play had the long and commercially successful theatrical run that it deserved.

Chapter 7

The "Obscure Subculture" of Art Writing

Oscar Wilde's famous quip that "The difference between literature and journalism is that journalism is unreadable and literature is unread" partially applies to art criticism. The problem with most art criticism is that it is both unreadable and unread. Paradoxically, however, as an obscure subculture of writing, art criticism appears in a truly large number of venues: several hundred international art magazines, numerous gallery and museum catalogues and daily newspaper reviews.

However, this glut does not mean the criticism is actually read. As James Elkins writes in What Happened to Art Criticism, "Art criticism is massively produced, and massively ignored" Art critics are the exception: they are paying attention. Criticism, to reference the title of a 2006 book of essays on the topic edited by Raphael Rubinstein, is in a "critical mess." This "mess," or crisis, a term several contributors similarly apply, has multiple causes. To begin with, much recent art criticism emphasizes description over evaluation-critical theorizing never even comes up. Too often such description presents an impenetrable wall of prose readers just do not want to climb.

That said, art critics face several major difficulties. Just to begin their practice they face the daunting task of acquiring knowledge in a range of disciplines, from art history to cultural studies.

As Elkins aptly puts it, "Art criticism has long been a

mongrel among academic pursuits, borrowing whatever it needed from other fields." But the borrowing must show more than a cursory grasp, and the only way to do so is to write criticism specific to a narrower field of knowledge in which the critic is an expert. Consider, for instance, Toronto critic Jeanne Randolph's training and practice as a psychiatrist, which has led to her cogent application of psychoanalytic theory to art.

Critics also receive ridiculously low pay; consequently, many have retired to academia to make a living, leaving them less time to concentrate on criticism. Meanwhile, the art market has taken over the evaluation of art in the United States and Europe, leaving critics without much influence. In Canada, where the market is smaller, local critics face another challenge: artists and curators often pass over their contributions, instead looking towards European and American theory.

As Critical Mess and a preceding 2002 roundtable by the journal October on the "condition" of criticism attest, concern about the state of the profession has resulted in a new era of reflection about criticism. October, first published in 1976, is an ideal forum to consider the state of criticism because it dates from an era when criticism was last influential: the late 70s to the early 90s.

Rigorously critical, Leftist response to the growing commercialism of Artforum, the magazine contained some of the most intelligent, radical criticism of the time—arguably of any time—featuring writers such as Craig Owens, Hal Foster, Benjamin Buchloh, Douglas Crimp and Rosalind Krauss. The October roster and other art critics from the downtown New York scene—notably, Peter Halley, Thomas Lawson, Walter Robinson and Rene Ricard—were integral to defining the art of the early 80s, at least in New York: the Metro Pictures generation—Jack Goldstein, Louise Lawlor and Cindy Sherman—and the neo-expressionist painters, Francesco Clemente, David Salle and Julian Schnabel.

"Then, however, came the "October Crisis," a backlash against the dense, complex art theory epitomized by October—more, in reality, a backlash against the various provincial emulations of October-style writing that employed difficult prose without rigorous theory. Around this time the dismissive term "artspeak" was coined to describe jargon-heavy art writing.

The conservative end of criticism's political spectrum—zealous modernist critics such as Peter Fuller (founder of the British art magazine Modern Painters), Robert Hughes and Hilton Kramer (publisher of the Right-leaning journal The New Criterion)—also didn't help. They remained stuck in perpetual nostalgic yearning for a pre-conceptual even pre-Pop past that they expressed in an ongoing diatribe, dismissing contemporary art with abdominal attacks.

Meanwhile, the global growth Of MFA programs ensured theory would not disappear, but that it would instead become institutionalized. These programs suffered the fate of being misunderstood and misapplied because, in producing art for thesis exhibitions, most fine arts graduate students do not have the time to gain the knowledge of philosophy and art history needed to properly comprehend art theory.

Simultaneously, critics were losing influence in the art world, the turning point arguably arriving along with the young British artists of the 90s (YBAS). Certainly Damien Hirst and Tracey Emin didn't need Derrida when Saatchi ensured their success.

As Buchloh wryly puts it, "You don't need criticism for an investment structure, you need experts. You don't have criticism of blue chip stocks either." Michael Duncan concurs: "a Julian Schnabel no longer needs a Rene Ricard. For a young artist, the imprimatur of Sotheby's or Chrisrie's is sufficient to substantiate a five-digit estimate."

If the market killed criticism, it is Damien Hirst's notorious skull made of diamonds (For the Love of God, 2007) that is its grave marker. Staring out against a stark black background on the cover of the ad-heavy, coffee-table-book-sized April 2008 issue of Artforum about the art market, it stands as ghoulish testimony to art criticism's loss of relevance. A controversial work arguably satirizing the excesses of the art market, For the Love of God is, however one views it, one of the most ostentatious pieces of art ever made. Its placement on the cover of an issue devoted to the art market in its current state of hypergreed shows how the commercial threatens the critical, even as the magazine proposes to reflect critically on the phenomenon.

Hal Foster goes further than Buchloh in his as sessment of criticism's irrelevance by pointing out that players in this market do not simply ignore critics, they actively avoid them: "a new nexus of dealers, collectors, and curators... [usually deem critics] an obstruction, and many managers of art now actively shun them, as do many artists."

Canadian critics, while facing no threat of removal by market forces (the contemporary art market in Canada is too small for that), do have to contend with being obscure. Yet, as elsewhere, Canada has no lack of magazines and gallery publications.

But the fees paid by these small publications, even for those writers that also receive Canada Council independent critics' grants, do not constitute a living. As a result, academia has become a definite alternative for some of Canada's best critics, including Dan Adler and Dot Tuer.

When I asked American critic Dave Hickey
what he thought was wrong with the state of
art criticism, he stressed its academicization.
"I think it's over... Academics will continue to
publish in academically funded publications,
invented so they might publish and not perish,
but no one will read them. I haven't read
an academic piece for years, and I used to do
so assiduously." Certainly, if one of the leading
critics internationally is not reading academic
criticism, academic criticism is rarely read.

Though academia is clearly failing to produce relevant criticism, critics have few other options. One possibility is curating—an increasingly popular option, not only because of the pay and security but also because curators have considerably more influence than critics. Nicolas Bourriaud best represents the transition of the critic to curator, as evidenced by his touchstone relational aesthetics essays of the 90s, to his co-directorship of the Palais de Tokyo between I999 and 2006, to his recent curation of international surveys including the Lyon Biennial 2007 and the upcoming Tate Triennial 2009. With the biennale count ever rising, art critics are falling further behind Bourriaud, and curators like Hans Ulrich Obrist, Chus Martinez, Robert Storr and Adriano Pedrosa, on the international circuit.

If the serious theoretical art critic and the influential groundbreaking art critic are anachronisms, can newspaper and magazine critics exploit this void? While many critics writing in large-circulation, mainstream publications dilute their rhetoric for non-art readers, critics from Baudelaire to Kenneth Baker, the long-practicing critic for the San Francisco Chronicle, have written important criticism for the general public.

Nevertheless, newspaper criticism overall is plagued by a failure to evaluate, as highlighted by a Columbia University National Arts Journalism Programme survey of 230 American art critics employed by the country's largest-circulation publications. The survey found that, of all their priorities, critics place the least emphasis on judgment while they place the most on description.

Similarly, with theory now cloistered, contributors to many art magazines, especially the glossiest ones, overemphasize description, concluding with a vague assessment of the artist's approach (e.g., "Bernstein follows her heart, especially when that heart is pissed off".

What's worse is this assessment is often penned in pseudo-hipster speak that may also be peppered with bogus neologisms such as "sci-fi historicism" symptomatic of a perpetual quest for something new to satisfy an art market suffering from information-age ADD.

American critic Carter Ratcliff offers a telling account of this tendency: "At most, the audience for art theory is adolescent, panting to keep up with new wrinkles in the orthodoxy as if they were fads manufactured by the entertainment industry.

And that is what they are... art theorists have found themselves as purveyors of high-end consumer goods." While I would be quicker to blame the writer than the audience, Ratcliff's lament provides an explanation for the mystery behind why the voguishly empty works of Vanessa Beecroft or the frat-boy humour of Maurizio Cattelan receive lavish attention in the art press.

Without a return to theoretical rigour and evaluative criticism, the critic will become irrelevant. However, this return is a tall order because the seeds of criticism's irrelevancy were sown in the 60s, when the Modernist criterion of "quality" was replaced with Judd's criterion of "interesting" and followed by a complete abandonment of the criterion of judgment in the Conceptual era.

While I am not advocating a return to judgment of aesthetic quality, I would propose the adoption of simple criteria, such as whether work provides a new way of looking at things more lasting than flavour-of-the-month novelty.

Likewise, Eleanor Hearmey suggests that her fellow art critics should be asking, "Can art today be anything more than just another entertainment option...? The task at hand is to produce challenging criticism that evaluates rather than neutrally introduces whatever new work is on the market. But certainly, with critics removed from the market, they are in the position to do this.

Art critics' lack of power may be a good thing, but they nevertheless need to retain some audience, which will require accepting the onus to improve their craft. Indeed, many occasional contributors to art magazines come from a literary discipline of some kind, and writers like Dave Hickey mix narrative and fiction to lively effect.

Yet most art magazines have difficulty finding regular contributors with writing skills beyond the grad-school level, so discerning art readers will continue to flip past sophomoric and soporific writing, emblematized by the following edit-worthy citations chosen randomly from periodicals lying around my house: Rosina Cazali's redundant lead in Flash Art, "Doubt constitutes a state of uncertainty;" Gary Michael

Dault's use of excessive alliteration in the Globe and Mail—think high school poetry contest—to show that New York-based artist Ryan McGinness' painting "can take its place in the sublimity sweepstakes beside big, black sepulchral paintings by Ad Reinhardt and Mark Rothko."

At the very least, critics should aim for the elimination of superfluous diction and content and, upon achieving that, they should seek the attainment of a rhythmic flow, a varied sentence structure, an only-if-necessary use of passive voice, and appropriate unmixed metaphor.

Another practical solution is to pay art critics more so that they can focus solely on criticism. At present, criticism is one of the lowest paying of all the visual arts offshoot fields—and that is a remarkable statement.

Non-journalistic critics are paid even less, if at all. Without fair pay for writing, the only choice is academia or another form of income support that stands to interfere with a writer's time and ability to cultivate ideas.

Yet as long as the "A-list" art magazines and daily newspapers favour ad sales over quality writing in this currently bullish art market, the situation will not change. While smaller, less commercial art magazines will never have the money to pay well, international art glossies such as Artforum and Flash Art need to take initiative. (One exception is the much thinner Contemporary, which despite its lack of ads, pays writers' fees at a rate comparable with large-circulation magazines.)

The formula is Grade I basic: if publications pay more, art critics will write better.

From superficiality and obscurity to poor
writing and low wages, art criticism has a long
way to go to regain credence and an audience.
Just the same, projects like the October roundtable
and Critical Mess are a tremendous start.
I share Buchloh's desire "to read criticism that
reflects on the current difficulties of writing
criticism and makes these one of its subjects."
There is no shortage of this kind of criticism.

After all, if one is writing through the "filter"
of the current tendencies threatening art criticism,
it is important to also address and, at
times, reassess these conditions. Even if the crisis
facing art criticism remains unsolved, assessing
what is wrong with it is a lively topic,
which will, if nothing else, stand as a sobre document
of this zeitgeist of diluted rigour and
record-breaking auction prices.

Chapter 8

The Relationship between Art and Life in Oscar Wilde's An Ideal Husband

After Oscar Wilde completed An Ideal Husband, his third drawing-room comedy, he said of it to a friend, the artist Charles Ricketts, "It was written for ridiculous puppets to play, and the critics will say, 'Ah, here is Oscar unlike himself!—' though in reality I became engrossed in writing it, and it contains a great deal of the real Oscar" (Ellmann 410). A careful reading of An Ideal Husband confirms this remark. It is a truism that every writer puts something of himself into everything he writes, but frequently it can be risky to try to determine which elements of a literary work come from the writer's psychology and personal experience and which elements are created mostly from his imagination.

In the case of Oscar Wilde, though imagination certainly plays a large role in his work, it is sometimes possible to link elements in it to his personal conflicts. Of all his drawing-room comedies, An Ideal Husband seems to have the most obvious link to the events of his life at the time of its creation, so much so that Rodney Shewan has described the plight of the Chilterns, the political couple who are the play's central characters, as identical to "the plight of the Wildes of Tite Street".

The similarity remarked on by Shewan is at first glance not apparent to the casual reader or playgoer. Like other literary works that reflect events in their creators' lives, the central situation in An Ideal Husband—the husband's fear that an old political misdeed that he had committed will be revealed—is only a transposition into more acceptable terms of Wilde's own trepidation about his secret homosexual life. Such transpositions in a writer's work of personal issues into something similar but less personal usually allow the writer to examine those issues more objectively, often finding discoveries and insights that he might otherwise not have.

In the case of An Ideal Husband, the appropriation of what was then a popular dramatic theme—the theme of the politician facing disgrace—allowed Wilde to deal with his guilt concerning his neglect of his wife, Constance, in favour of his young lover, Lord Alfred Douglas, and the rentboys both frequented. Most plays on the same subject had the politician appease public morality by resigning at the end; that Wilde does not have his main character, Sir Robert Chiltern, do the same shows, in my opinion, both his desire to continue with his double life and to retain the love of his wife in spite of it.

Kerry Powell in his book Oscar Wilde and the theatre of the 1890s notes that political plays of the time such as Arthur Wing Pinero's The Cabinet Minister (1890) reflected an ongoing debate about the different standards of conduct for the sexes and whether this ought to be resolved by eliminating notions of womanly "virtue," or by applying the same restrictive standards to men.

The advocates of doing the latter were not concerned only with male sexual conduct, but also with more general issues, in particular what they saw as the male misuse of power, both personal and political. Plays on the subject like Pinero's typically presented a husband who, while being idolized by his wife for his supposed virtue and honesty, is in fact hiding a past or present misdeed from her.

The dramatic tension resulting from the danger that he will be found out is typically resolved, as noted above, by the husband's withdrawal from public life, masculine waywardness thus coming under the control of the feminine virtue symbolized by the wife. In some of those plays, such as Sydney Grundy's A Bunch of Violets (1894) the husband pays for his misdeeds even more dearly by committing suicide, a device ironically reflecting traditional notions of what should befall an erring woman.

The motif of the erring husband can be seen as an attempt by the mostly male playwrights of the time to resolve the debate about male virtue in a way that accommodated those asking for a single standard while not displeasing more traditional playgoers. As Powell points out, Wilde's originality in adapting the same theme is to subvert the audience's expectations by having his erring husband consider retirement only to reject the idea, choosing instead to remain in public life and take the Cabinet post which has been offered to him. In doing so, Wilde was not only making an ironic comment on public morality but also offering a psychologically astute observation on the necessity of moral compromise from the standpoint of a man who had long had to perform a similar balancing act in his own life.

In this context even the play's title carries ironic implications, for the perfection Lady Chiltern expects from her husband is not humanly possible. Wilde extends the note of irony to the name of his main character: traditionally, the term "taking the Chiltern Hundreds" meant a politician had decided to resign. (Since British Parliament members technically cannot resign, certain Crown lands, called the "Chiltern Hundreds" are reserved for the nominal stewardship of members who are compelled to leave; after their release the lands are returned to the Crown for the next disgraced member to make use of).

The circumstances of his life during the time he composed An Ideal Husband suggested that Wilde was well aware of those ironies. He was into the second year of his affair with Douglas and was beginning to feel the strain of both Douglas's emotional instability and financial extravagance and of the ongoing quarrel between Douglas and his father, the Marquess of Queensberry, a quarrel in which Wilde found himself increasingly embroiled and which eventually would prove to be his undoing. An anecdote from the summer of 1893, when Wilde was beginning the play, illustrates the sense of unease he felt. At the time he was staying with Douglas at a summer house in Goring-on-Thames and entertaining a number of visitors, one of them being the young poet Theodore Wratislaw, who later recorded Wilde's words when, during a walk in the woods, the two men came to a blind turn in the path they were following.

Wilde stopped and said, "There! That is as far as I ever wish to see in life. Let me be satisfied with what I can see. I do not want to know what lies beyond the turning a few paces ahead" (qtd. in Ellmann 401). The anxiety Wilde clearly felt undoubtedly worked its way into the play, and despite the stagy conventions and stock situations on which the play is based, gives it much of its emotional force.

An analysis of the play, its events and structure, will illustrate both its relevance to the events in its creator's life and the differences between those events and those in the play, which are also telling. Sir Robert Chiltern, a wealthy, up-and-coming politician who has already attained the position of Under-Secretary for Foreign Affairs, finds this position threatened when Mrs. Cheveley, a notorious adventuress, uses her knowledge that Chiltern once sold a state secret to compel him to support a fraudulent canal scheme in which she has invested.

Chiltern knows that if the truth is revealed he risks losing the love of his wife, Gertrude (like Wilde's own wife, an active feminist), since it is based on her idea of him as the "ideal husband" of the title. Curiously, the Chilterns are described as being childless, unlike the Wildes, who in real life had two sons.

The plight of the fictional couple is thus freed from the complications that would ensue when scandal overtook Wilde and his family, and his wife and children, along with Wilde himself, were made to suffer for his sins. The absence of children is of course not the only difference between the Wildes and the Chilterns; the difference between Chiltern's public misdeed and the private homosexual transgressions of Wilde, which according to Victorian morality were literally unspeakable, has already been noted. Also notable is the fact that Chiltern's secret involves a single act that took place well in the past, before he married; except for that he really is the upstanding husband and public figure he appears to be.

Wilde, on the other hand, had to deal with an ongoing secret life that he could not reveal to his wife, but that had corroded the fabric of what had once seemed a happy marriage, to the extent that the two had become largely estranged even before the scandal that would destroy it. The problems the Chilterns face are thus a simplified and stylized version of the real-life dilemma Wilde was grappling with—a theoretical model, so to speak, which allowed Wilde to express his feelings and attitudes concerning trust in marriage.

The action of the play is compressed into twenty-four hours, during which time Chiltern is threatened by Mrs. Cheveley, is rejected by his wife when she discovers his secret, and finally is accepted by her again after she is persuaded to do so by Chiltern's friend, Lord Goring. The introductory description of Chiltern in the stage directions in the published version of the play, revised by Wilde after his release from prison, revealingly alludes to the "almost complete separation of passion and intellect" in his face.

It is tempting to connect this apparent proof of Chiltern's repression of his less socialized self to Wilde's belated realization of the similar split between his respectable roles as paterfamilias and literary lion and his secret sexual life. During the conversation later on in the first act between Chiltern and Mrs. Cheveley, who has accompanied another character, Lady Markby, to a party at the former's house, she reveals the fact that she and Chiltern have a common acquaintance, Baron Arhneim.

Baron Arhneim, it turns out, is the person to whom Chiltern, at the beginning of his career, sold information about the government's involvement in the Suez Canal project; his profit from this single dishonest act allowed Chiltern to set himself up in Parliament and established his later success. Mrs. Cheveley informs Chiltern that she has learned of this act and tells him she will expose him if he does not back her own scheme.

During her argument, she makes an astute comment about

the standards of public morality of the time: "Remember to what a point your Puritanism in England has brought you.... Scandals used to lend charm, or at least interest, to a man—now they crush him. And yours is a very nasty scandal. You couldn't survive it.... Sooner or later we have all to pay for what we do" (495-496). She goes on to predict what might happen if Chiltern's misdeed were leaked to the press in terms eerily prescient of what would in fact befall the playwright:

... Suppose that when I leave this house I drive down to some newspaper office, and give them this scandal and the proofs of it. Think of their loathsome joy, of the delight they would have in dragging you down, of the mud and mire they would plunge you in. Think of the hypocrite with his greasy smile penning his leading article, and arranging the foulness of the public placard.

Chiltern, understandably horrified by this picture, agrees to Mrs. Cheveley's terms. Later, in Act Two, he tells Lord Goring (who has warned him that "no man should, have a secret from his own wife. She invariably finds it out") about the circumstances surrounding his misdeed and the forces that had compelled him to commit it. He describes his meeting with Baron Arhneim at the latter's house in terms that seem curiously emotionally charged:

I remember so well how, with a strange smile on his pale, curved lips, he led me through his wonderful picture gallery, showed me his tapestries, his enamels, his jewels, his carved ivories, made me wonder at the strange loveliness of the luxury in which he lived; and then told me that luxury was nothing but a background, a painted scene in ca play, and that power, power over other men, power over the world, was the one thing worth having, the one supreme pleasure worth knowing, the one joy one never tired of, and that in our century only the rich possessed it.

Chiltern's account, phrased in the exotic language of Wilde's novel Dorian Gray, sounds more like a seduction than anything else; like Dorian Gray, the young, naive Chiltern, was initiated into forbidden pleasures by the older, more knowledgeable one, a process that made his eventual capitulation to the Baron's request for information inevitable. It is perhaps relevant at this point to note that in late-Victorian England the word strange, used twice by Wilde in the foregoing passage to describe the Baron and his way of life, often had homosexual overtones. Thus initiated by the Baron, Chiltern in his turn can enjoy the privileges that only money and rank can buy, privileges that Wilde in his own private life tried to buy with the literary fame and success he had craved—as he bought boys with silver watches and cigarette cases—learning too late that immunity from public judgment was reserved only for those born to privilege. Through Chiltern, Wilde unconsciously anticipates experience, and he also acknowledges in another speech of Chiltern's to Lord Goring his hidden conflicts in deciding to follow his desires:

> I tell you that there are terrible temptations that it requires strength, strength and courage, to yield to. To stake all one's life on a single moment, to risk everything on one throw, whether the stake be power or pleasure, I care not—there is no weakness in that. There is a horrible, a terrible courage.

Immediately after he counsels Chiltern to tell his secret to his wife, Lord Goring remarks, "Women have a wonderful instinct about things. They can discover everything except the obvious." Especially after he became involved with Lord Alfred Douglas, Wilde's conduct was increasingly reckless and obvious, but it is uncertain how much of the truth his wife suspected before the trials.

As noted earlier, husband and wife, who had been close and loving in the marriage's first years, had become increasingly estranged to the extent that Wilde had virtually moved out of the house living instead in a succession of hotel rooms and rented lodgings, ostensibly for privacy in his work, but really so that he could entertain Douglas and his other young companions.

By 1893, the year in which Wilde began An Ideal Husband, he and Constance had grown so far apart that one day when she arrived at the hotel where he was staying with Douglas (in a room with one double bed) to give him his mail and to ask him when he was coming home, he pretended to have forgotten the house number (Ellmann 394). This uncharacteristically cruel behavior on his part might have been inspired by guilt at his neglect of Constance.

After Sir Robert Chiltern upbraids his wife for rejecting him when she finds out the truth about him, he admits to Lord Goring, "I was brutal to her this evening. But I suppose when sinners talk to saints they are brutal always". Constance's own high morality, as well as her loyalty to her husband—which lasted until after his release from prison—must have made Wilde feel extremely guilty at times, causing him to attack her in much the same way that Chiltern attacks Gertrude.

What he could not admit in private, though, he put in his play, the observations of which about honesty in marriage were evidentally very important to him. When asked in an interview which point in the play he thought the critics had missed, he identified it as "the difference in the way in which a man loves a woman from that in which a woman loves a man"—that is, the ideal a wife has of her husband contrasted with "the weakness of a man who dares not show his imperfections to the thing he loves" (Mikhail 241). He described this point as comprising the "entire psychology" of the play (Burgess 241).

Chiltern's speech to Gertrude at the end of the second act is a plea for understanding, written by a man who knew he could not expect that from his own wife if she knew the truth about him: "Why can't you women love us, faults and all?... We have all feet of clay, women as well as men.... It is not the perfect, but the imperfect, who have need of love". He goes on to say, "You made your false idol of me, and I had not the courage to come down, show you my wounds, tell you my weaknesses".

Chiltern's speech is as much about Wilde's "inner torment," as E. H. Mikhail puts it, as it is about the now long-forgotten debate about male virtue. It is here that the irony of the play's title is underlined: like Chiltern, Wilde had to play the role in his public and family life of a person who in fact did not really exist, hiding his true self.

Up to a point Chiltern's dilemma closely resembles that of his creator. Wilde, however, is able to achieve in fiction what he could not in real life, allowing his politician at the end of the play to keep both his family and his career, after he has come perilously close to losing them. The incriminating letter that Mrs. Cheveley has in her possession, which forms the basis of her threat to expose Chiltern, is destroyed by Lord Goring—luckily for Chiltern, who has gone ahead and condemned her financial scheme in Parliament in defiance of her threat.

Though he considers resigning anyway, in the play's final scene he is dissuaded by his wife, who has been persuaded by Lord Goring that to do so would be playing into the hands of the moralists, and that Chiltern should be allowed to fulfill his ambitions. The speech in which he does so has attracted a fair deal of comment—much of it negative, since in it Wilde, in contradiction to the feminist statements he had made earlier in his career, has Goring make assertions about the roles of the sexes that were retrograde even in the 1890s:

> Women are not meant to judge US, but to forgive us when we need forgiveness. Pardon, not punishment, is their mission. Why should you scourge him with rods for a sin done in his youth, before he knew you, before he knew himself? A man's life is of more value than a woman's. It has larger issues, wider scope, greater ambitions. A woman's life revolves in curves of emotion. It is upon lines of intellect that a man's life progresses. Don't make any terrible mistake, Lady Chiltern. A woman who can keep a man's love, and love him in return, has done all the world wants of women, or should want of them.

Kerry Powell has suggested that this speech reflects Wilde's desire to oppose feminist demands that men reform to suit them with a "new masculinism" even if it meant having to assert old Victorian ideas about the separate spheres of the sexes. I believe that the impetus behind Goring's statement goes even deeper and is rooted in Wilde's experience as a homosexual man in the late nineteenth century, participating in both the visible heterosexual world and a secret, all-male world where women could not go and therefore could never fully understand. In this context, the political world in which Chiltern operates, also all-male in that time, may be a transposition into licit terms of Wilde's illicit homosexual world. Interpreted in this way, Goring's speech becomes a caution to Gertrude not to condemn or meddle in things she cannot understand as a woman; she can only accept them—and her husband—as they are. Gertrude's subsequent speech to her husband, though it is rendered not as convincingly as it might have been by her rote repetition of Goring's words, shows she has absorbed this lesson.

In doing so, she shows considerable courage, more than her husband has shown in fearing to expose himself to his wife. The new relationship between the spouses, based on a honest awareness of each other's faults and virtues, rather than false ideas, is illustrated in the play's last few lines:

LADY CHILTERN (leaning over the back of the chair): Aren't you coming in, Robert?

SIR ROBERT CHILTERN (taking her hand): Gertrude, is it love you feel for me, or is it pity merely?

LADY CHILTERN (kisses him): It is love, Robert. Love; and only love. For both of us a new life is beginning.

It is instructive to compare the Chiltern's fictional reconciliation with the estrangement in the Wilde's marriage, where such a "new life" was evidently not possible. Constance would not fully learn the truth about her husband until public scandal forced it on her.

To her credit, she displayed remarkable loyalty toward Wilde, who may have felt he did not deserve it. Even after family advisers had finally persuaded her to break with him emotionally if not legally, she forgave him. Constance's plight resembled that of the wife in another play Wilde planned and started to write but never finished, which also showed his understanding of their marriage. It is not clear when Wilde wrote the manuscript which he entitled "A Wife's Tragedy"; it might have been any time from the mid-eighties to the early nineties, the period when he wrote most of his plays. The play—what there is of it—portrays the disintegration of the marriage of Gerald and Nellie Lovel, a young couple living in

Venice. Gerald, a self-centered poet, is carrying on an affair with a European countess; when a visiting friend, Lord Mertoun, reproaches him for his neglect of Nellie, he retorts that he loves her.

When Mertoun says, "'You don't show it,'" Gerald replies, "'It's very vulgar to show one's love for one's wife'" (Mikhail 99). During a later scene between Nellie and Mertoun, she remarks in words that might have been Constance's, "'... my husband has lost all love for me. We stand apart. But I cannot leave him. It is my duty to remain'".

Despite this sense of duty, she finally decides to leave with Mertoun, who has declared his love for her, and lashes out at Gerald: "'Why should I wreck my life for you? You always think only of yourself'". The fragment ends with Gerald, by now abandoned by both Nellie and the Countess, longing for the wife whom he has lost.

The two plays, An Ideal Husband and the "Wife's Tragedy" fragment, thus illustrate the two contrasting scenarios in Wilde's mind when he imagined telling Constance the truth: either acceptance and reconciliation, or complete rejection.

"Ah, that is the great thing, to live the truth", Chiltern declares to Lord Goring after his confession to him, but the risks of "living the truth" were too great in Wilde's case for him to be able to consider it. Nevertheless, he was conscious of a regret that this was so, a regret that was connected to his understanding of the rift between him and Constance and the disadvantage her loyalty to him gave her in the face of his comparative indifference. "Loveless marriages are horrible," he has Chiltern say toward the end of An Meal Husband:

But there is one thing worse than an absolutely loveless marriage. A marriage in which there is love, but on one side only; faith, but on one side only; devotion, but on one side only and in which of the two hearts one is sure to be broken.

Constance' s heart may have been broken by her marriage to a man no longer able to give her the love she needed, but in her continuing affection for him, Oscar Wilde was perhaps luckier than he knew.

Chapter 9

The Ends of Satire in A Handful of Dust

One must have a heart of stone to read the death of Little Nell without laughing.

- Oscar Wilde

Wallace Stevens wrote that death is the mother of beauty, but for Evelyn Waugh death more often gives birth to comedy. In Decline and Fall, a schoolboy is killed by a stray bullet from a track official's misfired pistol. In Vile Bodies, a gossip columnist puts his head in an oven when he can no longer get into the right parties. In Black Mischief, the hero unwittingly consumes the stewed body of his lover during an African emperor's funeral rites. Such a casual acceptance of violent and untimely death has become an emblem of Waugh's sensibility, the signal characteristic of his dark humour. In Waugh's fiction, life is nasty, British, and short.

With an ambivalence characteristic of Waugh's critics, Conor Cruise O'Brien has called this apparent indifference to death a "schoolboy delight in cruelty", distancing himself morally and emotionally from Waugh's delight while still praising the author's peculiar talents. O'Brien discerns, even as he reproduces, a discrepancy in the fiction between ethics and pleasure, a gap that some theorists have argued is endemic to satire itself, which assumes a moral stance in defence of traditional, communal values, but exults in the representation of the vice and folly it excoriates.

As Michael Seidel has put it, despite his "curative, meliorative, or restorative role," the satirist is inevitably "implicated in the debasing form of his action". In order to clean up, you have to get dirty.

If Waugh's fiction offers a useful case study in the paradoxes of satire, it is equally valuable for the questions it opens in understanding modernism. For Waugh's attitudes toward both modernism and modernity more generally are similarly vexed. As George McCartney has written: "Waugh's response to the modern was marked by certain fruitful ambivalence. In his official pose he was the curmudgeon who despised innovation, but the anarchic artist in him frequently delighted in its formal and thematic possibilities" (Roaring 3).

Although Waugh later in life repeatedly denounced modernist formal experimentation, his early fiction nonetheless came to embody a modern sensibility in its apparent rejection of the novel's traditional ethical obligations. Even in matters of form, he didn't consider himself a traditionalist, but rather grouped himself with writers such as Firbank and Hemingway who deployed what Waugh sometimes called, following Wyndham Lewis, an "external method." Indeed, in Waugh, the satiric and the modern often look very much alike; while the author may claim to satirize a decadent modernity, the disruptive mechanism of his satire fosters the very modern decadence he decries.

A Handful of Dust brings to the fore this tension between Waugh's implicitly reformative, conservative impulse and his subversive and thoroughly modern-if not precisely modernist-enjoyment of the aesthetic possibilities of cruelty. The novel is the story of Tony Last, an English aristocrat thoroughly devoted to his family estate, Hetton, and to the unchanging routines that the decaying neo-Gothic country house embodies.

It tells of the dissolution of Tony's family, his beliefs, in a sense his entire world. But the novel also tells the story of the dissolution of satire; in it Waugh both thematizes and enacts the breakdown of the comic-ironic sensibility that characterizes his early work. Understanding this breakdown, in fact, can explain a longstanding and unresolved critical conundrum-the abrupt tonal shift of the novel's concluding chapters, which modulate away from the comic into the mode Freud called the uncanny. What I argue in the following pages, in short, is that in A Handful of Dust Waugh pushes his satire to such limits that it must take another form.

Early in the novel, Waugh gives his readers a kind of object lesson in the ethics of comedy. While Tony and his young son, John Andrew, walk to church, John tells his father a story he has heard from the stable manager Ben about a mule named Peppermint "who had drunk his company's rum ration" in the First World War and subsequently died. Tony finds the story "very sad", but John Andrew responds: "Well I thought it was sad too, but it isn't. Ben said it made him laugh fit to bust his pants".

What seems important here is not merely the difference in the men's reactions-Ben finds comedy where Tony finds pathos-but the hierarchy among them. If Waugh is joking about the simplicity of John's logic, he is also using the boy to comment critically on Tony's easy sympathy for a long-dead mule. John's acceptance of Ben as the authority in such aesthetic judgments, in other words, indicates not only Tony's parental neglect (Drewry 6)-a failure to instill in his son the values of his social class-but also the outmoded nature of those very values. Waugh expects his readers to understand that, in this case at least, a cruel reaction trumps a sympathetic one.

Like the death of Little Nell for Oscar Wilde, the death of Peppermint for Waugh forces a choice between laughter and tears. Wilde presumably laughs at Dickens's literary treatment of the death of Nell, his manipulation of his readers' emotions, not the child's death per se. (Little Nell, being fictional, has no death per se.) By laughing, and boasting about his laughter, Wilde rejects the entire system of values embedded in Dickens's novel and the culture from which it springs. Thus Lionel Trilling claims that Wilde's target is not merely "insincerity" (claiming virtuous feelings one does not experience), but the Victorian value of sincerity itself-the obedience to the social code that demands these virtuous feelings. Quoting another of Wilde's famous maxims-"all bad poetry springs from genuine feeling" (qtd. in Trilling 119)-

Trilling takes Wilde's oppositional attitude to imply "that the direct conscious confrontation of experience and the direct public expression of it do not necessarily yield the truth and indeed that they are likely to pervert it". Feeling not only fails to guarantee aesthetic quality, but becomes itself the very object of Wilde's suspicion.

This suspicion of the authority of feeling situates Wilde as an important precursor to Waugh and a key figure in an influential strain of modernism. Wilde has become, Eve Kosofsky Sedgwick notes, "the very embodiment of... a modernist antisentimentality", and it is this specific flaw of sentimentality that modernist aesthetics after Wilde-as articulated by writers ranging from D. H. Lawrence and T. S. Eliot to Flannery O'Connor and James Baldwin-often sought vigorously to repudiate. (Indeed, with the recent re-estimation of popular sentimental modes of literature, modernism, or a convenient idea of it, has suffered among critics for this repudiation.) 1 will return to the troublesome, even paradoxical, problem of delimiting the sentimental as an aesthetic category; my point for now is that the shift Trilling describes away from sincerity-and toward a more elusive standard he calls "authenticity"-corresponds to, and even compels, a shift in the meaning of the word sentimental from positive overtones of sensitivity and compassion toward negative connotations of excess, falseness, and laxity.

The loss of faith in emotion as a guarantee of moral or aesthetic value thus generates a very powerful idea of what it is to be modern. If we understand "modernism" less as a school or movement (as the "ism" invariably suggests) than as a sensibility-the more colloquial sense of "the modern"-then the term becomes a synonym, or near-synonym, for words such as sophistication, urbanity, refinement, even aloofness.

The value that antisentimental writers like Wilde and Waugh placed on qualities such as wit and even ethical indifference becomes a sign not merely of cultural distinction but of a deep skepticism toward inherited ideas of what it means to know and feel.

Placed in this theoretical context, A Handful of Dust

becomes a much more significant novel for understanding modernism than its somewhat orthodox formal surface might suggest. Ben's laughter at the death of Peppermint can now be understood as a refusal to let the kind of "genuine feelings" that Wilde scorns deprive the mule's rum binge of its inherent comedy, a rejection of Tony's reflexive sentimentality. Indeed, Ben's laughter is only one of many instances in the novel that bring to the fore a case of suffering only to undercut or move past the ostensible sympathy the situation appears to elicit. Take the very first words of the book:

"Was anyone hurt?"

"No one I am thankful to say," said Mrs. Beaver, "except two housemaids who lost their heads and jumped through a glass roof into the paved court. They were in no danger. The fire never properly reached the bedrooms I am afraid. Still they are bound to need doing up, everything black with smoke and drenched in water and luckily they had that old-fashioned sort of extinguisher that ruins everything." (3; Waugh's emphasis)

Before we even know the topic of conversation, we hear an apparent expression of compassion that provokes a deceptively complex response. Mrs. Beaver voices sympathy for the victims of the fire but her concern is immediately revealed as insubstantial, since she cares only for those of her own class. The injured (or dead?) housemaids are an afterthought; Mrs. Beaver implicitly dismisses their fates as deserved, since their injuries resulted from foolish panic. The reader, moreover, makes a second correction in understanding Mrs. Beaver's initial sentence.

When she says the maids "lost their heads," the reader, still unaware of the fire, can easily take this phrase literally. How indifferent is Mrs. Beaver to the maids' suffering? Cold-hearted enough to dismiss their decapitation? And even when we learn that they "lost their heads" in only a figurative sense, we never discover the women's ultimate fates. Did they survive? How badly were they injured? Was anyone hurt? Mrs. Beaver moves onto her true concern, the property damage that her business can financially exploit.

Mrs. Beaver's initial concern with human suffering is

revealed as mere conversational reflex, or idle curiosity, soon forgotten. The novel, to be sure, does not cultivate our sadism toward the housemaids; if anything, Mrs. Beaver's cava lier treatment of them arouses a little sympathy. Yet the narrative seems content to let the Beavers' conversation unfold and to leave the residual question of the housemaids unaddressed. Instead, we laugh at the virtual nakedness of Mrs. Beaver's greed, or the shabbiness of her effort to cloak this greed in false compassion.

The novel's concern is less with who is hurt, or how badly, as with how some people respond when others are hurt. This book is not about the housemaids or about Peppermint the mule, but about our responses to their fates.

A Handful of Dust is full of such small avoidances. Jenny Abdul-Akbar, the former wife of a Moroccan prince, bears "the most terrible scars" from her husband's abuse but comes off as a comic figure, absurdly eager to confess the details of her "frightful nightmare" to near-strangers. The prostitute Milly is absolutely blase when telling Tony about the circumstances that led to the birth of her daughter: "I was only sixteen when I had her. I was the youngest of the family and our stepfather wouldn't leave any of us girls alone. That's why I have to work for a living".

When Brenda reads to Tony from the morning papers, her disengaged chatter runs together nightmarish grotesqueries and social gossip:

Reggie's been making another speech... There's such an extraordinary picture of Babe and Jock...a woman in America has had twins by two different husbands. Would you have thought that possible?... Two more chaps in gas ovens...a little girl has been strangled in a cemetery with a bootlace... that play we went to about a farm is coming off.

In all three of these cases abuse or murder remains a mild disruption on the surface of the text, troubling a reader briefly but remaining infused with the comic-ironic tone that pervades the novel. If the novel does hold any sympathy for the suffering of Jenny, Milly, or the girl in the cemetery, it refuses to make a direct plea for compassion. Such a plea, presumably, would only give way to something resembling Tony's naive and sentimental affection for a mule poisoned by rum. Instead, the material of "frightful nightmare" (to use Jenny's phrase) is converted, through a kind of emotional alchemy, into social comedy.

Such moments, frequent as they are, may lead the reader to expect a kind of moral failure in Waugh's characters, yet they hardly prepare her for the novel's most shocking instance of a troublesome response to pain-Brenda's reaction to her son's death. (John dies in a hunting accident.) Tony's friend Jock Grant-Menzies travels to London to tell her the news, and when Brenda hears that "John" has died she mistakenly assumes Jock to be speaking of her lover, John Beaver.

When she learns it is her son who has died, she is stunned: "John... John Andrew... I... Oh thank God...". That Brenda feels relief and thanks God that her son has died instead of her obnoxious lover clearly reveals her depravity. Her response to the news-unlike her reaction to the report of the strangled girl-is so shocking that whatever laughter it might provoke is overwhelmed by the revulsion a reader likely experiences. Even more significantly, however, Brenda's reaction validates Mrs. Rattery's earlier comment to Tony that the death might not upset Brenda as much as he fears: "You can't ever tell what's going to hurt people".

Echoing the novel's opening question-or obliquely answering it-Mrs. Rattery's remark intimates not only that Tony's faith in Brenda's decency will lead him astray, but also that in Waugh's universe all human passions are too thickly disguised for others to assess accurately. Waugh's external method does not so much deny the interiority of the self, but rather suggests that it is oddly unknowable, buried beneath layers of social custom and ritualized expression.

Unlike the death of Little Nell, or Lord Tangent in Decline and Fall, or the schoolgirl in the cemetery, John Andrew's is one fictional child's death at which no one can laugh. Yet the comedy manages to proceed. Brenda's friends see the death as gossip for their circle, and Jenny narcissistically blames herself: "O God.... What have I done to deserve it?" The most ridiculous response is that of Brenda's mother, who writes what Brenda calls "a sweet letter":

...I shall not come down to Hetton for the funeral, but I shall be thinking of you both all the time and my dear grandson. I shall think of you as 1 saw you all three, together, at Christmas. Dear children, at a time like this only yourselves can be any help to each other. Love is the only thing that is stronger than sorrow....

The grandmother's cliched expressions of grief, contradicted by her refusal to be inconvenienced by travel, bear no more weight than Mrs. Beaver's professed concern for the victims of the fire. The platitudes of Brenda's mother return us to a world where narrator and reader are both more comfortable: we again laugh at the moral inadequacy of the novel's characters.

Tony, of course, cannot assume the indifference, to the death and to Brenda's affair, that comes so easily to Brenda and her friends; the middle of the novel focuses on the clash between his pain and the nonchalance of those around him. Thus, when Brenda's mother urges Tony to take Brenda back, the reader begins to feel what must be Tony's outrage:

I will tell you exactly how it happened, Tony. Brenda must have felt a tiny bit neglected-people often do at that stage of marriage have known countless cases-and it was naturally flattering to her to find a young man to beg and carry for her. That's all it was, nothing wrong. And then the terrible shock of little John's accident unsettled her and she didn't know what she was saying or writing. You'll both laugh over this little fracas in years to come. (174-75; Waugh's emphasis)

The suggestion that the death (safely euphemized as "little John's accident") and the break-up of the marriage ("this little fracas") might be the subject of laughter is outrageous-an outrageousness remarkable in the work of a novelist who so often displays his own modernity by laughing at death and suffering.

We have arrived at a paradox: Waugh, whose "schoolboy delight in cruelty" seems to owe so much to Wilde's stance of laughing at the death of Little Nell, directs his greatest indignation at the character who trivializes the death of John Andrew and laughs at the subsequent dissolution of his parents' marriage.

Waugh's own attitude toward Wilde embodies this paradox. he repeatedly derided Wilde as a figure of fashion, and described him as "at heart radically sentimental", even though the anti-Dickensian Wilde seems most influential on Waugh in his rejection of sentimental poses. Likewise, the modernity of Brenda and her friends, which, in its delightfully extreme nonchalance, shares much with the indifferent postures of Waugh the satirist, itself becomes subject to the author's ironic inflections. Brenda and her clique transform life into a kind of art to be judged only on aesthetic, not moral, grounds:

[Brenda's] very choice of partner gave the affair an appropriate touch of fantasy; Beaver, the joke figure they had all known and despised, suddenly caught up to her among the luminous clouds of deity. If, after seven years looking neither to right nor left, she had at last broken away with Jock Grant-Menzies or Robin Beasley... it would have been thrilling no doubt, but straightforward, drawing-room comedy. The choice of Beaver raised the whole escapade into a realm of poetry for Polly and Daisy and Angela and all the gang of gossips.

Drawing-room comedy is the genre through which Brenda and her friends usually view their world, a genre populated by "joke figure[s]" such as Beaver. But the invocation of the "realm of poetry" and the "touch of fantasy," echoing Tony's private vocabulary of English Romance, suggests that Brenda's own worldview is also built on fantasy. Brenda's Wildean equanimity may stand in contrast to Tony's more overtly outmoded devotion to a Victorian way of life, but both characters understand the world through a set of aesthetic forms at once grandiose and cliched. Ironic postures of indifference, so often characteristic of Waugh's own narrative tone, become Waugh's target every bit as much as sentimental affectations of feeling.

Those such aggressively antisentimental postures,

whether Wilde's or Brenda's, reveal themselves as susceptible to the charge of sentimentality suggests a larger contradiction within the idea of sentimentality that Sedgwick has discussed at length: the collapse of the distinction "between sentimentality and its denunciation".

Sedgwick notes that accusations of sentimentality tend to expose the accuser to similar charges, according to the logic of "it takes one to know one": "[O]nly those who are themselves prone to these vicariating impulses... are equipped to detect them in the writing or being of others". As a result, merely "to enter into the discourse of sentimentality... is almost inevitably to be caught up in a momentum of... scapegoating attribution" -trying to expose the "real" sentimentalist. Yet that act of exposure is specifically what the paradoxes of the term "sentimental" imply cannot be done, since naming or denouncing a "real" or "closet" sentimentalist only adds one more link to a potentially endless chain.

Waugh, I suggest, runs up against precisely this paradox. His own satiric sensibility, so acute in detecting the sentimental in others-including literary precursors such as Wilde-cultivates readerly sympathy for Tony in a decidedly unsatiric, even sentimental manner; moreover, he indicts those characters whose accents of indifference most closely echo the authorial-narratorial voice itself.

A brief look at Waugh's personal biography might help to make the point. Waugh's biographers have noted that Tony's situation resembles Waugh's own after his first wife (also named Evelyn) left him for a lover. In a letter to Harold Acton, Waugh expressed frustration that friends and relatives urged him not to make too much of the affair:

Everyone is talking so much nonsense on all sides of me about my affairs, that my wits reel. Evelyn's family & mine join in asking me to "forgive" her whatever that may mean...I did not know it was possible to be so miserable & live but I am told that this is a common experience. (Letters 39)

In a letter to Henry Yorke, furthermore, Waugh voiced a desire to find solace in the humorous reactions of others to his plight: "If you hear any amusing opinions about my divorce do tell me. Particularly from the older generation. The Gardner line is that I am very 'unforgiving'" (Letters 40). Finally, a few months later, Waugh again wrote to Yorke:

I have decided that I have gone on for too long in that fog of sentimentality & I am going to stop hiding away from everyone. I was getting into a sort of Charlie Chaplinish Pagliacci attitude to myself as the man with a tragedy in his life and a tender smile for children. (Letters 41)

The parallels are significant: like Tony, Waugh felt pressure to affect a blase sophistication others seemed to possess quite naturally, and, like the narrator of his novel, he shifts attention from the experience of pain to the amusement derived from the responses of others.

Yet the differences between the letters and the novel are equally instructive. Most obviously, the glaring asymmetry that there was no dead son in Waugh's life implies that the author felt he needed a dramatic incident to precipitate the collapse of the Lasts' marriage. Indeed it suggests that Waugh was loading the dice in favour of Tony, manipulating his reader's emotions in a manner worthy of Wilde's Dickens. More subtly, however, Tony never expresses the dissatisfaction with, and persecution by, the responses of others that Waugh articulates in his letters; these feelings are only implied, left for the reader to experience.

Nor does Tony seek solace by mocking those who respond to his fate in "amusing" ways; this too is left to the reader. Finally, Tony never assumes enough self-consciousness to regard his own feeling of victimization as sentimental; in the novel, it is Brenda's piggish brother Reggie who suggests that Tony is merely "taking the line of the injured husband".

In short, the whole range of feelings that Waugh articulated in his letters-anger, self-pity, self-reproach-are in the novel either left implicit or put into the mouths of unreliable characters. This is wholly in keeping with Waugh's adherence to a Lewisian external method that refrains from rendering the interior lives of characters, but it also suggests that certain reactions are suppressed for the sake of the aesthetic demands of the genre.

There is, moreover, an important exception to Waugh's external method in the novel, and it is the ultimate indication of the author's sympathy for Tony that he violates his aesthetic principles in order to render his hero's interior mental state. When Tony is compelled to stage an affair to justify his divorce legally, the madness of his circumstances begins to terrify him:

For a month now he had lived in a world suddenly bereft of order; it was as though the whole reasonable and decent constitution of things, the sum of all he had experienced or learned to expect, were an inconspicuous, inconsiderable object mislaid somewhere on the dressing table; no outrageous circumstance in which he found himself, no new mad thing brought to his notice could add a jot to the all-encompassing chaos that shrieked about his ears.

While the episode at Brighton, in which Tony is forced into increasingly ridiculous behavior, appears farcical to the reader, to Tony it seems "phantasmagoric, and even gruesome". This rift between the comic and the "phantasmagoric" and "gruesome," visible in the narrator's departure from principle in order to enter Tony's mind, points up the limitations of the "drawing-room comedy" genre epitomized by the mock-affair. Waugh explicitly tells us that the events are phantasmagoric and gruesome because the protocols of his method demand that he represent these same events as comic.

However effective Waugh's satire may be as a critique of sentimentality, then, it also appears incapable of rendering certain emotional states. In drawing-room comedy, phantasmagoria will always appear as silly, never gruesome. The problem Waugh's satire faces thus may be the paradigmatic challenge of all literature. Roland Barthes has written:

A friend has just lost someone he loves, and I want to express my sympathy. I proceed to write him a letter. Yet the words I find do not satisfy me: they are "phrases": I make up "phrases" out of the most affectionate part of myself; I then realise that the message I want to send this friend, the message which is my sympathy itself, could after all be reduced to a simple word: condolences. Yet the very purpose of communication is opposed to this, for it would be a cold and consequently inverted message, since what I want to communicate is the very warmth of my sympathy.

I conclude that in order to correct my message (that is, in order for it to be exact), I must not only vary it, but also that this variation must be original and apparently invented. This fatal succession of constraints will be recognized as literature itself.

For Barthes, the aim of literature is not to express the inexpressible, but rather, working with a received, public language, to "unexpress the expressible", to render an essentially banal emotion in an original language. As Trilling put it, genuine feeling juxtaposed with direct expression fails to yield truth. Hence the indirectness of literature, hence the ironic representation of grief.

One could of course dismiss the problem altogether, and dispense with the effort to render grief; to do this might be to realise the theoretical possibilities suggested by Lewis, who insists that "perfect laughter, if there could be such a thing, would be inhuman", or by other champions of modernist abstraction, such as Jose Ortega y Gasset, who urged the "progressive elimination of the human, all too human, elements predominant in romantic and naturalistic production".

But Waugh rejects this option and presses upon his reader the ethical dimension of his characters' struggles. What results is a satiric attack on ironic attitudes-a satire that ceases to look like a satire, a drawing-room comedy that flees the drawing room for the jungle.

Tony's flight to South America in the novel's final chapters, and the fate he meets there, provide a drastic change from the rest of A Handful of Dust, not only in setting but also in tone, even genre. Henry Yorke wrote to Waugh in 1934:

I feel the end is so fantastic that it throws the rest out of proportion. Aren't you mixing two things together? The first part of the book is convincing, a real picture of people one has met.... But then to let Tony be detained by some madman introduces an entirely fresh note and we are with phantasy with a ph at once.

Yorke's complaint, that the story undergoes a tonal shift which destroys the integrity of the novel, has a clear explanation in the genesis of the book. Waugh initially composed and published the episode of Tony at "Chez Todd"-in which Tony is rescued but then held captive by an old man, Mr. Todd, who forces him to read aloud, over and over, the complete works of Dickens-as a free-standing story entitled "The Man Who Liked Dickens"; only later, curious about his character's history, did he write the rest of the novel.

The "fantastic" short story, by this argument, possessed unity on its own, but clashed with the comic-satiric tone of the novel that was appended to it. Waugh, however, insisted to Yorke that the episode was necessary: "[T]he Amazon stuff had to be there. The scheme was a Gothic man in the hands of savages-first Mrs. Beaver etc. then the real ones, finally the silver foxes at Hetton" (Letters 88).

Yet Yorke objected to tonal, not thematic discord; Waugh never answered his complaint. Is it possible, then, to go beyond a merely genetic explanation of this tonal shift? Rather than seeing "mixing two things together" as a flaw resulting from the creative process, might we see the disjunction as essential to the novel?

In calling the final episode "phantasy with a ph," Yorke situates the story within an aesthetic tradition that dwells on the "phantasmagoric" and the "gruesome"-to use the terms from Tony's interior monologue in Brighton. Freud famously called this tradition "the uncanny," and Wolfgang Kayser after him called it "the grotesque." The term "grotesque" has a long history of shifting meanings, but contemporary critics tend to agree in seeing the grotesque as characterized by a duality or ambivalence that goes back to Ruskin's analysis of Venetian gargoyles.

For Ruskin, the grotesque combines "two elements, one ludicrous, the other fearful". In the ludicrous aspect of the grotesque lies its affinities to satire and caricature; in the fearful side, its relation to Freud's uncanny. The conclusion of

Waugh's novel, then, moves from one face of the grotesque to another, from laughter to fear.

"I will show you fear in a handful of dust," wrote T. S. Eliot in the line that gave Waugh his title (Eliot 4), and in this ending the "phantasmagoric" and the "gruesome," the materials of "frightful nightmare," are no longer converted into comedy. Of course, the idea that reading Dickens interminably-a lifetime of reading the death of Little Nell-might be a Dantean punishment indicates that Waugh has not entirely abandoned the comic, and I will return to the comic undertones of these concluding chapters. But the reader's laughter, as Yorke's response attests, becomes increasingly uneasy.

Curiously, criticism of A Handful of Oust has neglected to link the novel's ending with Freud's uncanny, whether because Waugh's readers have obediently followed the author in their distaste for psychoanalysis, or because such concerns have not seemed germane to their efforts to locate in the novel a stable system of moral and religious beliefs.

In the most widely accepted reading, Richard Wasson and others after him have argued that it is a kind of poetic justice that Tony should live out his days endlessly reading the author so deeply associated with the Victorian values that have led him astray.

Without wholly rejecting Wasson's argument, I want to suggest that a psychoanalytic reading can help not only to establish thematic parallels between the two parts of the novel, but also to explain why Waugh's novel breaks out of the confines of the drawing room, literally and figuratively. If, as I have argued, the satiric mode of the opening chapters of the novel stages a failure of feeling, as it relentlessly works to avoid excessive sentiment by allowing reader and narrator to laugh at the moral inadequacy of its characters, these final fantastic chapters reintroduce sentiment, only in an estranged, uncanny guise.

Like both satire and the sentimental, the uncanny as a literary category has been the subject of significant theoretical work. For some years it functioned as a minor buzzword of deconstructive criticism, whose dead authors so often left ghostly traces. Some critics went so far as to identify literature and narrative themselves as uncanny.

But Freud used the term in a much less metaphorical sense; in defending his foray into aesthetics, he defined that field as "the theory of the qualities of feeling" ("Uncanny" 219), and wrote of the uncanny: "It is undoubtedly related to what is frightening-to what arouses dread and horror.... Yet we may expect that a special core of feeling is present which justifies the use of a special conceptual term" ("Uncanny" 219). Freud himself has some trouble describing the feeling further, as his descriptions tend to slide into psychoanalytic explanation of the origins of the feeling. But in his literary discussion he reserves the term for those works-most extensively, E. T. A. Hoffmann's "The Sandman"-that elicit in readers this feeling of anxiety or dread.

Ghost stories, tales of the supernatural, Gothic novels, horror movies, and the like are thus natural, although not necessary, loci of the uncanny. Used in this sense, the uncanny as a generic term complements both the sentimental and the satiric, which I have also discussed in terms of their effects (pity, laughter) on an implied reader.

A brief review of Freud's theory may be useful. For Freud, the experience of the uncanny derives from either the revival of repressed infantile complexes, or the confirmation of surmounted primitive beliefs ("Uncanny" 249).

The category of "infantile complexes" includes such Freudian favourites as the castration complex and "womb-phantasies," while "primitive beliefs"-for example, in animism, magic, or evil spirits-entail a failure to demarcate psychical from material reality. This failure in turn stems from an overvaluation of the power of one's own thoughts, or a projection of those thoughts onto the external world. In short, it is the regression to magical thinking, linked to the childhood of the individual or the species, which induces the feeling of the uncanny. But there is a second condition necessary for the production of the uncanny in fiction, a condition less psychological than narratological. The phenomenon that produces the uncanny must survive the process of "reality-testing," that is, scrutiny to determine whether it is real or illusory.

An author can deliberately create supernatural fictional events that do not stand up to reality-testing (e.g., fairy tales), and therefore do not seem uncanny. By the same token, however, an author can manipulate the reader to believe more fully in the reality of supernatural phenomena than she would in real life by first establishing a reader's faith in the reality of the characters; as a result, fiction can, more easily than life, induce the feeling of the uncanny ("Uncanny" 250). The uncanniness of Waugh's conclusion is thus enhanced by the author's having first created, in Yorke's words, "a real picture of people one has met."

What is it, then, in "Du Cote de Chez Todd" that induces the feeling of the uncanny? Where is the fear in A Handful of Dust? To begin, we might recognize in Tony's exile a variation on the modernist paradigm of the voyage as a return to beginnings. Like Conrad in Heart of Darkness, Waugh uses the barbarism of the wilderness to comment ironically on the savagery of "civilization."

A latter-day Marlow exploring the blank spaces on the map, Tony finds himself at the remotest reaches of European exploration: "The stream which watered [Mr. Todd's land] was not marked on any map". For both authors, too, the journey to the ends of empire is a temporal regression; Marlow explicitly calls his voyage a trip back in time, and Tony returns to a world of animistic belief in which, Todd suggests, there exist magic potions for every purpose, including raising the dead. Even in Waugh's composition of the novel, the tale "began at the end" with the short story about reading Dickens ("Fan-Fare" 303).

In typically modernist fashion, moreover, Tony's regression is psychological as well as anthropological. He travels back to a land of childhood as well as precivilization; geographical dislocation becomes the occasion for, or literalization of, a metaphorical exploration of the self. Deep in the Amazon jungles, Tony finds himself seeking an idealized version of his childhood home.

Spurred by Dr. Messinger's tales, he imagines the City of their quest as "Gothic in character, all vanes and pinnacles, gargoyles, battlements, groining and tracery, pavilions and terraces, a transfigured Hetton". He traverses the ocean in search of the Hetton that eluded him in England. But when Tony finally finds the city of his quest, it is no medieval fantasy, but Mr. Todd's Yeatsian house "of mud and wattle".

In The Uses of Enchantment, Bruno Bettelheim writes that in fairy tales, "the house in the woods and the parental home are the same place, experienced quite differently because of a change in the psychological situation". Positive and negative associations are split between the safe parental home and the dangerous house in the woods in order to organize the ambivalent feelings attached to domesticity and family.

And lest we apply Bettelheim's symbolic code too freely, the text has already pointed us in this direction with its references to Hetton; the hut is indeed "a transfigured Hetton," although not transfigured as Tony imagined. It is a space at once home and not home, familiar and unfamiliar-precisely the terrain that Freud called the unheimlich. For, in Freud's theory, the uncanny is familiar but appears as unfamiliar because our knowledge of it has been repressed: "the prefix 'un' is the token of repression" ("Uncanny" 245).

Tony has traveled from the drawing-room comedy of England, through a jungle of confusion, and emerged into a clearing. This enclosed space is both the unconscious psychic space of childhood and the literary space of "phantasy with a ph."

Discerning the parallels between the stately country home of Hetton and the little house in the jungle makes clear that the two parts of the novel share thematic concerns beyond the rather obvious analogies Waugh himself described between savagery at home and abroad. And while the fear provoked by Tony's powerlessness at the hands of Todd can be understood on a merely psychological plane, a psychoanalytic reading accounts for a number of otherwise peculiar details.

For example, Tony relies on Todd for his daily food; when Tony refuses to read to him, the old man deprives Tony of his supper. Todd provides medicine too, which Tony drinks down like a little boy: '"Nasty medicine/ [Tony] said, and began to cry". Most strikingly, Todd first begins to appear as menacing when he describes his neighbors to Tony: "The Pie-wie women are ugly but very devoted. I have had many. Most of the men and women living in this savannah are my children.

That is why they obey-for that reason and because I have the gun". The little old man's surprising and unsettling sexual potency makes him the father of the whole community around him, and the gun, while offering a joke about the obedience of children, serves as a garish emblem of phallic power. Supplying food and medicine, fathering children, enforcing his will as the law, Todd's behavior makes perfect sense if his hut is understood as a dreamlike, transfigured Hetton and Todd himself as a transfigured father. In the original short story, "The Man Who Liked Dickens," Mr. Todd was called "Mr. McMaster," and Tony turns out to be a prisoner at this master's house just as he for so many years was unable to leave his father's estate.

But in spite of the paternal role that Todd often assumes, much of his behavior fails to fit such a model. Todd is illiterate, infantile, and needy; he demands to be read to like a stubborn child. In fact, it is Todd who explicitly compares Tony to his father: "You read beautifully.... It is almost as though my father were here again". Like a child, Todd habitually strikes a pose of mock-innocence when he knows he is doing wrong. This childlike old man, moreover, constitutes "a unique audience" for Tony to read to, in a passage that is oddly disturbing despite lacking any suggestion of supernaturalism:

The old man sat astride his hammock opposite Tony... following the words, soundlessly, with his lips. Often when a new character was introduced he would say, "Repeat the name, I have forgotten him," or "Yes, yes, I remember her well. She dies, poor woman." he would frequently interrupt with questions.... He laughed loudly at all the jokes and at some passages which did not seem humorous to Tony, asking him to repeat them two or three times; and later at the description of the sufferings of the outcasts in "Tom-all-alones" tears ran down his cheeks into his beard. His comments on the story were usually simple. "I think that Dedlock is a very proud man," or, "Mrs. Jellyby does not take enough care of her children."

The simplicity of Todd's concerns, his unsophisticated diction, his attempt to follow along silently, and, above all, the utter excess of his emotional-indeed sentimental-reactions seem much more appropriate to a young child than to an old man. Thus, if Todd's earlier name, McMaster, suggests his paternal authority, it also might suggest his role as son; like the "un" in unheimlich, the "Mc" in McMaster is "the token of repression," indicating a deeper and more contradictory significance.

Todd, then, with the emotional reactions of a child, but the sexual and punitive power of a father, can be said to represent the son's usurpation of paternal authority; he is Tony's triumphant rival in an oedipal struggle. For Tony's captivity evokes a complex of desires and fears bound up with succession and inheritance, impotence and generativity, usurpation and punishment, which have been latent throughout the novel.

Tony's surname, Last, signals the extinction of his line, and John's death leaves him without an heir. After the death, in fact, Tony tries to convince his adulterous wife that their generativity has not reached its end: "Brenda, sweet, I don't understand. We're both young. Of course we can never forget John. He'll always be our eldest son but...". Brenda doesn't let him finish his sentence. The death and the divorce bring about the end of Tony's procreative life.

The emergence of Mr. Todd in the novel's final episode is then a defamiliarizing, a rendering un-homely, of the family romance already operating among Tony, Brenda, and John Andrew. For young as he may be, John Andrew is a sexual rival of his father, and Waugh's insights into childhood sexuality are wonderfully Freudian. When Brenda, to assuage her own guilt, tries to engineer an affair between Tony and Jenny, it is the son, not the father, who falls for the "Princess": "She's more beautiful than Miss Tendril, even. I think she's the most beautiful lady I've ever seen.... D'you think she'd like to watch me have my bath?" Later, when Jenny says good-night, he is even more forward:

They sat on John's small bed in the night-nursery. he threw the clothes back and crawled out, nestling against Jenny. "Back to bed," she said, "or I shall spank you."

"Would you do it hard? I shouldn't mind. "

"Oh dear," said Brenda.

To recognize the sexual rivalry between Tony and John is to see that it is more than mere coincidence-indeed more than the author's rigging up a joke at Brenda's expense-that John Beaver and John Andrew Last share a first name.

For while John Andrew might be Tony's rival in an intrapsychic struggle, John Beaver is both a secondary and more literal sexual rival.

We have another case of a psychoanalytic "splitting," where the potentially patricidal agent is symbolically divided into a good figure and an evil one, between an innocent victim, John A., and a loathsome perpetrator, John B. Brenda's mistaking one for the other, while manifestly displaying her own misplaced affections, also voices a latent textual desire to kill off the evil rival and spare the good one. In other words, her mistaken conclusion that John Beaver has died summons an alternative situation with which the reader and author would probably be much happier, given their implied sympathy for Tony.

But the psychoanalytic content of Tony's situation is only one source of the uncanny anxiety that Waugh's phantasmagoria produces. For Freud's essay on the uncanny, as Neil Hertz observes, contains an important ambiguity. Hertz notes that Freud wrote "The Uncanny" while he was working out the theory of the repetition compulsion in Beyond the Pleasure Principle and viewed the repetition compulsion as a source of the uncanny.

But, Hertz argues, Freud is not always clear whether it is the content of the repetition or the mere fact of repetition that arouses anxiety; often the former seems trivial in comparison to the latter: "Whatever it is that is repeated-an obsessive ritual, perhaps, or a bit of acting-out in relation to one's analyst-will... feel most compellingly uncanny when it is seen as merely coloring, that is, when it comes to seem most gratuitously rhetorical". Hertz's point is that when involuntary repetition appears uncanny, the particular act that one finds oneself repeating might seem utterly benign-as benign, say, as reading a novel by Dickens.

For in a peculiar way, the triviality, even the silliness of Tony's fate-the fact that it feels like a sick joke-is exactly what makes the scene so disturbing, giving it a power over readers that even Marlow's confrontation with Kurtz no longer quite possesses. Indeed, Todd's demand for reading echoes, a little uncannily, Beyond the Pleasure Principle, where Freud cites the child's desire to hear a familiar story repeated as an example of the repetition compulsion par excellence:

If a child has been told a nice story, he will insist on hearing it over and over again rather than a new one; and he will remorselessly stipulate that the repetition shall be an identical one.

When Mr. Todd articulates a desire for repetition he is every bit as "remorseless":

You see, they are the only books I have ever heard. My father used to read them and then later the black man... and now you. I have heard them all several times by now but I never get tired.

Mr. Todd quite literally is the compulsion to repeat; he forces Tony to read and reread to him, in what has seemed to many readers an endless repetition. As his name would indicate then, Todd is an externalization of Tony's own unconscious death-drive, the drive that gives rise to the repetition compulsion, which Freud describes as "the inertia inherent in organic life" in relation to the instincts that "tend towards the restoration of an earlier state of things" (Beyond 43-44). The novel's title, in fact, while directly invoking The Waste Land, may also, through Eliot, allude to Genesis 3:19. There God announces the mortality of Adam in language that perfectly illustrates the phenomenon of which Freud spoke, the tendency of life to regress to an inorganic state: "Dust thou art, and unto dust shalt thou return." (Lacan makes the same point: "Thanatos... is the reduction to dust".)

As an externalized agent of Tony's own unconscious instinct, Todd/McMaster is Tony's master, the law that "overrides the pleasure principle" (Beyond 24), the law that Tony must obey even as he recognizes the absurdity of such obedience. With the loss of his watch, Tony is stranded in the province of the unconscious, which, as psychoanalytic theory has it, knows no sense of time. Tony's enslavement to the repetition compulsion is thus eternal; any hope of return to England is destroyed.

In this estranged form, Todd's arbitrary exercise of authority very literally assumes the "'daemonic' force" (Beyond 41) that Freud attributes to the repetition compulsion. Of course, before and after Freud, literary works have embodied elements of the unconscious as devils, vampires, evil spirits, or little old men in the jungle. As Hertz notes, the relation between "demonic" and "psychological" explanations of uncanny experience is, in psychoanalytic theory, one of manifest to latent.

Within a given fictional world, there may indeed exist "real" demons or spirits, but their affective power still derives from their psychodynamic origin (Hertz 108,105). Moreover, the idea of the unconscious as demonic reminds us of what Slavoj Zizek, following Lacan, takes to be a central Freudian idea-"the status of the unconscious as radically external". To see ourselves as the puppets of unconscious forces is to realise the automatism of our own selves, the stubborn unconsciousness of the unconscious.

Interestingly, recognizing the automatism of our behavior is also the source of laughter in Bergson's famous theory of the comic as "something mechanical encrusted on the living"; similarly, it is essential to Lewis's externalist prescriptions for satire. The uncanny thus shares this fundamental perception with the comic, and the proximity of the two modes in Waugh's work is no accident. But of course there is a difference. Freud himself, discussing none other than Oscar Wilde, notes that the comic tends to work against the production of uncanny anxiety: "Even a 'real' ghost, as in Oscar Wilde's Canterville Ghost, loses all power of at least arousing gruesome feelings in us as soon as the author begins to amuse himself by being ironical about it and allows liberties to be taken with it" ("Uncanny" 252; Freud's italics). Laughter serves as a corrective force, rescuing us from pure mechanism, whereas the uncanny fails to restore us to ourselves.

In the novel's uncanny conclusion, then, the reader not only confronts the violent psychodynamics underlying the novel's social comedy, but also glimpses the phantasmagoric underside of the novel's disavowal of sentimentality. Sentiment, combated so aggressively in the novel's earlier episodes, returns-and literally with a vengeance. Waugh's use of Dickens thus offers a variation on Wilde's laughter at the death of Nell.

This time around, the sentimentality of the Victorian author induces not laughter but horror; Dickens is not aesthetically laughable, as he was for Wilde, but aesthetically dreadful. For Waugh, the heart of darkness, the savage core of man's being, is revealed to be not brutal barbarism but the sentimental pieties of culture.

Shifting a discussion of modernism away from both the formal/technical and the social/historical questions that have driven so much work in the field, and raising alongside them questions of sensibility and genre, not only situates Waugh much closer to the centre of important trends in Anglo-American modernism, but also suggests the importance of understanding how modernist literature serves to structure and model the ways in which we respond emotionally to the pain of others.

The collapse of Waugh's satire into the uncanny suggests that the efforts of so many modernists to escape the sentimental might necessarily give rise to an undertow in which the claims of feeling reassert themselves, although in negative form. Rather than write off modernist antisentimentality as a politically reactionary effort of highbrows to distinguish themselves from an increasingly literate populace, we might critically examine it as a new problem in the representation of suffering based in a fundamental reorientation toward the way that feeling itself is understood.24 Set beside the work of other modernists, such as Djuna Barnes, Samuel Beckett, and Nathanael West, whose satiric impulses also tend to produce moments of uncanny dread or anxiety, 25 Waugh's fiction offers a vantage point from which to re-examine relations of ethics and aesthetics, sympathy and detachment, reality and representation, and to ask why this sort of dark and unstable comedy has proved such an enduring mode throughout the twentieth century.

In an interesting footnote to Todd's encounter with Dickens, Waugh, in 1953, reviewed a study of Dickens in which he, not surprisingly, referred to Dickens as a "tear jerker." Yet he also recognized the novelist's "unique genius," and in Dickens's habit of mesmerism saw an apt metaphor for the author's peculiarly compelling power over his readers ("Apotheosis" 447). Strikingly, Waugh compared Dickens to Chaplin, the same figure of sentimentality to whom he had likened himself, disparagingly, two decades before:

The happiest comparison perhaps is to Mr Charles Chaplin, in particular to the film City Lights. There we have scenes of appalling sentimentality and unreality,... but we have a unique genius in full exuberance.... We all have our moods when Dickens sickens us. In a lighter, looser and perhaps higher mood we fall victim to his "magnetism." Like Mme de la Rue we unroll from our sensible ball and do what the Master orders. ("Apotheosis" 447)

Without entirely dropping his ironic tone, Waugh concedes that however "unreal" the emotion that Dickens and Chaplin elicit, it retains its pull on even the most sophisticated of readers. Here the sentimental itself appears as uncanny: the tearjerker captivates us just as the hypnotist does; the "Master" Dickens forces us to obey his will just as Mr. McMaster forces Tony. If satire points out to us the ludicrousness of our sentimental impulses by reducing human character to the laughably rigid operation of mechanized emotions, then the uncanny holds up this reduced character as something more disquieting: a dumb puppet in thrall to forces outside itself.

A decade later, Waugh testified a third time to this uncanny power. In his autobiography, A Little Learning, he recounts how his father, another man who loved Dickens, would read to his sons:

For some eight years of my life for some three or four evenings a week...he read to me, my brother and to whatever friends might be in the house, for an hour or more from his own old favourites-most of Shakespeare, most of Dickens, most of Tennyson.... Had it not been so well done, there might have been something ludicrous about the small, elderly, stout figure impersonating the heroines of forgotten comedies with such vivacity. In fact he held us enthralled.

Although the experience is recounted as pleasurable-even bordering on the "ludicrous" so amenable to Waugh's satire-this Dickensian scene of domestic novel-reading curiously anticipates (or echoes) Tony's encounter with Mr. Todd. Indeed, in Ninety-Two Days, the account of his South American travels that furnished material for A Handful of Dust, Waugh conceded that while reading Dickens in the jungle he recovered a pleasure in reading he had not experienced since childhood. Like the novel, the autobiographical accounts suggest that the engagement with Dickens is a situation of supernatural enthrallment to a master with uncanny powers-uncanny because, as in childhood, the sentimental pull of the novel can still possess us.

Chapter 10

The Spectacle of Criticism

Wilde's power to arouse fantasies in others - and to fulfill them - is seemingly inexhaustible. Everyone has an opinion about Oscar Wilde. It is also true that opinions about no other author have been so ill-informed. From the beginning, there appeared to be about Wilde something slightly slant. Earlier in the century the fantasies perhaps might have been dispelled. Now, as the century draws to a close, the same fantasies continue to circulate.

It is impossible to say exactly when Wilde became a public figure. In 1878 he won the prestigious Newdigate prize at Oxford for the "best poem in English verse" and he gave the winner's ceremonial reading at the Sheldonian Theatre. Relatives, friends, and his former teacher in classics, J. P. Mahaffy, came across from Dublin to attend. Shortly thereafter, Wilde went to London to pursue an as yet undecided career. About a dozen of his poems had been published in Dublin magazines. In London he added additional poems to those already in print and in 1881 he published them.

Critics who reviewed the volume were divided in their opinions, as they generally are. His poetry was associated with a movement that had been identified at least a decade earlier as "Aestheticism," by which was meant, according to one of its most popular critics, Robert Buchanan, art that was degenerate in making public its explicit attentiveness to private emotions, barbaric in its preoccupation with ritual, and Jacobin-inclined to violent excess-in its politics. The latter allusion evoked recurrent English fears of Anglo-Irish and Anglo-French collusion in real or imagined "papist plots."

When Wilde's poems were published his name was linked to Dante Gabriel Rossetti and Algernon Swinburne and Charles Baudelaire. Accusations of "plagiarism," a subject which was then, as it is now, complex and controversial, were probably more damaging.

Despite the mixed response to Wilde's poems, in 1881 he was invited by the Librarian of the Oxford Union, Oxford's undergraduate debating society, to present a copy of the volume as a gift, which he inscribed: "To the Oxford Union, My first volume of poems." There can be no doubt that Wilde's career - as a social critic and as a dramatist - pivoted downward after the scandalous trials that convicted him in 1895 of "gross indecency" and sent hi m to prison for two years. What is nearly always forgotten is that although he was not yet a public figure in 1881, the scandal that arose from the Union's rejection of his *Poems* and the accusation of plagiarism ensured that he was on his way to becoming one.

Never before had a book been presented that had not been accepted: in this case the Oxford Union established the more indecorous precedent of rejecting a gift that an author had been invited to present. The Union sent a letter of apology to Wilde to which he replied that he regretted its decision, his "chief regret indeed being that there should still be at Oxford such a large number of young men who are ready to accept their own ignorance as an index, and their own conceit a criterion of any imaginative and beautiful work" and he expressed the hope that "no other poet or writer of English will ever be subjected to what I feel sure you as well as myself are conscious of, the coarse impertinence of having a work officially rejected which has been no less officially sought for."

Punch, which devoted itself to verbal and visual caricature, attended with pleasure to the fray at Oxford and contributed to drawing attention to the young "aesthete" from Dublin even as it continued to draw attention to vexed political issues: Home Rule for Ireland; Gladstone's Land Reform Bills; and Irish nationalist agitation. Wilde had opinions about Irish nationalism, about Home Rule, and about the history of Anglo-Irish relations which he would soon convey to audiences in

North America that numbered in the thousands, of whom many belonged to the emigrant millions who fled earlier in the century during the Famine years. In one review of James Anthony Froude's writings on England, he wrote: "Blue-Books are generally dull reading, but Blue-Books on Ireland have always been interesting.

They form the record of one of the great tragedies of modern Europe. In them England has written her own indictment against herself and has given the world this history of her shame." This voice, as audible in Wilde's early as in his later writings, is less familiar. Legend has prevailed in favouring the flamboyant, self-absorbed "dandy" - for "dandy" read homosexual - in pursuit of notoriety.

We have always known that the early studies of Wilde are unreliable. Often, readings of his work have depended on questionable texts. More often, readings of his life have depended on apocryphal anecdotes. Although the need for a complete and authoritative edition of Wilde's work has been apparent for nearly a century, scholars have been slow to respond.

Wilde has inspired, nevertheless, a flourishing bibliography of critical studies, biographies, novels, plays, poems, and films. In his recent bibliographical study of Wilde, Ian Small concurs with two other Englishmen, Ian Fletcher and John Stokes, who, in the mid- 1970s, in an extensive review of Anglo-Irish writing, declared that "in all their dealings with Wilde, the English have been wrong about practically everything." Small points optimistically to the promise of scholarship during the 1980s. In the mid-nineties there is reason for greater optimism. Yet, in studies of Wilde, even the most scholarly critics have proceeded without their habitual caution.

Richard Ellmann, in his *Oscar Wilde* (1987), might have revised this view in his magisterial biography. Instead, his detailed narrative discloses Wilde's secret: Wilde had a secret life. In this view, Wilde enacted his secret before he was aware of the forces that impelled him to behave one way rather than another way, forces that drove him to self-destruction.

Ellmann brings to his reading of Wilde a particular notion of "the homosexual" as a "self" at once stable, opaque, and obsessive (rather than, for example, volatile, porous, and fluctuating, as the "self" might be regarded). Invariably, Ellmann finds in nearly every episode of Wilde's life traces of the insuppressible "homosexual impulse" or, as he sometimes refers to it, Wilde's "homosexual drive."

According to Ellmann's reading, that is the same impulse that accounts for Wilde's public displays and his simultaneous private liaisons. One particular photograph with the caption, "Wilde in costume as Salome," is falsely identified as Wilde. It was not until 1992, five years after Ellmann's biography was published, that John Stokes and, subsequently in 1994, Merlin Holland, Oscar Wilde's grandson, acknowledging the scholarly pursuit of Horst Schroeder, corrected and explained the error.

In *The Times Literary Supplement* Merlin Holland alerted readers that this photograph is not of Wilde but of Alice Guszalewicz, a Hungarian actress who, in 1906, played Salome in Richard Strauss's opera. It should be noted, as Merlin Holland points out, it is likely that Ellmann, so near to the end of his own life, did not personally verify the source of the photograph. Ellmann might have prevented the error had circumstances been different. Nevertheless, the elision of Oscar Wilde with Alice Guszalewicz is telling. Perhaps there is something to be gained from the error: it alerts us to the force of our fantasies.

Photographs seldom coincide with the mental images we carry of ourselves or of others. This photograph is an exception. How perfectly it coincides with a certain image of Wilde. Here we are meant to see the "homosexual impulse" - Ellmann's myth - actualized in the fullness of its remarkable simplicity.

Wilde is presented to us cross-dressed, bedecked with jewelry in the costume of Salome. He has cast himself in the leading role for a private performance of his own censored play - the Lord Chamberlain denied a license, which in 1893 prevented the performance of *Salome* in London. Here Wilde displays his public self and, at the same time, reveals to us his lurid secret self, the "self" that Ellmann's narrative discloses sympathetically. That is the myth. In the biography, this photograph is ringed round with the various episodes that constitute Ellmann's life of Wilde. In this poised moment the camera - and the biographer - has captured the profoundly narcissistic gesture, the single gesture, that is meant to evoke the entire life.

According to this reading that considers homoeroticism to be a variety of "narcissism," the figure kneeling, his hands outstretched, is about to embrace the severed head of John the Baptist. Once the head is raised Wilde will press his lips against John's lips as Herod will look on in horror.

There is more to be observed about this scene, but not now. What remains to be said here is this: as in the play Herod views the behavior of Salome, so in this photograph we see, or imagine we see, the behavior of Wilde. Like so many anecdotes that constitute the legend, this photographic anecdote turns Wilde into a lurid spectacle.

How was it possible for this photograph of Alice Guszalewicz to pass as Wilde? When we bring to bear on the legend of Wilde a more supple conception of our own affective lives than the prevailing view of our late nineteenth-century forebears, we are likely to see Wilde as well as ourselves somewhat differently. Then it may well turn out that we will learn more about our own fantasies than about Wilde. Then we will look upon the spectacle of Wilde criticism with wonder.

The importance of Oscar Wilde resides both in his art and in his personality. He is one of the most accomplished writers of his generation, but quite apart from his actual literary achievement, he is significant as a symbolic figure who exemplified a way of being homosexual at a pivotal moment in the emergence of gay consciousness, the crucial final decade of the nineteenth century.

Actually, however, Wilde's literary significance is inseparable from his function as a symbolic figure. Although he frequently asserted the impersonality of art, his own art is irreparably bound to his personality.

In fact, his greatest artistic creation is the complex and contradictory persona reflected in his work and in his life. Ultimately, that persona became transfigured from a witty aesthete into a figure as poignant as it was unpredictable, Saint Oscar, the homosexual martyr.

Born to accomplished but eccentric parents in Ireland in 1854, Wilde was educated at Trinity College, Dublin, and Magdalen College, Oxford, where he was almost equally influenced by the practically incompatible artistic doctrines of the moralistic John Ruskin and the epicurean Walter Pater.

Leaving Oxford in 1878, he declared prophetically, "Somehow or other I'll be famous, and if not famous, I'll be notorious." A master of drawing attention to himself, he quickly became known as the high priest of aestheticism, the intimate of artists, and the companion of actresses.

A superb conversationalist and a flamboyant dandy, he became a celebrity by virtue of his outrageousness as much as through his actual accomplishments.

Wilde's penchant for self-advertisement and for audacious posing ought not to obscure the seriousness behind his apparent flippancy, however.

The apostle of aestheticism and decadence, the dandy addicted to gold-tipped cigarettes and exquisite objets d'art, the social butterfly who cultivated the lords and ladies of the aristocracy, and the witty epigrammatist who delighted in deflating Victorian pomposity while celebrating the trivial at the expense of the earnest was also a penetrating social critic who defended individualism and pluralism and attacked economic and social exploitation and injustice.

Chapter 11

Wilde as a Social Critic

In The Soul of Man under Socialism (1891), for example, he enunciated a doctrine of libertarian socialism quite at variance with his mask of frivolity. For all its utopian idealism and arch wit, the pamphlet acutely dissects the harmful effects of private property on rich and poor alike.

It is also filled with subtle insights into the nature of oppression, as when it redefines selfishness in terms of authoritarian morality: "Selfishness is not living as one wishes to live, it is asking others to live as one wishes to live. And unselfishness is letting other people's lives alone, not interfering with them."

Wilde's antiauthoritarianism and his scorn for the philistinism of his late Victorian age are particularly important aspects of his persona and of his emergence as a symbolic figure, even as they are qualified by his almost equally strong need for social acceptance.

WILDE'S HOMOSEXUALITY

Wilde's need for social acceptance may have been a factor in his 1884 marriage to a young, somewhat conventional and naive socialite, Constance Lloyd, a union that quickly produced two sons.

Although he had flirted with homosexuality for many years and had aroused the suspicions and gossip of many (and later came to regard himself as having always been homosexual), he seems to have begun the sustained practice of homosexuality in 1886, when he met a young Canadian, Robbie Ross, who was to be his lifelong and faithful friend and eventually his literary executor. In 1891, Wilde met Lord Alfred Douglas, the twenty-one-year-old son of the ninth Marquess of Queensberry, who was to hound Wilde to his spectacular fall.

Douglas apparently introduced Wilde to the Victorian homosexual underground of male brothels and procurers and prostitutes who were to figure prominently in the sensational trials of 1895. Although Douglas appears to have been a thoroughly undisciplined young man, utterly unworthy of Wilde's devotion, the writer became so infatuated as to lose all sense of proportion and finally to embark on the course of action that was to culminate in his sentence to two years' penal servitude at hard labour.

HIS HOMOSEXUALITY AND HIS LITERARY ACHIEVEMENT

In hindsight, Wilde's association with Douglas seems a disaster. At the same time, however, the tumultuous affair may have inspired Wilde to some of his best work. Unquestionably, the discovery of his homosexuality liberated his art and marks a major breakthrough in his artistic maturity.

Indeed, Wilde's brief period of serious achievement, which began in 1888 with the publication of his collection of fairy tales, The Happy Prince, coincides with his period of homosexual activity.

Over the next seven years, he was to produce important prose works such as The Picture of Dorian Gray (1890, 1891), The Soul of Man under Socialism, Intentions (1891), Lord Arthur Savile's Crime and Other Stories (1891), and House of Pomegranates (1891), as well as the five successful plays: Salomé (1893), Lady Windermere's Fan (1892), A Woman of No Importance (1893), An Ideal Husband (1895), and The Importance of Being Earnest (1895).

WILDE'S FALL AND ITS CONSEQUENCES

This brief period of genuine accomplishment ended abruptly on February 18, 1895, only four days after the triumphant opening of The Importance of Being Earnest, when the Marquess of Queensberry left a card for Wilde at his club: "To Oscar Wilde, posing somdomite [sic]."

Encouraged by Douglas, who loathed his father, Wilde sued Queensberry for criminal libel: a suit that was won by the bitter and unstable Marquess and that was to culminate in Wilde's own prosecutions for "gross indecency between males."

The severity of Wilde's sentence--which contributed to his premature death in exile in Paris in 1900--and the extremity of his suffering rendered him a martyr in the struggle for homosexual emancipation.

Yet Wilde is, it must be acknowledged, an unlikely martyr and an ambiguous one. His martyrdom, after all, resulted as much from his own folly as from the viciousness of his persecutors, who were not eager to prosecute him or other homosexuals of high social standing or artistic prominence.

Indeed, his trials and conviction may fairly be blamed on his (and Alfred Douglas's) willed stupidity and penchant for self-dramatization, and perhaps as well on his unconscious need for exposure and punishment.

The theme of martyrdom runs through much of his work, early and late, and probably reflects the strong masochistic element in his personality, even as it also mirrors his sense of alienation. Moreover, his disastrous decision to prosecute Queensberry for alleging that he posed as a sodomite was itself reactionary rather than defiant.

Even after the debacle of his libel suit against Queensberry, Wilde could have escaped his own prosecution by fleeing to the Continent, a solution tacitly suggested by the magistrate, who apparently delayed issuing the warrant for his arrest in order to permit him to go abroad.

That he did not go into exile, as so many prominent Victorian homosexuals had done when faced with the prospect of scandal and prison, is a measure less of his rebelliousness than of his felt need to maintain his position in society.

Even the eloquent defence in his second trial of "the Love that dare not speak its name"--"a great affection of an elder for a younger man as there was between David and Jonathan, such as Plato made the very basis of his philosophy, and such as you will find in the sonnets of Michael Angelo and Shakespeare. . . . that deep, spiritual affection which is as pure as it is perfect"--is sharply undercut by the fact that the speech, largely untrue and certainly misleading, was designed to deny the physical expression of his homosexuality rather than to defend it.

The only hero of the Wilde trials was the procurer Alfred Taylor, who loyally refused to testify against his client and consequently shared his harsh punishment.

Wilde's own folly and masochism may have brought him into the prisoner's dock at Old Bailey, but once there he was victimized by the bigotry and hypocrisy of a society that he had ridiculed and exposed and yet could never completely reject. He became the scapegoat for his society's sexual and moral insecurities.

WILDE'S PRETRIAL RETICENCE IN DEPICTING HOMOSEXUALITY

Not surprisingly, however, those insecurities were also Wilde's own, as indicated by the reticence and coyness of his depictions of homosexuality in texts such as "The Portrait of Mr. W.H." and The Picture of Dorian Gray.

Although Wilde deserves enormous credit for bravery in even broaching gay themes at a time when it was dangerous to do so, his gay texts before his fall tend to be divided against themselves. Heir to a homosexual aesthetic tradition that stretches from Winckelmann to Pater and the centre in England of fin de siècle dandyism and decadence, Wilde still remains surprisingly moralistic in these works.

Wilde's homosexuality leaves its mark on most of his canon, usually expressed indirectly in the form of a recurrent interest in scandalous secrets, mysterious pasts, and divided lives, though he may have contributed to the explicitly homosexual erotic novel Teleny, or The Reverse of the Medal (1893), which was apparently written by several members of his circle.

In a play like The Importance of Being Earnest, Wilde

translates the ambivalence he felt toward his homosexuality--epitomized by the very notion of "Bunburying," the need to lead a double life--into a complex parody of both himself and his society and thereby creates a masterpiece, perhaps the greatest comedy in the language.

Without ever mentioning homosexuality, Wilde in Importance creates the quintessentially gay play. He turns Victorian values on their heads and discovers in the comedy of camp a means of covertly attacking his society's prejudices and discreetly defending his own nonconformity.

The farce brilliantly depicts the liminal position that Wilde occupied in relation to his homophobic society, in it, yet not of it. Perhaps the most poignant aspect of Importance is the fact that its comedy is fueled by Wilde's desperate desire to be accepted by the very society he lampoons.

In his earlier works that approach the homosexual theme more directly, however, the author's ambivalence fails to achieve resolution, and the result is a kind of imaginative paralysis: a rueful suspension between idealism and realism in "The Portrait of Mr. W.H." and a melodramatic moralism in The Picture of Dorian Gray.

Only after his dizzying fall, in the painful but sly De Profundis does Wilde achieve a vision at once unified and capacious enough to contain his contradictoriness.

"THE PORTRAIT OF MR. W.H."

"The Portrait of Mr. W.H." is a work on which Wilde expended great time and effort, and it is one of the most revealing of his stories.

The original version was published as an article of 12,000 words in 1889, but Wilde became more and more obsessed with the subject of Shakespeare's Sonnets, and during the next four years, he revised and augmented the story, in the process more than doubling its length.

The manuscript of the revised story, actually a novelette, was thought to have been lost in the chaos that accompanied the sale of Wilde's property after his arrest; many years later, it was discovered in the offices of Wilde's publisher, John Lane, and the revised version finally achieved print in 1921. On one level, the story is merely a pleasant speculation on the identity of the young man of Shakespeare's Sonnets, whom Wilde identifies as a boy actor named Willie Hughes, and a detailed interpretation of the sequence and its relationship to Shakespeare's plays.

But on another level, the work is also a meditation on homosexuality and a foiled coming out story, Nabokovian in its complexity and irony.

"The Portrait of Mr. W.H." is divided into five sections, the middle three of which are devoted almost entirely to analyses of Shakespeare's poems and his relationship with the young man of the Sonnets, whereas the first and final sections are devoted to the contemporary frame story. Significantly, both the middle and the framing sections are self-consciously homosexual in tone.

Whereas the Shakespeare material deals specifically with the poet's attachment to a young man, Willie Hughes, who becomes the symbol of an idealized homosexuality, the framing sections are concerned with characters who are sketched in terms of an easily recognizable homosexual style--one that Wilde more than anyone else helped establish in the popular imagination. Cyril Graham, Erskine, and the unnamed narrator are effete connoisseurs who interpret high culture to the middle classes.

Central to both sections is the association of homosexual Eros and creativity and the motif of an older man inspired by the beauty of a younger one.

"The Portrait of Mr. W.H." can be read as a cautious defence of homosexuality in terms very similar to the defence that Wilde would later offer for "the Love that dare not speak its name." Associating Willie Hughes with Gaveston in Marlowe's Edward II and linking the love of the Sonnets with the neoplatonism of Ficino and Michelangelo and the Hellenism of Winckelmann, the story presents homosexual passion as transcending but not denying the physical.

At the same time, however, the narrator frankly acknowledges that the idealistic sixteenth-century philosophy that explains Shakespeare's attachment to Willie Hughes would be denounced as immoral and criminal in his own age. In answer to critics who see in the Sonnets "something dangerous, something unlawful even," he defiantly asserts the superiority of the soul's affections to man-made law.

Most tellingly, he recognizes both peril and potential in the kind of love that Shakespeare felt for Willie Hughes: "It is no doubt true that to be filled with an absorbing passion is to surrender the security of one's lower life, and yet in such surrender there may be gain."

This notion that there may be gain in embracing a truth higher than the security of everyday reality reverberates throughout the story, finally mocking the narrator himself when he rejects his own soul's truth, his homosexuality.

Perhaps even more important than its idealization and cautious defence of homosexuality is the novelette's emphasis on the continuity of homosexual feeling from the past to the present, even as that recognition culminates in an acknowledgment of the dangers of self-discovery and an awareness of gay oppression.

This continuity, rather than the identity of Mr. W.H., is the real secret of the Sonnets and the real connection between the frame-story and the critical sections. In "The Portrait of Mr. W.H.," to study the Sonnets is to recognize a personal affinity with the homoerotic passion of Shakespeare and Willie Hughes. As a result of his absorption with Shakespeare's poems, Cyril, Erskine, and the narrator each finds reflected in the Sonnets an image of his own homosexuality. More accurately, they project onto their reading of Shakespeare's sequence their own homosexual sensibilities, discovering in the text the mirror of their own desire.

Thus, the search for the solution "to the greatest mystery of modern literature" finally reveals less about the Sonnets than about Cyril, Erskine, and especially the narrator.

The narrator's ultimate repudiation of the Willie Hughes hypothesis is usually regarded merely as a witty Wildean narrative twist, illustrating the paradox "that in convincing someone else of a belief you lose the belief yourself."

But the narrator's repudiation is also a response to the dangers of self-discovery. More specifically, it symbolizes his sublimation of his homosexual nature, reflecting his awareness and fear of gay oppression.

In "The Portrait of Mr. W.H.," Wilde enacts a parable about the difficulty of maintaining homosexual idealism in the late nineteenth century (particularly in contrast to the Renaissance, which is presented as a romantic, Hellenistic era), illustrating how the age was--in Cyril's words--"afraid to turn the key that unlocked the mystery of the poet's heart."

Although implicated in Cyril's forgery and Erskine's fraud, this idealism nevertheless represents a higher truth than the security of the life of everyday consciousness. But the narrator, prizing safety above honesty, chooses to live in the mundane reality of a philistine world rather than accept his own deepest nature. Thus, "The Portrait of Mr. W.H." both defends homosexuality and regretfully--perhaps prophetically--rejects it.

THE PICTURE OF DORIAN GRAY

"The Portrait of Mr. W.H." and Wilde's flawed yet haunting experiment in the gothic novel, The Picture of Dorian Gray, share a number of similarities, including an ambivalence toward homosexuality.

The similarities may be because Wilde probably revised the story at the same time as he revised the novel, which was originally published in Lippincott's Monthly Magazine in July 1890 then expanded and reissued as a book in 1891. In a real sense, however, The Picture of Dorian Gray is even more ambivalent about homosexuality than "The Portrait of Mr. W.H."

Whereas the novelette depicts regretfully the failure to attempt a potentially liberating self-realization, the novel risks satirizing the very notion of self-realization by (perhaps unintentionally) equating it with mere dissipation and self-indulgence.

The novel's fascination resides in the discrepancy between its obvious moral and its contradictory tone. The moralism of the novel is apparent from its plot structure, which emphasizes the fall and punishment of a narcissistic young man who makes a Faustian bargain to preserve his youthful beauty.

Wilde himself explained the story as a condemnation of excess. But such moralism is undercut by the fact that the good characters in the novel are weak and passive, whereas the corrupt ones are glamorous and strong. In addition, the ambiguous narrator makes the hedonistic doctrine enunciated by Sir Henry Wotton and embraced by Dorian Gray seductive indeed.

Notwithstanding the retributive ending of the book, the Faustian dream of an escape from human limitations and moral strictures is rendered more appealingly than the superimposed morals condemning narcissism and excess. It is no wonder that in the popular imagination, the name Dorian Gray conjures not an image of evil but of supernaturally extended youth bought at the trivial price of a disfigured portrait.

Homosexuality is an important aspect of The Picture of Dorian Gray, and the novel deserves credit as a pioneering depiction of homosexual relationships in serious English fiction. But it is important to emphasize that Wilde hints at homosexuality rather than expresses it directly.

Homosexual readers would certainly have responded to the book's undercurrent of gay feeling and may have found the very name "Dorian" suggestive of Greek homosexuality, since it was Dorian tribesmen who allegedly introduced homosexuality into Greece.

But Wilde purposely leaves the exact nature of the sins of Dorian Gray mysterious and vague; his dissipations are by no means exclusively or even primarily homosexual. More clearly homoerotic, however, is the competition of Basil Hallward and Lord Henry Wotton for the attentions of Dorian.

Wilde's attitude toward homosexuality in the novel may best be seen in his portrayal of Basil. The character most clearly defined as homosexual, Hallward is also the most morally sensitive character. He represents an idealized, platonized homosexuality, linked to a long tradition of art and philosophy.

Tellingly, however, Basil's love for Dorian is presented ambiguously. On the one hand, its power is confirmed by the transformation of Basil's art that it effects. On the other hand, it is the source of guilt and fear, and the very art that it inspires is ominous, for that art culminates in the sinister portrait.

By presenting the naive and unformed Dorian with an image of himself (the artist's own image of him), by awakening him to his beauty and thereby encouraging his vanity, Basil may even be said to initiate the entire tragedy.

The diabolism of the painting may be dismissed as a gothic plot device, but Wilde's serious purpose in implicating Basil in the corruption of Dorian Gray is to underline the major theme of the work, the wickedness of using others.

This theme is clearest in Dorian's heartless exploitation of others and in the amused, detached voyeurism of Lord Henry, but it is involved as well in Basil's reduction of Dorian to "simply a motive in art" found "in the curves of certain lines, in the loveliness and subtleties of certain colours."

If Basil is to blame for objectifying Dorian, so too is Lord Henry. Although Basil and Henry are at first glance extremely dissimilar--the one earnest and idealistic, the other cynical and disillusioned--the rivals share an artistic impulse. They both want to transform and re-present reality, a desire that may be a psychological compensation for their essential passivity. Basil's artistry finds expression in painting, Henry's in the exercise of influence.

Tellingly, Henry's homoerotic attraction to Dorian is whetted voyeuristically by Basil's worship of the young man, and Henry is thereby roused from his characteristic languor to a desire to influence Dorian, a process that is itself a sublimated expression of homosexuality. The worldly cynic undertakes as his goal the "making" of Dorian much as a poet or sculptor might shape a work of art.

The central irony of The Picture of Dorian Gray is that the Hellenic ideal of "the harmony of soul and body" pursued by Basil and Henry alike, and localized in their separate visions of Dorian, is not realized largely because they project onto the young man their own unbalanced and fragmentary images.

Moreover, in the corrupt and materialistic world of late-nineteenth-century London, Dorian's project of self-realization amounts simply to a self-indulgence that mocks both Basil's idealism and Henry's tendentious (mis)interpretation of Pateresque epicureanism.

Rather than harmonizing, in the course of the novel, Dorian's soul and body become increasingly disconnected and finally separated entirely, as symbolized in the increasing disjunction between the unaging beauty of Dorian's body and the hideous representation of his soul (that is, the picture).

This irony suggests that the Faustian theme is by no means confined to the gothic diabolism of Dorian's supernatural bargain for a youthful appearance. By assuming godlike powers of creation, Basil and Henry also partake in the Faustian desire to escape human limitations.

But if Basil and Henry are finally condemned for their objectification of Dorian and for their Faustian aspirations, the romantic dream of an idealized harmony of body and soul nevertheless survives the moralistic conclusion to protest against an unsatisfactory reality and a tragic history.

The Picture of Dorian Gray is a text divided against itself, but its creative tensions yield both a poignant sense of loss that the world cannot be recreated and made whole and an implied vision of a world at ease with homosexuality, a world in which sensual enjoyment has been made an element of "a new spirituality, of which a fine instinct for beauty was to be the dominant characteristic."

Perhaps more responsible than any other single English work in forging the stereotypical link between art, decadence, and homosexuality, The Picture of Dorian Gray--for all its moralistic posturing--mourns the loss of a golden age and art's inability to recreate that homoerotic harmony of flesh and spirit nostalgically associated with Hellenism.

DE PROFUNDIS

Wilde's most important and least ambivalent contribution to gay literature is the remarkable letter written in prison, De Profundis, a work that creatively transmutes the disaster of his prosecution and imprisonment into a ludic triumph. Written over a period of three months in 1897, after he had been imprisoned for some eighteen months, and addressed to Lord Alfred Douglas, De Profundis is far more than the recriminatory attack of a disenchanted lover or a self-serving, self-pitying tract.

It might best be described as Wilde's attempt to create and present a complex and contradictory but nevertheless authentic self, one to displace or qualify the masks he had himself created earlier and the ugly images attributed to him in the popular press.

The importance of Wilde's prison letter for gay literature is that in it the writer breaks out of the bourgeois mold he had so frequently attacked yet to which he so tenaciously clung. As a result of his imprisonment, he discovers a new freedom and emerges as Saint Oscar, the victim of gay oppression who finally triumphs over a philistine society.

The key faculty of the authentic self that Wilde creates in De Profundis is imagination. Imagination, as used in the work, is a preexistentialist term for the individual's attentiveness to received ideas and relationships; it indicates a liveliness of the spirit, an awareness of the meaning of experience, a critical alertness to the nature of one's relationships both to others and to social institutions, and a constant questioning of established social codes.

In De Profundis, imagination is Wilde's means of liberating himself from his problematic relationship to society.

The most daring aspect of De Profundis is Wilde's simultaneous depictions of Christ in his image and himself in Christ's image. Christ is presented not as a supernatural being but as a fascinating artist whose power of imagination "makes him the palpitating centre of romance."

The embodiment of agape, Christ understands the sufferings of others. He is also the proponent of radical individualism, and rather than consisting of moralistic prohibitions, Christ's "morality is all sympathy."

Wilde also depicts Christ as an imaginative social critic, alert to the injustices of society and waging a war against social tyranny. Christ's antagonists are the philistines, who never question the dehumanizing and limiting social codes that they enforce, codes that have created a thoroughly inhumane prison system, incarcerated Wilde for his homosexuality, and robbed him of his children.

The portrait of Christ as the romantic artist martyred by a philistine society functions for Wilde not merely as self-aggrandizement but also as a means of attacking the religious base of philistine morality.

In De Profundis, Wilde defends his homosexuality, or Uranianism, obliquely but strongly, and the work deserves a prominent place in the literature of homosexual apologias. Wilde's frank admission of his homosexuality as "a fact about me" translates his sexual identity into an element of the new self-knowledge he has gained in the crucible of suffering and one that he will not willingly deny or surrender.

Skeptical of the medical model of homosexuality emerging in the late nineteenth century, he refers dismissively to Cesare Lomboroso, an Italian criminologist who believed homosexuality was a congenital dysfunction, to be treated in insane asylums rather than prisons.

Although open to a theoretical connection between homosexuality and artistic creativity, as implied by homosexual apologists like John Addington Symonds and Edward Carpenter and endorsed in "The Portrait of Mr. W.H." and The Picture of Dorian Gray, Wilde observes laconically that "the pathological phenomenon in question is also found among those who have not genius."

Rather than belaboring the causes of homosexuality, he is defiant of those who would condemn him. He resolutely denounces the "wrong and unjust laws" of the "wrong and unjust system" that convicted him, and confesses that "The one disgraceful, unpardonable, and to all time contemptible action of my life was my allowing myself to be forced into appealing to Society for help and protection. . . . " This new awareness of his relation to a society whose code he violated yet naively looked to for protection is an important measure of his growth in imagination as a result of his experience.

The most moving aspect of De Profundis is Wilde's graphic account of the mental and physical pain he has undergone in prison. Deserted by Douglas, humiliated by a vengeful public, branded and cast out from society, he describes his life as a veritable "Symphony of Sorrow."

But the supreme theme of the work is the meaningfulness of suffering. Wilde declares that suffering "is really a revelation. One discerns things that one never discerned before." He concludes that "to have become a deeper man is the privilege of those who have suffered."

It is this deeper man who triumphs in De Profundis. As a result of seeing the world differently, he is able to accept himself and his plight without bitterness. He emerges as a kind of Harlequin Christ-figure, a martyred clown who enjoys the last laugh. He exercises his imagination to translate his martyrdom into a triumph analogous to the Christian comedy implicit in Good Friday and the Resurrection.

The new self that triumphs at the end of De Profundis revels defiantly in his exclusion from society, his marginality as homosexual pariah. Thus, Wilde rejects the artificial society that has condemned him and looks to nature for comfort and consolation:

Society, as we have constituted it, will have no place for me, has none to offer; but Nature, whose sweet rains fall on unjust and just alike, will have clefts in the rocks where I may hide and secret valleys in whose silence I may weep undisturbed. She will hang the night with stars so that I may walk abroad in the darkness without stumbling, and send the wind over my footprints so that none may track me to my hurt: she will cleanse me in great waters, and with bitter herbs make me whole.

This passage, with its defiant assertion of Wilde's status as a child of nature, its criticism of a shallow society, its yearning for an Arcadian retreat, its faint but deliberate echoes of Ecclesiastes, and its self-dramatization that approaches parody, is at once slyly comic and deeply moving, expressing in little the complex comic tone of the whole, where tragedy and comedy not only coexist but deepen each other.

It may be true, as W. H. Auden observed, that the Wilde scandal had a disastrous effect on the arts "because it allowed the philistine man to identify himself with the decent man," but it is also true, as John Cowper Powys remarked, that Wilde consequently became "a sort of rallying cry to all those writers and artists who suffer, in one degree or other, from the persecution of the mob."

For homosexuals, he became a martyr figure, a haunting symbol of gay vulnerability and gay resistance. Responsible more than anyone else for forming the popular stereotype of the homosexual as a dandiacal wit who flaunts middle-class mores, he is also most responsible for exemplifying the political realities of gay oppression.

He is a symbolic figure not only because his imprisonment is the political reality that all subsequent considerations of homosexuality must confront, but also because his defiance and his painfully earned self-realization are important lessons in the struggle for gay liberation.

Chapter 12

The Rise of Historical Criticism

Historical criticism nowhere occurs as an isolated fact in the civilisation or literature of any people. It is part of that complex working towards freedom which may be described as the revolt against authority. It is merely one facet of that speculative spirit of an innovation, which in the sphere of action produces democracy and revolution, and in that of thought is the parent of philosophy and physical science; and its importance as a factor of progress is based not so much on the results it attains, as on the tone of thought which it represents, and the method by which it works.

Being thus the resultant of forces essentially revolutionary, it is not to be found in the ancient world among the material despotisms of Asia or the stationary civilisation of Egypt. The clay cylinders of Assyria and Babylon, the hieroglyphics of the pyramids, form not history but the material for history. The Chinese annals, ascending as they do to the barbarous forest life of the nation, are marked with a soberness of judgment, a freedom from invention, which is almost unparalleled in the writings of any people; but the protective spirit which is the characteristic of that people proved as fatal to their literature as to their commerce.

Free criticism is as unknown as free trade. While as regards the Hindus, their acute, analytical and logical mind is directed rather to grammar, criticism and philosophy than to history or chronology. Indeed, in history their imagination seems to have run wild, legend and fact are so indissolubly mingled together that any attempt to separate them seems vain.

If we except the identification of the Greek Sandracottus with the Indian Chandragupta, we have really no clue by which we can test the truth of their writings or examine their method of investigation. It is among the Hellenic branch of the Indo-Germanic race that history proper is to be found, as well as the spirit of historical criticism; among that wonderful offshoot of the primitive Aryans, whom we call by the name of Greeks and to whom, as has been well said, we owe all that moves in the world except the blind forces of nature.

For, from the day when they left the chill table-lands of Tibet and journeyed, a nomad people, to AEgean shores, the characteristic of their nature has been the search for light, and the spirit of historical criticism is part of that wonderful Aufklarung or illumination of the intellect which seems to have burst on the Greek race like a great flood of light about the sixth century B.C. L'ESPRIT D'UN SIECLE NE NAIT PAS ET NE MEURT PAS E JOUR FIXE, and the first critic is perhaps as difficult to discover as the first man.

It is from democracy that the spirit of criticism borrows its intolerance of dogmatic authority, from physical science the alluring analogies of law and order, from philosophy the conception of an essential unity underlying the complex manifestations of phenomena. It appears first rather as a changed attitude of mind than as a principle of research, and its earliest influences are to be found in the sacred writings.

For men begin to doubt in questions of religion first, and then in matters of more secular interest; and as regards the nature of the spirit of historical criticism itself in its ultimate development, it is not confined merely to the empirical method of ascertaining whether an event happened or not, but is concerned also with the investigation into the causes of events, the general relations which phenomena of life hold to one another, and in its ultimate development passes into the wider question of the philosophy of history.

Now, while the workings of historical criticism in these two spheres of sacred and uninspired history are essentially manifestations of the same spirit, yet their methods are so different, the canons of evidence so entirely separate, and the motives in each case so unconnected, that it will be necessary for a clear estimation of the progress of Greek thought, that we should consider these two questions entirely apart from one another. I shall then in both cases take the succession of writers in their chronological order as representing the rational order - not that the succession of time is always the succession of ideas, or that dialectics moves ever in the straight line in which Hegel conceives its advance.

In Greek thought, as elsewhere, there are periods of stagnation and apparent retrogression, yet their intellectual development, not merely in the question of historical criticism, but in their art, their poetry and their philosophy, seems so essentially normal, so free from all disturbing external influences, so peculiarly rational, that in following in the footsteps of time we shall really be progressing in the order sanctioned by reason.

At an early period in their intellectual development the Greeks reached that critical point in the history of every civilised nation, when speculative invades the domain of revealed truth, when the spiritual ideas of the people can no longer be satisfied by the lower, material conceptions of their inspired writers, and when men find it impossible to pour the new wine of free thought into the old bottles of a narrow and a trammelling creed.

From their Aryan ancestors they had received the fatal legacy of a mythology stained with immoral and monstrous stories which strove to hide the rational order of nature in a chaos of miracles, and to mar by imputed wickedness the perfection of God's nature - a very shirt of Nessos in which the Heracles of rationalism barely escaped annihilation.

Now while undoubtedly the speculations of Thales, and the alluring analogies of law and order afforded by physical science, were most important forces in encouraging the rise of the spirit of scepticism, yet it was on its ethical side that the Greek mythology was chiefly open to attack. It is difficult to shake the popular belief in miracles, but no man will admit sin and immorality as attributes of the Ideal he worships; so the first symptoms of a new order of thought are shown in the passionate outcries of Xenophanes and Heraclitos against the evil things said by Homer of the sons of God; and in the story told of Pythagoras, how that he saw tortured in Hell the 'two founders of Greek theology,' we can recognise the rise of the Aufklarung as clearly as we see the Reformation foreshadowed in the INFERNO of Dante.

Any honest belief, then, in the plain truth of these stories soon succumbed before the destructive effects of the A PRIORI ethical criticism of this school; but the orthodox party, as is its custom, found immediately a convenient shelter under the aegis of the doctrine of metaphors and concealed meanings. To this allegorical school the tale of the fight around the walls of Troy was a mystery, behind which, as behind a veil, were hidden certain moral and physical truths.

The contest between Athena and Ares was that eternal contest between rational thought and the brute force of ignorance; the arrows which rattled in the quiver of the 'Far Darter' were no longer the instruments of vengeance shot from the golden bow of the child of God, but the common rays of the sun, which was itself nothing but a mere inert mass of burning metal.

Modern investigation, with the ruthlessness of Philistine analysis, has ultimately brought Helen of Troy down to a symbol of the dawn. There were Philistines among the Greeks also who saw in the [Greek text which cannot be reproduced] a mere metaphor for atmospheric power.

Now while this tendency to look for metaphors and hidden meanings must be ranked as one of the germs of historical criticism, yet it was essentially unscientific. Its inherent weakness is clearly pointed out by Plato, who showed that while this theory will no doubt explain many of the current legends, yet, if it is to be appealed to at all, it must be as a universal principle; a position he is by no means prepared to admit.

Like many other great principles it suffered from its disciples, and furnished its own refutation when the web of Penelope was analysed into a metaphor of the rules of formal logic, the warp representing the premises, and the woof the conclusion. Rejecting, then, the allegorical interpretation of the sacred writings as an essentially dangerous method, proving either too much or too little, Plato himself returns to the earlier mode of attack, and re-writes history with a didactic purpose, laying down certain ethical canons of historical criticism. God is good; God is just; God is true; God is without the common passions of men.

These are the tests to which we are to bring the stories of the Greek religion. 'God predestines no men to ruin, nor sends destruction on innocent cities; He never walks the earth in strange disguise, nor has to mourn for the death of any well-beloved son. Away with the tears for Sarpedon, the lying dream sent to Agamemnon, and the story of the broken covenant!'

Similar ethical canons are applied to the accounts of the heroes of the days of old, and by the same A PRIORI principles Achilles is rescued from the charges of avarice and insolence in a passage which may be recited as the earliest instance of that 'whitewashing of great men,' as it has been called, which is so popular in our own day, when Catiline and Clodius are represented as honest and far-seeing politicians, when EINE EDLE UND GUTE NATUR is claimed for Tiberius, and Nero is rescued from his heritage of infamy as an accomplished DILETTANTE whose moral aberrations are more than excused by his exquisite artistic sense and charming tenor voice.

But besides the allegorising principle of interpretation, and the ethical reconstruction of history, there was a third theory, which may be called the semi-historical, and which goes by the name of Euhemeros, though he was by no means the first to propound it.

Appealing to a fictitious monument which he declared that he had discovered in the island of Panchaia, and which purported to be a column erected by Zeus, and detailing the incidents of his reign on earth, this shallow thinker attempted to show that the gods and heroes of ancient Greece were 'mere ordinary mortals, whose achievements had been a good deal exaggerated and misrepresented,' and that the proper canon of historical criticism as regards the treatment of myths was to rationalise the incredible, and to present the plausible residuum as actual truth. To him and his school, the centaurs, for instance, those mythical sons of the storm, strange links between the lives of men and animals, were merely some youths from the village of Nephele in Thessaly, distinguished for their sporting tastes; the 'living harvest of panoplied knights,' which sprang so mystically from the dragon's teeth, a body of mercenary troops supported by the profits on a successful speculation in ivory; and Actaeon, an ordinary master of hounds, who, living before the days of subscription, was eaten out of house and home by the expenses of his kennel.

Now, that under the glamour of myth and legend some substratum of historical fact may lie, is a proposition rendered extremely probable by the modern investigations into the workings of the mythopoeic spirit in post-Christian times.

Charlemagne and Roland, St. Francis and William Tell, are none the less real personages because their histories are filled with much that is fictitious and incredible, but in all cases what is essentially necessary is some external corroboration, such as is afforded by the mention of Roland and Roncesvalles in the chronicles of England, or (in the sphere of Greek legend) by the excavations of Hissarlik. But to rob a mythical narrative of its kernel of supernatural elements, and to present the dry husk thus obtained as historical fact, is, as has been well said, to mistake entirely the true method of investigation and to identify plausibility with truth.

And as regards the critical point urged by Palaiphatos, Strabo, and Polybius, that pure invention on Homer's part is inconceivable, we may without scruple allow it, for myths, like constitutions, grow gradually, and are not formed in a day. But between a poet's deliberate creation and historical accuracy there is a wide field of the mythopoeic faculty.

This Euhemeristic theory was welcomed as an essentially philosophical and critical method by the unscientific Romans, to whom it was introduced by the poet Ennius, that pioneer of cosmopolitan Hellenicism, and it continued to characterise the tone of ancient thought on the question of the treatment of mythology till the rise of Christianity, when it was turned by such writers as Augustine and Minucius Felix into a formidable weapon of attack on Paganism. It was then abandoned by all those who still bent the knee to Athena or to Zeus, and a general return, aided by the philosophic mystics of Alexandria, to the allegorising principle of interpretation took place, as the only means of saving the deities of Olympus from the Titan assaults of the new Galilean God.

In what vain defence, the statue of Mary set in the heart of the Pantheon can best tell us. Religions, however, may be absorbed, but they never are disproved, and the stories of the Greek mythology, spiritualised by the purifying influence of Christianity, reappear in many of the southern parts of Europe in our own day. The old fable that the Greek gods took service with the new religion under assumed names has more truth in it than the many care to discover.

Having now traced the progress of historical criticism in the special treatment of myth and legend, I shall proceed to investigate the form in which the same spirit manifested itself as regards what one may term secular history and secular historians. The field traversed will be found to be in some respects the same, but the mental attitude, the spirit, the motive of investigation are all changed.

There were heroes before the son of Atreus and historians before Herodotus, yet the latter is rightly hailed as the father of history, for in him we discover not merely the empirical connection of cause and effect, but that constant reference to Laws, which is the characteristic of the historian proper. For all history must be essentially universal; not in the sense of comprising all the synchronous events of the past time, but through the universality of the principles employed.

And the great conceptions which unify the work of Herodotus are such as even modern thought has not yet rejected. The immediate government of the world by God, the nemesis and punishment which sin and pride invariably bring with them, the revealing of God's purpose to His people by signs and omens, by miracles and by prophecy; these are to Herodotus the laws which govern the phenomena of history.

He is essentially the type of supernatural historian; his

eyes are ever strained to discern the Spirit of God moving over the face of the waters of life; he is more concerned with final than with efficient causes. Yet we can discern in him the rise of that HISTORIC SENSE which is the rational antecedent of the science of historical criticism, the [Greek text which cannot be reproduced], to use the words of a Greek writer, as opposed to that which comes either [Greek text which cannot be reproduced]. He has passed through the valley of faith and has caught a glimpse of the sunlit heights of Reason; but like all those who, while accepting the supernatural, yet attempt to apply the canons of rationalism, he is essentially inconsistent.

For the better apprehension of the character of this historic sense in Herodotus it will be necessary to examine at some length the various forms of criticism in which it manifests itself. Such fabulous stories as that of the Phoenix, of the goat-footed men, of the headless beings with eyes in their breasts, of the men who slept six months in the year ([Greek text which cannot be reproduced]), of the wer-wolf of the Neuri, and the like, are entirely rejected by him as being opposed to the ordinary experience of life, and to those natural laws whose universal influence the early Greek physical philosophers had already made known to the world of thought.

Other legends, such as the suckling of Cyrus by a bitch, or the feather-rain of northern Europe, are rationalised and explained into a woman's name and a fall of snow. The supernatural origin of the Scythian nation, from the union of Hercules and the monstrous Echidna, is set aside by him for the more probable account that they were a nomad tribe driven by the Massagetae from Asia; and he appeals to the local names of their country as proof of the fact that the Kimmerians were the original possessors.

But in the case of Herodotus it will be more instructive to pass on from points like these to those questions of general probability, the true apprehension of which depends rather on a certain quality of mind than on any possibility of formulated rules, questions which form no unimportant part of scientific history; for it must be remembered always that the canons of historical criticism are essentially different from those of judicial evidence, for they cannot, like the latter, be made plain to every ordinary mind, but appeal to a certain historical faculty founded on the experience of life.

Besides, the rules for the reception of evidence in courts of law are purely stationary, while the science of historical probability is essentially progressive, and changes with the advancing spirit of each age. Now, of all the speculative canons of historical criticism, none is more important than that which rests on psychological probability.

Arguing from his knowledge of human nature, Herodotus rejects the presence of Helen within the walls of Troy. Had she been there, he says, Priam and his kinsmen would never have been so mad ([Greek text which cannot be reproduced]) as not to give her up, when they and their children and their city were in such peril (ii. 118); and as regards the authority of Homer, some incidental passages in his poem show that he knew of Helen's sojourn in Egypt during the siege, but selected the other story as being a more suitable motive for an epic.

Similarly he does not believe that the Alcmaeonidae family, a family who had always been the haters of tyranny ([Greek text which cannot be reproduced]), and to whom, even more than to Harmodios and Aristogeiton, Athens owed its liberty, would ever have been so treacherous as to hold up a shield after the battle of Marathon as a signal for the Persian host to fall on the city.

A shield, he acknowledges, was held up, but it could not possibly have been done by such friends of liberty as the house of Alcmaeon; nor will he believe that a great king like Rhampsinitus would have sent his daughter [Greek text which cannot be reproduced]. Elsewhere he argues from more general considerations of probability; a Greek courtesan like Rhodopis would hardly have been rich enough to build a pyramid, and, besides, on chronological grounds the story is impossible (ii. 134).

In another passage (ii. 63), after giving an account of the forcible entry of the priests of Ares into the chapel of the god's mother, which seems to have been a sort of religious faction fight where sticks were freely used ([Greek text which cannot be reproduced]), 'I feel sure,' he says, 'that many of them died from getting their heads broken, notwithstanding the assertions of the Egyptian priests to the contrary.' There is also something charmingly naive in the account he gives of the celebrated Greek swimmer who dived a distance of eighty stadia to give his countrymen warning of the Persian advance. 'If, however,' he says, 'I may offer an opinion on the subject, I would say that he came in a boat.'

There is, of course, something a little trivial in some of the instances I have quoted; but in a writer like Herodotus, who stands on the borderland between faith and rationalism, one likes to note even the most minute instances of the rise of the critical and sceptical spirit of inquiry. How really strange, at base, it was with him may, I think, be shown by a reference to those passages where he applies rationalistic tests to matters connected with religion.

He nowhere, indeed, grapples with the moral and scientific difficulties of the Greek Bible; and where he rejects as incredible the marvellous achievements of Hercules in Egypt, he does so on the express grounds that he had not yet been received among the gods, and so was still subject to the ordinary conditions of mortal life ([Greek text which cannot be reproduced]).

Even within these limits, however, his religious conscience seems to have been troubled at such daring rationalism, and the passage (ii. 45) concludes with a pious hope that God will pardon him for having gone so far, the great rationalistic passage being, of course, that in which he rejects the mythical account of the foundation of Dodona. 'How can a dove speak with a human voice?' he asks, and rationalises the bird into a foreign princess.

Similarly he seems more inclined to believe that the great storm at the beginning of the Persian War ceased from ordinary atmospheric causes, and not in consequence of the incantations of the MAGIANS. He calls Melampos, whom the majority of the Greeks looked on as an inspired prophet, 'a clever man who had acquired for himself the art of prophecy';

and as regards the miracle told of the AEginetan statues of the primeval deities of Damia and Auxesia, that they fell on their knees when the sacrilegious Athenians strove to carry them off, 'any one may believe it,' he says, 'who likes, but as for myself, I place no credence in the tale.'

So much then for the rationalistic spirit of historical criticism, as far as it appears explicitly in the works of this great and philosophic writer; but for an adequate appreciation of his position we must also note how conscious he was of the value of documentary evidence, of the use of inscriptions, of the importance of the poets as throwing light on manners and customs as well as on historical incidents.

No writer of any age has more vividly recognised the fact that history is a matter of evidence, and that it is as necessary for the historian to state his authority as it is to produce one's witnesses in a court of law.

While, however, we can discern in Herodotus the rise of an historic sense, we must not blind ourselves to the large amount of instances where he receives supernatural influences as part of the ordinary forces of life.

Compared to Thucydides, who succeeded him in the development of history, he appears almost like a mediaeval writer matched with a modern rationalist. For, contemporary though they were, between these two authors there is an infinite chasm of thought. The essential difference of their methods may be best illustrated from those passages where they treat of the same subject.

The execution of the Spartan heralds, Nicolaos and Aneristos, during the Peloponnesian War is regarded by Herodotus as one of the most supernatural instances of the workings of nemesis and the wrath of an outraged hero; while the lengthened siege and ultimate fall of Troy was brought about by the avenging hand of God desiring to manifest unto men the mighty penalties which always follow upon mighty sins. But Thucydides either sees not, or desires not to see, in either of these events the finger of Providence, or the punishment of wicked doers.

The death of the heralds is merely an Athenian retaliation

for similar outrages committed by the opposite side; the long agony of the ten years' siege is due merely to the want of a good commissariat in the Greek army; while the fall of the city is the result of a united military attack consequent on a good supply of provisions.

Now, it is to be observed that in this latter passage, as well as elsewhere, Thucydides is in no sense of the word a sceptic as regards his attitude towards the truth of these ancient legends. Agamemnon and Atreus, Theseus and Eurystheus, even Minos, about whom Herodotus has some doubts, are to him as real personages as Alcibiades or Gylippus.

The points in his historical criticism of the past are, first, his rejection of all extra-natural interference, and, secondly, the attributing to these ancient heroes the motives and modes of thought of his own day. The present was to him the key to the explanation of the past, as it was to the prediction of the future. Now, as regards his attitude towards the supernatural he is at one with modern science.

We too know that, just as the primeval coal- beds reveal to us the traces of rain-drops and other atmospheric phenomena similar to those of our own day, so, in estimating the history of the past, the introduction of no force must be allowed whose workings we cannot observe among the phenomena around us.

To lay down canons of ultra-historical credibility for the explanation of events which happen to have preceded us by a few thousand years, is as thoroughly unscientific as it is to intermingle preternatural in geological theories. Whatever the canons of art may be, no difficulty in history is so great as to warrant the introduction of a spirit of spirit [Greek text which cannot be reproduced], in the sense of a violation of the laws of nature.

Upon the other point, however, Thucydides falls into an anachronism. To refuse to allow the workings of chivalrous and self-denying motives among the knights of the Trojan crusade, because he saw none in the faction-loving Athenian of his own day, is to show an entire ignorance of the various characteristics of human nature developing under different circumstances, and to deny to a primitive chieftain like Agamemnon that authority founded on opinion, to which we give the name of divine right, is to fall into an historical error quite as gross as attributing to Atreus the courting of the populace ([Greek text which cannot be reproduced]) with a view to the Mycenean throne.

The general method of historical criticism pursued by Thucydides having been thus indicated, it remains to proceed more into detail as regards those particular points where he claims for himself a more rational method of estimating evidence than either the public or his predecessors possessed. 'So little pains,' he remarks, 'do the vulgar take in the investigation of truth, satisfied with their preconceived opinions,' that the majority of the Greeks believe in a Pitanate cohort of the Spartan army and in a double vote being the prerogative of the Spartan kings, neither of which opinions has any foundation in fact.

But the chief point on which he lays stress as evincing the 'uncritical way with which men receive legends, even the legends of their own country,' is the entire baselessness of the common Athenian tradition in which Harmodios and Aristogeiton were represented as the patriotic liberators of Athens from the Peisistratid tyranny. So far, he points out, from the love of freedom being their motive, both of them were influenced by merely personal considerations, Aristogeiton being jealous of Hipparchos' attention to Harmodios, then a beautiful boy in the flower of Greek loveliness, while the latter's indignation was aroused by an insult offered to his sister by the prince.

Their motives, then, were personal revenge, while the result of their conspiracy served only to rivet more tightly the chains of servitude which bound Athens to the Peisistratid house, for Hipparchos, whom they killed, was only the tyrant's younger brother, and not the tyrant himself. To prove his theory that Hippias was the elder, he appeals to the evidence afforded by a public inscription in which his name occurs immediately after that of his father, a point which he thinks shows that he was the eldest, and so the heir. This view he further corroborates by another inscription, on the altar of Apollo, which mentions the children of Hippias and not those of his brothers; 'for it was natural for the eldest to be married first'; and besides this, on the score of general probability he points out that, had Hippias been the younger, he would not have so easily obtained the tyranny on the death of Hipparchos. Now, what is important in Thucydides, as evinced in the treatment of legend generally, is not the results he arrived at, but the method by which he works.

The first great rationalistic historian, he may be said to have paved the way for all those who followed after him, though it must always be remembered that, while the total absence in his pages of all the mystical paraphernalia of the supernatural theory of life is an advance in the progress of rationalism, and an era in scientific history, whose importance could never be over-estimated, yet we find along with it a total absence of any mention of those various social and economical forces which form such important factors in the evolution of the world, and to which Herodotus rightly gave great prominence in his immortal work. The history of Thucydides is essentially one-sided and incomplete.

The intricate details of sieges and battles, subjects with which the historian proper has really nothing to do except so far as they may throw light on the spirit of the age, we would readily exchange for some notice of the condition of private society in Athens, or the influence and position of women.

There is an advance in the method of historical criticism; there is an advance in the conception and motive of history itself; for in Thucydides we may discern that natural reaction against the intrusion of didactic and theological considerations into the sphere of the pure intellect, the spirit of which may be found in the Euripidean treatment of tragedy and the later schools of art, as well as in the Platonic conception of science. History, no doubt, has splendid lessons for our instruction, just as all good art comes to us as the herald of the noblest truth.

But, to set before either the painter or the historian the

inculcation of moral lessons as an aim to be consciously pursued, is to miss entirely the true motive and characteristic both of art and history, which is in the one case the creation of beauty, in the other the discovery of the laws of the evolution of progress: IL NE FAUT DEMANDER DE L'ART QUE L'ART, DU PASSE QUE LE PASSE. Herodotus wrote to illustrate the wonderful ways of Providence and the nemesis that falls on sin, and his work is a good example of the truth that nothing can dispense with criticism so much as a moral aim.

Thucydides has no creed to preach, no doctrine to prove. He analyses the results which follow inevitably from certain antecedents, in order that on a recurrence of the same crisis men may know how to act. His object was to discover the laws of the past so as to serve as a light to illumine the future. We must not confuse the recognition of the utility of history with any ideas of a didactic aim.

Two points more in Thucydides remain for our consideration: his treatment of the rise of Greek civilisation, and of the primitive condition of Hellas, as well as the question how far can he be said really to have recognised the existence of laws regulating the complex phenomena of life.

The investigation into the two great problems of the origin of society and the philosophy of history occupies such an important position in the evolution of Greek thought that, to obtain any clear view of the workings of the critical spirit, it will be necessary to trace at some length their rise and scientific development as evinced not merely in the works of historians proper, but also in the philosophical treatises of Plato and Aristotle.

The important position which these two great thinkers occupy in the progress of historical criticism can hardly be over-estimated. I do not mean merely as regards their treatment of the Greek Bible, and Plato's endeavours to purge sacred history of its immorality by the application of ethical canons at the time when Aristotle was beginning to undermine the basis of miracles by his scientific conception of law, but with reference to these two wider questions of the rise of civil institutions and the philosophy of history. And first, as regards the current theories of the primitive condition of society, there was a wide divergence of opinion in Hellenic society, just as there is now.

For while the majority of the orthodox public, of whom Hesiod may be taken as the representative, looked back, as a great many of our own day still do, to a fabulous age of innocent happiness, a BELL' ETE DELL' AURO, where sin and death were unknown and men and women were like Gods, the foremost men of intellect such as Aristotle and Plato, AEschylus and many of the other poets (1) saw in primitive man 'a few small sparks of humanity preserved on the tops of mountains after some deluge,' 'without an idea of cities, governments or legislation,' 'living the lives of wild beasts in sunless caves,' 'their only law being the survival of the fittest.'

And this, too, was the opinion of Thucydides, whose ARCHAEOLOGIA as it is contains a most valuable disquisition on the early condition of Hellas, which it will be necessary to examine at some length. Now, as regards the means employed generally by Thucydides for the elucidation of ancient history, I have already pointed out how that, while acknowledging that 'it is the tendency of every poet to exaggerate, as it is of every chronicler to seek to be attractive at the expense of truth; he yet assumes in the thoroughly euhemeristic way, that under the veil of myth and legend there does yet exist a rational basis of fact discoverable by the method of rejecting all supernatural interference as well as any extraordinary motives influencing the actors.

It is in complete accordance with this spirit that he appeals, for instance, to the Homeric epithet of [Greek text which cannot be reproduced], as applied to Corinth, as a proof of the early commercial prosperity of that city; to the fact of the generic name HELLENES not occurring in the ILIAD as a corroboration of his theory of the essentially disunited character of the primitive Greek tribes; and he argues from the line 'O'er many islands and all Argos ruled,' as applied to Agamemnon, that his forces must have been partially naval, 'for Agamemnon's was a continental power, and he could not have been master of any but the adjacent islands, and these would not be many but through the possession of a fleet.' Anticipating in some measure the comparative method of research, he argues from the fact of the more barbarous Greek tribes, such as the AEtolians and Acarnanians, still carrying arms in his own day, that this custom was the case originally over the whole country. 'The fact,' he says, 'that the people in these parts of Hellas are still living in the old way points to a time when the same mode of life was equally common to all.'

Similarly, in another passage, he shows how a corroboration of his theory of the respectable character of piracy in ancient days is afforded by 'the honour with which some of the inhabitants of the continent still regard a successful marauder,' as well as by the fact that the question, 'Are you a pirate?' is a common feature of primitive society as shown in the poets; and finally, after observing how the old Greek custom of wearing belts in gymnastic contests still survived among the more uncivilised Asiatic tribes, he observes that there are many other points in which a likeness may be shown between the life of the primitive Hellenes and that of the barbarians to-day.'

As regards the evidence afforded by ancient remains, while adducing as a proof of the insecure character of early Greek society the fact of their cities being always built at some distance from the sea, yet he is careful to warn us, and the caution ought to be borne in mind by all archaeologists, that we have no right to conclude from the scanty remains of any city that its legendary greatness in primitive times was a mere exaggeration. 'We are not justified,' he says, 'in rejecting the tradition of the magnitude of the Trojan armament, because Mycenae and the other towns of that age seem to us small and insignificant.

For, if Lacedaemon was to become desolate, any antiquarian judging merely from its ruins would be inclined to regard the tale of the Spartan hegemony as an idle myth; for the city is a mere collection of villages after the old fashion of Hellas, and has none of those splendid public buildings and temples which characterise Athens, and whose remains, in the case of the latter city, would be so marvellous as to lead the superficial observer into an exaggerated estimate of the Athenian power.' Nothing can be more scientific than the archaeological canons laid down, whose truth is strikingly illustrated to any one who has compared the waste fields of the Eurotas plain with the lordly monuments of the Athenian acropolis.

On the other hand, Thucydides is quite conscious of the value of the positive evidence afforded by archaeological remains. He appeals, for instance, to the character of the armour found in the Delian tombs and the peculiar mode of sepulture, as corroboration of his theory of the predominance of the Carian element among the primitive islanders, and to the concentration of all the temples either in the Acropolis, or in its immediate vicinity, to the name of [Greek text which cannot be reproduced] by which it was still known, and to the extraordinary sanctity of the spring of water there, as proof that the primitive city was originally confined to the citadel, and the district immediately beneath it (ii. 16).

And lastly, in the very opening of his history, anticipating one of the most scientific of modern methods, he points out how in early states of civilisation immense fertility of the soil tends to favour the personal aggrandisement of individuals, and so to stop the normal progress of the country through 'the rise of factions, that endless source of ruin'; and also by the allurements it offers to a foreign invader, to necessitate a continual change of population, one immigration following on another.

He exemplifies his theory by pointing to the endless political revolutions that characterised Arcadia, Thessaly and Boeotia, the three richest spots in Greece, as well as by the negative instance of the undisturbed state in primitive time of Attica, which was always remarkable for the dryness and poverty of its soil.

Now, while undoubtedly in these passages we may recognise the first anticipation of many of the most modern principles of research, we must remember how essentially limited is the range of the ARCHAEOLOGIA, and how no theory at all is offered on the wider questions of the general conditions of the rise and progress of humanity, a problem which is first scientifically discussed in the REPUBLIC of Plato.

And at the outset it must be premised that, while the study of primitive man is an essentially inductive science, resting rather on the accumulation of evidence than on speculation, among the Greeks it was prosecuted rather on deductive principles. Thucydides did, indeed, avail himself of the opportunities afforded by the unequal development of civilisation in his own day in Greece, and in the places I have pointed out seems to have anticipated the comparative method.

But we do not find later writers availing themselves of the wonderfully accurate and picturesque accounts given by Herodotus of the customs of savage tribes. To take one instance, which bears a good deal on modern questions, we find in the works of this great traveller the gradual and progressive steps in the development of the family life clearly manifested in the mere gregarious herding together of the Agathyrsi, their primitive kinsmanship through women in common, and the rise of a feeling of paternity from a state of polyandry. This tribe stood at that time on that borderland between umbilical relationship and the family which has been such a difficult point for modern anthropologists to find.

The ancient authors, however, are unanimous in insisting that the family is the ultimate unit of society, though, as I have said, an inductive study of primitive races, or even the accounts given of them by Herodotus, would have shown them that the [Greek text which cannot be reproduced] of a personal household, to use Plato's expression, is really a most complex notion appearing always in a late stage of civilisation, along with recognition of private property and the rights of individualism. Philology also, which in the hands of modern investigators has proved such a splendid instrument of research, was in ancient days studied on principles too unscientific to be of much use.

Herodotus points out that the word ERIDANOS is essentially Greek in character, that consequently the river supposed to run round the world is probably a mere Greek invention. His remarks, however, on language generally, as in the case of PIROMIS and the ending of the Persian names, show on what unsound basis his knowledge of language rested. In the BACCHAE of Euripides there is an extremely interesting passage in which the immoral stories of the Greek mythology are accounted for on the principle of that misunderstanding of words and metaphors to which modern science has given the name of a disease of language.

In answer to the impious rationalism of Pentheus - a sort of modern Philistine - Teiresias, who may be termed the Max Muller of the Theban cycle, points out that the story of Dionysus being inclosed in Zeus' thigh really arose from the linguistic confusion between [Greek text which cannot be reproduced] and [Greek text which cannot be reproduced].

On the whole, however - for I have quoted these two instances only to show the unscientific character of early philology - we may say that this important instrument in recreating the history of the past was not really used by the ancients as a means of historical criticism.

Nor did the ancients employ that other method, used to such advantage in our own day, by which in the symbolism and formulas of an advanced civilisation we can detect the unconscious survival of ancient customs: for, whereas in the sham capture of the bride at a marriage feast, which was common in Wales till a recent time, we can discern the lingering reminiscence of the barbarous habit of exogamy, the ancient writers saw only the deliberate commemoration of an historical event.

Aristotle does not tell us by what method he discovered that the Greeks used to buy their wives in primitive times, but, judging by his general principles, it was probably through some legend or myth on the subject which lasted to his own day, and not, as we would do, by arguing back from the marriage presents given to the bride and her relatives.

The origin of the common proverb 'worth so many beeves,' in which we discern the unconscious survival of a purely pastoral state of society before the use of metals was known, is ascribed by Plutarch to the fact of Theseus having coined money bearing a bull's head. Similarly, the Amathusian festival, in which a young man imitated the labours of a woman in travail, is regarded by him as a rite instituted in Ariadne's honour, and the Carian adoration of asparagus as a simple commemoration of the adventure of the nymph Perigune.

In the first of these WE discern the beginning of agnation and kinsmanship through the father, which still lingers in the 'couvee' of New Zealand tribes: while the second is a relic of the totem and fetish worship of plants. Now, in entire opposition to this modern inductive principle of research stands the philosophic Plato, whose account of primitive man is entirely speculative and deductive.

The origin of society he ascribes to necessity, the mother of all inventions, and imagines that individual man began deliberately to herd together on account of the advantages of the principle of division of labour and the rendering of mutual need. It must, however, be borne in mind that Plato's object in this whole passage in the REPUBLIC was, perhaps, not so much to analyse the conditions of early society as to illustrate the importance of the division of labour, the shibboleth of his political economy, by showing what a powerful factor it must have been in the most primitive as well as in the most complex states of society; just as in the LAWS he almost rewrites entirely the history of the Peloponnesus in order to prove the necessity of a balance of power.

He surely, I mean, must have recognised himself how essentially incomplete his theory was in taking no account of the origin of family life, the position and influence of women, and other social questions, as well as in disregarding those deeper motives of religion, which are such important factors in early civilisation, and whose influence Aristotle seems to have clearly apprehended, when he says that the aim of primitive society was not merely life but the higher life, and that in the origin of society utility is not the sole motive, but that there is something spiritual in it if, at least, 'spiritual' will bring out the meaning of that complex expression [Greek text which cannot be reproduced]. Otherwise, the whole account in the REPUBLIC of primitive man will always remain as a warning against the intrusion of A PRIORI speculations in the domain appropriate to induction.

Now, Aristotle's theory of the origin of society, like his philosophy of ethics, rests ultimately on the principle of final causes, not in the theological meaning of an aim or tendency imposed from without, but in the scientific sense of function corresponding to organ. 'Nature maketh no thing in vain' is the text of Aristotle in this as in other inquiries. Man being the only animal possessed of the power of rational speech is, he asserts, by nature intended to be social, more so than the bee or any other gregarious animal.

He is [Greek text which cannot be reproduced], and the national tendency towards higher forms of perfection brings the 'armed savage who used to sell his wife' to the free independence of a free state, and to the [Greek text which cannot be reproduced], which was the test of true citizenship. The stages passed through by humanity start with the family first as the ultimate unit.

The conglomeration of families forms a village ruled by that patriarchal sway which is the oldest form of government in the world, as is shown by the fact that all men count it to be the constitution of heaven, and the villages are merged into the state, and here the progression stops. For Aristotle, like all Greek thinkers, found his ideal within the walls of the [Greek text which cannot be reproduced], yet perhaps in his remark that a united Greece would rule the world we may discern some anticipation of that 'federal union of free states into one consolidated empire' which, more than the [Greek text which cannot be reproduced], is to our eyes the ultimately perfect polity. How far Aristotle was justified in regarding the family as the ultimate unit, with the materials afforded to him by Greek literature, I have already noticed.

Besides, Aristotle, I may remark, had he reflected on the meaning of that Athenian law which, while prohibiting marriage with a uterine sister, permitted it with a sister-german, or on the common tradition in Athens that before the time of Cecrops children bore their mothers' names, or on some of the Spartan regulations, could hardly have failed to see the universality of kinsmanship through women in early days, and the late appearance of monandry. Yet, while he missed this point, in common, it must be acknowledged, with many modern writers, such as Sir Henry Maine, it is essentially as an explorer of inductive instances that we recognise his improvement on Plato.

The treatise [Greek text which cannot be reproduced], did it remain to us in its entirety, would have been one of the most valuable landmarks in the progress of historical criticism, and the first scientific treatise on the science of comparative politics. A few fragments still remain to us, in one of which we find Aristotle appealing to the authority of an ancient inscription on the 'Disk of Iphitus,' one of the most celebrated Greek antiquities, to corroborate his theory of the Lycurgean revival of the Olympian festival; while his enormous research is evinced in the elaborate explanation he gives of the historical origin of proverbs such as [Greek text which cannot be reproduced], of religious songs like the [Greek text which cannot be reproduced] of the Botticean virgins, or the praises of love and war.

And, finally, it is to be observed how much wider than Plato's his theory of the origin of society is. They both rest on a psychological basis, but Aristotle's recognition of the capacity for progress and the tendency towards a higher life shows how much deeper his knowledge of human nature was. In imitation of these two philosophers, Polybius gives an account of the origin of society in the opening to his philosophy of history.

Somewhat in the spirit of Plato, he imagines that after one of the cyclic deluges which sweep off mankind at stated periods and annihilate all pre-existing civilisation, the few surviving members of humanity coalesce for mutual protection, and, as in the case with ordinary animals, the one most remarkable for physical strength is elected king. In a short time, owing to the workings of sympathy and the desire of approbation, the moral qualities begin to make their appearance, and intellectual instead of bodily excellence becomes the qualification for sovereignty.

Other points, as the rise of law and the like, are dwelt on in a somewhat modern spirit, and although Polybius seems not to have employed the inductive method of research in this question, or rather, I should say, of the hierarchical order of the rational progress of ideas in life, he is not far removed from what the laborious investigations of modern travellers have given us.

And, indeed, as regards the working of the speculative faculty in the creation of history, it is in all respects marvellous how that the most truthful accounts of the passage from barbarism to civilisation in ancient literature come from the works of poets. The elaborate researches of Mr. Tylor and Sir John Lubbock have done little more than verify the theories put forward in the PROMETHEUS BOUND and the DE NATURA RERUM; yet neither AEschylus nor Lucretias followed in the modern path, but rather attained to truth by a certain almost mystic power of creative imagination, such as we now seek to banish from science as a dangerous power, though to it science seems to owe many of its most splendid generalities.

Leaving then the question of the origin of society as treated by the ancients, I shall now turn to the other and the more important question of how far they may he said to have attained to what we call the philosophy of history. Now at the outset we must note that, while the conceptions of law and order have been universally received as the governing principles of the phenomena of nature in the sphere of physical science, yet their intrusion into the domain of history and the life of man has always been met with a strong opposition, on the ground of the incalculable nature of two great forces acting on human action, a certain causeless spontaneity which men call free will, and the extra-natural interference which they attribute as a constant attribute to God.

Now, that there is a science of the apparently variable phenomena of history is a conception which WE have perhaps only recently begun to appreciate; yet, like all other great thoughts, it seems to have come to the Greek mind spontaneously, through a certain splendour of imagination, in the morning tide of their civilisation, before inductive research had armed them with the instruments of verification.

For I think it is possible to discern in some of the mystic speculations of the early Greek thinkers that desire to discover what is that 'invariable existence of which there are variable states,' and to incorporate it in some one formula of law which may serve to explain the different manifestations of all organic bodies, MAN INCLUDED, which is the germ of the philosophy of history; the germ indeed of an idea of which it is not too much to say that on it any kind of historical criticism, worthy of the name, must ultimately rest.

For the very first requisite for any scientific conception of history is the doctrine of uniform sequence: in other words, that certain events having happened, certain other events corresponding to them will happen also; that the past is the key of the future. Now at the birth of this great conception science, it is true, presided, yet religion it was which at the outset clothed it in its own garb, and familiarised men with it by appealing to their hearts first and then to their intellects; knowing that at the beginning of things it is through the moral nature, and not through the intellectual, that great truths are spread.

So in Herodotus, who may be taken as a representative of the orthodox tone of thought, the idea of the uniform sequence of cause and effect appears under the theological aspect of Nemesis and Providence, which is really the scientific conception of law, only it is viewed from an ETHICAL standpoint. Now in Thucydides the philosophy of history rests on the probability, which the uniformity of human nature affords us, that the future will in the course of human things resemble the past, if not reproduce it. He appears to contemplate a recurrence of the phenomena of history as equally certain with a return of the epidemic of the Great Plague. Notwithstanding what German critics have written on the subject, we must beware of regarding this conception as a mere reproduction of that cyclic theory of events which sees in the world nothing but the regular rotation of Strophe and Antistrophe, in the eternal choir of life and death.

For, in his remarks on the excesses of the Corcyrean Revolution, Thucydides distinctly rests his idea of the recurrence of history on the psychological grounds of the general sameness of mankind. 'The sufferings,' he says, 'which revolution entailed upon the cities were many and terrible, such as have occurred and always will occurs as long as human nature remains the same, though in a severer or milder form, and varying in their symptoms according to the variety of the particular cases.

'In peace and prosperity states and individuals have better sentiments, because they are not confronted with imperious necessities; but war takes away the easy supply of men's wants, and so proves a hard taskmaster, which brings most men's characters to a level with their fortunes.' It is evident that here Thucydides is ready to admit the variety of manifestations which external causes bring about in their workings on the uniform character of the nature of man.

Yet, after all is said, these are perhaps but very general statements: the ordinary effects of peace and war are dwelt on, but there is no real analysis of the immediate causes and general laws of the phenomena of life, nor does Thucydides seem to recognise the truth that if humanity proceeds in circles, the circles are always widening.

Perhaps we may say that with him the philosophy of history is partly in the metaphysical stage, and see, in the progress of this idea from Herodotus to Polybius, the exemplification of the Comtian Law of the three stages of thought, the theological, the metaphysical, and the scientific: for truly out of the vagueness of theological mysticism this conception which we call the Philosophy of History was raised to a scientific principle, according to which the past was explained and the future predicted by reference to general laws. Now, just as the earliest account of the nature of the progress of humanity is to be found in Plato, so in him we find the first explicit attempt to found a universal philosophy of history upon wide rational grounds.

Having created an ideally perfect state, the philosopher proceeds to give an elaborate theory of the complex causes which produce revolutions, of the moral effects of various forms of government and education, of the rise of the criminal classes and their connection with pauperism, and, in a word, to create history by the deductive method and to proceed from A PRIORI psychological principles to discover the governing laws of the apparent chaos of political life.

There have been many attempts since Plato to deduce from a single philosophical principle all the phenomena which experience subsequently verifies for us. Fichte thought he could predict the world-plan from the idea of universal time.

Hegel dreamed he had found the key to the mysteries of life in the development of freedom, and Krause in the categories of being. But the one scientific basis on which the true philosophy of history must rest is the complete knowledge of the laws of human nature in all its wants, its aspirations, its powers and its tendencies: and this great truth, which Thucydides may be said in some measure to have apprehended, was given to us first by Plato.

Now, it cannot be accurately said of this philosopher that either his philosophy or his history is entirely and simply A PRIORI. ON EST DE SON SIECLE MEME QUAND ON Y PROTESTE, and so we find in him continual references to the Spartan mode of life, the Pythagorean system, the general characteristics of Greek tyrannies and Greek democracies. For while, in his account of the method of forming an ideal state, he says that the political artist is indeed to fix his gaze on the sun of abstract truth in the heavens of the pure reason, but is sometimes to turn to the realisation of the ideals on earth: yet, after all, the general character of the Platonic method, which is what we are specially concerned with, is essentially deductive and A PRIORI.

And he himself, in the building up of his Nephelococcygia, certainly starts with a [Greek text which cannot be reproduced], making a clean sweep of all history and all experience; and it was essentially as an A PRIORI theorist that he is criticised by Aristotle, as we shall see later.

To proceed to closer details regarding the actual scheme of the laws of political revolutions as drawn out by Plato, we must first note that the primary cause of the decay of the ideal state is the general principle, common to the vegetable and animal worlds as well as to the world of history, that all created things are fated to decay - a principle which, though expressed in the terms of a mere metaphysical abstraction, is yet perhaps in its essence scientific.

For we too must hold that a continuous redistribution of matter and motion is the inevitable result of the nominal persistence of Force, and that perfect equilibrium is as impossible in politics as it certainly is in physics. The secondary causes which mar the perfection of the Platonic 'city of the sun' are to be found in the intellectual decay of the race consequent on injudicious marriages and in the Philistine elevation of physical achievements over mental culture; while the hierarchical succession of Timocracy and Oligarchy, Democracy and Tyranny, is dwelt on at great length and its causes analysed in a very dramatic and psychological manner, if not in that sanctioned by the actual order of history.

And indeed it is apparent at first sight that the Platonic succession of states represents rather the succession of ideas in the philosophic mind than any historical succession of time. Aristotle meets the whole simply by an appeal to facts. If the theory of the periodic decay of all created things, he urges, be scientific, it must be universal, and so true of all the other states as well as of the ideal.

Besides, a state usually changes into its contrary and not to the form next to it; so the ideal state would not change into Timocracy; while Oligarchy, more often than Tyranny, succeeds Democracy. Plato, besides, says nothing of what a Tyranny would change to.

According to the cycle theory it ought to pass into the ideal state again, but as a fact one Tyranny is changed into another as at Sicyon, or into a Democracy as at Syracuse, or into an Aristocracy as at Carthage. The example of Sicily, too, shows that an Oligarchy is often followed by a Tyranny, as at Leontini and Gela. Besides, it is absurd to represent greed as the chief motive of decay, or to talk of avarice as the root of Oligarchy, when in nearly all true oligarchies money-making is forbidden by law. And finally the Platonic theory neglects the different kinds of democracies and of tyrannies.

Now nothing can be more important than this passage in Aristotle's POLITICS (v. 12.), which may he said to mark an era in the evolution of historical criticism. For there is nothing on which Aristotle insists so strongly as that the generalisations from facts ought to be added to the data of the A PRIORI method - a principle which we know to be true not merely of deductive speculative politics but of physics also: for are not the residual phenomena of chemists a valuable source of improvement in theory? His own method is essentially historical though by no means empirical.

On the contrary, this far-seeing thinker, rightly styled IL MAESTRO DI COLOUR CHE SANNO, may be said to have apprehended clearly that the true method is neither exclusively empirical nor exclusively speculative, but rather a union of both in the process called Analysis or the Interpretation of Facts, which has been defined as the application to facts of such general conceptions as may fix the important characteristics of the phenomena, and present them permanently in their true relations.

He too was the first to point out, what even in our own day is incompletely appreciated, that nature, including the development of man, is not full of incoherent episodes like a bad tragedy, that inconsistency and anomaly are as impossible in the moral as they are in the physical world, and that where the superficial observer thinks he sees a revolution the philosophical critic discerns merely the gradual and rational evolution of the inevitable results of certain antecedents.

And while admitting the necessity of a psychological basis for the philosophy of history, he added to it the important truth that man, to be apprehended in his proper position in the universe as well as in his natural powers, must be studied from below in the hierarchical progression of higher function from the lower forms of life.

The important maxim, that to obtain a clear conception of anything we must 'study it in its growth from the very beginning,' is formally set down in the opening of the

POLITICS, where, indeed, we shall find the other characteristic features of the modern Evolutionary theory, such as the 'Differentiation of Function' and the 'Survival of the Fittest' explicitly set forth. What a valuable step this was in the improvement of the method of historical criticism it is needless to point out.

By it, one may say, the true thread was given to guide one's steps through the bewildering labyrinth of facts. For history (to use terms with which Aristotle has made us familiar) may be looked at from two essentially different standpoints; either as a work of art whose [Greek text which cannot be reproduced] or final cause is external to it and imposed on it from without; or as an organism containing the law of its own development in itself, and working out its perfection merely by the fact of being what it is.

Now, if we adopt the former, which we may style the theological view, we shall be in continual danger of tripping into the pitfall of some A PRIORI conclusion - that bourne from which, it has been truly said, no traveller ever returns.

The latter is the only scientific theory and was apprehended in its fulness by Aristotle, whose application of the inductive method to history, and whose employment of the evolutionary theory of humanity, show that he was conscious that the philosophy of history is nothing separate from the facts of history but is contained in them, and that the rational law of the complex phenomena of life, like the ideal in the world of thought, is to be reached through the facts, not superimposed on them - [Greek text which cannot be reproduced].

And finally, in estimating the enormous debt which the science of historical criticism owes to Aristotle, we must not pass over his attitude towards those two great difficulties in the formation of a philosophy of history on which I have touched above. I mean the assertion of extra-natural interference with the normal development of the world and of the incalculable influence exercised by the power of free will.

Now, as regards the former, he may be said to have neglected it entirely. The special acts of providence proceeding from God's immediate government of the world, which Herodotus saw as mighty landmarks in history, would have been to him essentially disturbing elements in that universal reign of law, the extent of whose limitless empire he of all the great thinkers of antiquity was the first explicitly to recognise.

Standing aloof from the popular religion as well as from the deeper conceptions of Herodotus and the Tragic School, he no longer thought of God as of one with fair limbs and treacherous face haunting wood and glade, nor would he see in him a jealous judge continually interfering in the world's history to bring the wicked to punishment and the proud to a fall. God to him was the incarnation of the pure

Intellect, a being whose activity was the contemplation of his own perfection, one whom Philosophy might imitate but whom prayers could never move, to the sublime indifference of whose passionless wisdom what were the sons of men, their desires or their sins? While, as regards the other difficulty and the formation of a philosophy of history, the conflict of free will with general laws appears first in Greek thought in the usual theological form in which all great ideas seem to be cradled at their birth.

It was such legends as those of OEdipus and Adrastus, exemplifying the struggles of individual humanity against the overpowering force of circumstances and necessity, which gave to the early Greeks those same lessons which we of modern days draw, in somewhat less artistic fashion, from the study of statistics and the laws of physiology. In Aristotle, of course, there is no trace of supernatural influence.

The Furies, which drive their victim into sin first and then punishment, are no longer 'viper-tressed goddesses with eyes and mouth aflame,' but those evil thoughts which harbour within the impure soul. In this, as in all other points, to arrive at Aristotle is to reach the pure atmosphere of scientific and modern thought.

But while he rejected pure necessitarianism in its crude form as essentially a REDUCTIO AD ABSURDUM of life, he was fully conscious of the fact that the will is not a mysterious and ultimate unit of force beyond which we cannot go and whose special characteristic is inconsistency, but a certain creative attitude of the mind which is, from the first, continually influenced by habits, education and circumstance; so absolutely modifiable, in a word, that the good and the bad man alike seem to lose the power of free will; for the one is morally unable to sin, the other physically incapacitated for reformation.

And of the influence of climate and temperature in forming the nature of man (a conception perhaps pressed too far in modern days when the 'race theory' is supposed to be a sufficient explanation of the Hindoo, and the latitude and longitude of a country the best guide to its morals) Aristotle is completely unaware. I do not allude to such smaller points as the oligarchical tendencies of a horse-breeding country and the democratic influence of the proximity of the sea (important though they are for the consideration of Greek history), but rather to those wider views in the seventh book of his POLITICS, where he attributes the happy union in the Greek character of intellectual attainments with the spirit of progress to the temperate climate they enjoyed, and points out how the extreme cold of the north dulls the mental faculties of its inhabitants and renders them incapable of social organisation or extended empire; while to the enervating heat of eastern countries was due that want of spirit and bravery which then, as now, was the characteristic of the population in that quarter of the globe.

Thucydides has shown the causal connection between political revolutions and the fertility of the soil, but goes a step farther and points out the psychological influences on a people's character exercised by the various extremes of climate - in both cases the first appearance of a most valuable form of historical criticism.

To the development of Dialectic, as to God, intervals of time are of no account. From Plato and Aristotle we pass direct to Polybius. The progress of thought from the philosopher of the Academe to the Arcadian historian may be best illustrated by a comparison of the method by which each of the three writers, whom I have selected as the highest expression of the rationalism of his respective age, attained to his ideal state: for the latter conception may be in a measure regarded as representing the most spiritual principle which they could discern in history.

Now, Plato created his on A PRIORI principles; Aristotle formed his by an analysis of existing constitutions; Polybius found his realised for him in the actual world of fact. Aristotle criticised the deductive speculations of Plato by means of inductive negative instances, but Polybius will not take the 'Cloud City' of the REPUBLIC into account at all. He compares it to an athlete who has never run on 'Constitution Hill,' to a statue so beautiful that it is entirely removed from the ordinary conditions of humanity, and consequently from the canons of criticism.

The Roman state had attained in his eyes, by means of the mutual counteraction of three opposing forces, that stable equilibrium in politics which was the ideal of all the theoretical writers of antiquity. And in connection with this point it will be convenient to notice here how much truth there is contained in the accusation often brought against the ancients that they knew nothing of the idea of Progress, for the meaning of many of their speculations will be hidden from us if we do not try and comprehend first what their aim was, and secondly why it was so.

Now, like all wide generalities, this statement is at least inaccurate. The prayer of Plato's ideal City - [Greek text which cannot be reproduced], might be written as a text over the door of the last Temple to Humanity raised by the disciples of Fourier and Saint-Simon, but it is certainly true that their ideal principle was order and permanence, not indefinite progress. For, setting aside the artistic prejudices which would have led the Greeks to reject this idea of unlimited improvement, we may note that the modern conception of progress rests partly on the new enthusiasm and worship of humanity, partly on the splendid hopes of material improvements in civilisation which applied science has held out to us, two influences from which ancient Greek thought seems to have been strangely free.

For the Greeks marred the perfect humanism of the great men whom they worshipped, by imputing to them divinity and its supernatural powers; while their science was eminently speculative and often almost mystic in its character, aiming at culture and not utility, at higher spirituality and more intense reverence for law, rather than at the increased facilities of locomotion and the cheap production of common things about which our modern scientific school ceases not to boast.

And lastly, and perhaps chiefly, we must remember that the 'plague spot of all Greek states,' as one of their own writers has called it, was the terrible insecurity to life and property which resulted from the factions and revolutions which ceased not to trouble Greece at all times, raising a spirit of fanaticism such as religion raised in the middle ages of Europe.

These considerations, then, will enable us to understand first how it was that, radical and unscrupulous reformers as the Greek political theorists were, yet, their end once attained, no modern conservatives raised such outcry against the slightest innovation. Even acknowledged improvements in such things as the games of children or the modes of music were regarded by them with feelings of extreme apprehension as the herald of the DRAPEAU ROUGE of reform.

And secondly, it will show us how it was that Polybius found his ideal in the commonwealth of Rome, and Aristotle, like Mr. Bright, in the middle classes. Polybius, however, is not content merely with pointing out his ideal state, but enters at considerable length into the question of those general laws whose consideration forms the chief essential of the philosophy of history. He starts by accepting the general principle that all things are fated to decay (which I noticed in the case of Plato), and that 'as iron produces rust and as wood breeds the animals that destroy it, so every state has in it the seeds of its own corruption.' He is not, however, content to rest there, but proceeds to deal with the more immediate causes of revolutions, which he says are twofold in nature, either external or internal.

Now, the former, depending as they do on the synchronous conjunction of other events outside the sphere of scientific estimation, are from their very character incalculable; but the latter, though assuming many forms, always result from the over-great preponderance of any single element to the detriment of the others, the rational law lying at the base of all varieties of political changes being that stability can result only from the statical equilibrium produced by the counteraction of opposing parts, since the more simple a constitution is the more it is insecure. Plato had pointed out before how the extreme liberty of a democracy always resulted in despotism, but Polybius analyses the law and shows the scientific principles on which it rests.

The doctrine of the instability of pure constitutions forms an important era in the philosophy of history. Its special applicability to the politics of our own day has been illustrated in the rise of the great Napoleon, when the French state had lost those divisions of caste and prejudice, of landed aristocracy and moneyed interest, institutions in which the vulgar see only barriers to Liberty but which are indeed the only possible defences against the coming of that periodic Sirius of politics, the [Greek text which cannot be reproduced].

There is a principle which Tocqueville never wearies of explaining, and which has been subsumed by Mr. Herbert Spencer under that general law common to all organic bodies which we call the Instability of the Homogeneous.

The various manifestations of this law, as shown in the normal, regular revolutions and evolutions of the different forms of government, are expounded with great clearness by Polybius, who claimed for his theory, in the Thucydidean spirit, that it is a [Greek text which cannot be reproduced], not a mere [Greek text which cannot be reproduced], and that a knowledge of it will enable the impartial observer to discover at any time what period of its constitutional evolution any particular state has already reached and into what form it will be next differentiated, though possibly the exact time of the changes may be more or less uncertain. Now in this necessarily incomplete account of the laws of political revolutions as expounded by Polybius enough perhaps has been said to show what is his true position in the rational development of the

'Idea' which I have called the Philosophy of History, because it is the unifying of history.

Seen darkly as it is through the glass of religion in the pages of Herodotus, more metaphysical than scientific with Thucydides, Plato strove to seize it by the eagle- flight of speculation, to reach it with the eager grasp of a soul impatient of those slower and surer inductive methods which Aristotle, in his trenchant criticism of his greater master, showed were more brilliant than any vague theory, if the test of brilliancy is truth. What then is the position of Polybius? Does any new method remain for him? Polybius was one of those many men who are born too late to be original.

To Thucydides belongs the honour of being the first in the history of Greek thought to discern the supreme calm of law and order underlying the fitful storms of life, and Plato and Aristotle each represents a great new principle.

To Polybius belongs the office - how noble an office he made it his writings show - of making more explicit the ideas which were implicit in his predecessors, of showing that they were of wider applicability and perhaps of deeper meaning than they had seemed before, of examining with more minuteness the laws which they had discovered, and finally of pointing out more clearly than any one had done the range of science and the means it offered for analysing the present and predicting what was to come.

His office thus was to gather up what they had left, to give their principles new life by a wider application. Polybius ends this great diapason of Greek thought. When the Philosophy of history appears next, as in Plutarch's tract on 'Why God's anger is delayed,' the pendulum of thought had swung back to where it began. His theory was introduced to the Romans under the cultured style of Cicero, and was welcomed by them as the philosophical panegyric of their state. The last notice of it in Latin literature is in the pages of Tacitus, who alludes to the stable polity formed out of these elements as a constitution easier to commend than to produce and in no case lasting.

Yet Polybius had seen the future with no uncertain eye,

and had prophesied the rise of the Empire from the unbalanced power of the ochlocracy fifty years and more before there was joy in the Julian household over the birth of that boy who, born to power as the champion of the people, died wearing the purple of a king. No attitude of historical criticism is more important than the means by which the ancients attained to the philosophy of history.

The principle of heredity can be exemplified in literature as well as in organic life: Aristotle, Plato and Polybius are the lineal ancestors of Fichte and Hegel, of Vico and Cousin, of Montesquieu and Tocqueville.

As my aim is not to give an account of historians but to point out those great thinkers whose methods have furthered the advance of this spirit of historical criticism, I shall pass over those annalists and chroniclers who intervened between Thucydides and Polybius. Yet perhaps it may serve to throw new light on the real nature of this spirit and its intimate connection with all other forms of advanced thought if I give some estimate of the character and rise of those many influences prejudicial to the scientific study of history which cause such a wide gap between these two historians.

Foremost among these is the growing influence of rhetoric and the Isocratean school, which seems to have regarded history as an arena for the display either of pathos or paradoxes, not a scientific investigation into laws. The new age is the age of style. The same spirit of exclusive attention to form which made Euripides often, like Swinburne, prefer music to meaning and melody to morality, which gave to the later Greek statues that refined effeminacy, that overstrained gracefulness of attitude, was felt in the sphere of history.

The rules laid down for historical composition are those relating to the aesthetic value of digressions, the legality of employing more than one metaphor in the same sentence, and the like; and historians are ranked not by their power of estimating evidence but by the goodness of the Greek they write. I must note also the important influence on literature exercised by Alexander the Great; for while his travels encouraged the more accurate research of geography, the very splendour of his achievements seems to have brought history again into the sphere of romance.

The appearance of all great men in the world is followed invariably by the rise of that mythopoeic spirit and that tendency to look for the marvellous, which is so fatal to true historical criticism. An Alexander, a Napoleon, a Francis of Assisi and a Mahomet are thought to be outside the limiting conditions of rational law, just as comets were supposed to be not very long ago.

While the founding of that city of Alexandria, in which Western and Eastern thought met with such strange result to both, diverted the critical tendencies of the Greek spirit into questions of grammar, philology and the like, the narrow, artificial atmosphere of that University town (as we may call it) was fatal to the development of that independent and speculative spirit of research which strikes out new methods of inquiry, of which historical criticism is one.

The Alexandrines combined a great love of learning with an ignorance of the true principles of research, an enthusiastic spirit for accumulating materials with a wonderful incapacity to use them. Not among the hot sands of Egypt, or the Sophists of Athens, but from the very heart of Greece rises the man of genius on whose influence in the evolution of the philosophy of history I have a short time ago dwelt.

Born in the serene and pure air of the clear uplands of Arcadia, Polybius may be said to reproduce in his work the character of the place which gave him birth. For, of all the historians - I do not say of antiquity but of all time - none is more rationalistic than he, none more free from any belief in the 'visions and omens, the monstrous legends, the grovelling superstitions and unmanly craving for the supernatural' ([Greek text that cannot be reproduced]) which he himself is compelled to notice as the characteristics of some of the historians who preceded him. Fortunate in the land which bore him, he was no less blessed in the wondrous time of his birth.

For, representing in himself the spiritual supremacy of the Greek intellect and allied in bonds of chivalrous friendship to the world-conqueror of his day, he seems led as it were by the hand of Fate 'to comprehend,' as has been said, 'more clearly than the Romans themselves the historical position of Rome,' and to discern with greater insight than all other men could those two great resultants of ancient civilisation, the material empire of the city of the seven hills, and the intellectual sovereignty of Hellas. Before his own day, he says, the events of the world were unconnected and separate and the histories confined to particular countries. Now, for the first time the universal empire of the Romans rendered a universal history possible.

This, then, is the august motive of his work: to trace the gradual rise of this Italian city from the day when the first legion crossed the narrow strait of Messina and landed on the fertile fields of Sicily to the time when Corinth in the East and Carthage in the West fell before the resistless wave of empire and the eagles of Rome passed on the wings of universal victory from Calpe and the Pillars of Hercules to Syria and the Nile.

At the same time he recognised that the scheme of Rome's empire was worked out under the aegis of God's will. For, as one of the Middle Age scribes most truly says, the [Greek text which cannot be reproduced] of Polybius is that power which we Christians call God; the second aim, as one may call it, of his history is to point out the rational and human and natural causes which brought this result, distinguishing, as we should say, between God's mediate and immediate government of the world.

With any direct intervention of God in the normal development of Man, he will have nothing to do: still less with any idea of chance as a factor in the phenomena of life. Chance and miracles, he says, are mere expressions for our ignorance of rational causes.

The spirit of rationalism which we recognised in Herodotus as a vague uncertain attitude and which appears in Thucydides as a consistent attitude of mind never argued about or even explained, is by Polybius analysed and formulated as the great instrument of historical research. Herodotus, while believing on principle in the supernatural, yet was sceptical at times. Thucydides simply ignored the supernatural. He did not discuss it, but he annihilated it by explaining history without it. Polybius enters at length into the whole question and explains its origin and the method of treating it. Herodotus would have believed in Scipio's dream. Thucydides would have ignored it entirely.

Polybius explains it. He is the culmination of the rational progression of Dialectic. 'Nothing,' he says, 'shows a foolish mind more than the attempt to account for any phenomena on the principle of chance or supernatural intervention.

History is a search for rational causes, and there is nothing in the world - even those phenomena which seem to us the most remote from law and improbable - which is not the logical and inevitable result of certain rational antecedents.'

Some things, of course, are to be rejected A PRIORI without entering into the subject: 'As regards such miracles,' he says, 'as that on a certain statue of Artemis rain or snow never falls though the statue stands in the open air, or that those who enter God's shrine in Arcadia lose their natural shadows, I cannot really be expected to argue upon the subject.

For these things are not only utterly improbable but absolutely impossible.' 'For us to argue reasonably on an acknowledged absurdity is as vain a task as trying to catch water in a sieve; it is really to admit the possibility of the supernatural, which is the very point at issue.' What Polybius felt was that to admit the possibility of a miracle is to annihilate the possibility of history: for just as scientific and chemical experiments would be either impossible or useless if exposed to the chance of continued interference on the part of some foreign body, so the laws and principles which govern history, the causes of phenomena, the evolution of progress, the whole science, in a word, of man's dealings with his own race and with nature, will remain a sealed book to him who admits the possibility of extra-natural interference.

The stories of miracles, then, are to be rejected on A PRIORI rational grounds, but in the case of events which we know to have happened the scientific historian will not rest till he has discovered their natural causes which, for instance, in the case of the wonderful rise of the Roman Empire - the most marvellous thing, Polybius says, which God ever brought about - are to be found in the excellence of their constitution ([Greek text which cannot be reproduced]), the wisdom of their advisers, their splendid military arrangements, and their superstition ([Greek text which cannot be reproduced]).

For while Polybius regarded the revealed religion as, of course, objective reality of truth, he laid great stress on its moral subjective influence, going, in one passage on the subject, even so far as almost to excuse the introduction of the supernatural in very small quantities into history on account of the extremely good effect it would have on pious people. But perhaps there is no passage in the whole of ancient and modern history which breathes such a manly and splendid spirit of rationalism as one preserved to us in the Vatican - strange resting-place for it! - in which he treats of the terrible decay of population which had fallen on his native land in his own day, and which by the general orthodox public was regarded as a special judgment of God sending childlessness on women as a punishment for the sins of the people.

For it was a disaster quite without parallel in the history of the land, and entirely unforeseen by any of its political-economy writers who, on the contrary, were always anticipating that danger would arise from an excess of population overrunning its means of subsistence, and becoming unmanageable through its size.

Polybius, however, will have nothing to do with either priest or worker of miracles in this matter. He will not even seek that 'sacred Heart of Greece,' Delphi, Apollo's shrine, whose inspiration even Thucydides admitted and before whose wisdom Socrates bowed.

How foolish, he says, were the man who on this matter would pray to God. We must search for the rational causes, and the causes are seen to be clear, and the method of prevention also. He then proceeds to notice how all this arose from the general reluctance to marriage and to bearing the expense of educating a large family which resulted from the carelessness and avarice of the men of his day, and he explains on entirely rational principles the whole of this apparently supernatural judgment.

Now, it is to be borne in mind that while his rejection of miracles as violation of inviolable laws is entirely A PRIORI - for discussion of such a matter is, of course, impossible for a rational thinker - yet his rejection of supernatural intervention rests entirely on the scientific grounds of the necessity of looking for natural causes. And he is quite logical in maintaining his position on these principles.

For, where it is either difficult or impossible to assign any rational cause for phenomena, or to discover their laws, he acquiesces reluctantly in the alternative of admitting some extra-natural interference which his essentially scientific method of treating the matter has logically forced on him, approving, for instance, of prayers for rain, on the express ground that the laws of meteorology had not yet been ascertained. He would, of course, have been the first to welcome our modern discoveries in the matter.

The passage in question is in every way one of the most interesting in his whole work, not, of course, as signifying any inclination on his part to acquiesce in the supernatural, but because it shows how essentially logical and rational his method of argument was, and how candid and fair his mind. Having now examined Polybius's attitude towards the supernatural and the general ideas which guided his research, I will proceed to examine the method he pursued in his scientific investigation of the complex phenomena of life.

For, as I have said before in the course of this essay, what is important in all great writers is not so much the results they arrive at as the methods they pursue. The increased knowledge of facts may alter any conclusion in history as in physical science, and the canons of speculative historical credibility must be acknowledged to appeal rather to that subjective attitude of mind which we call the historic sense than to any formulated objective rules.

But a scientific method is a gain for all time, and the true if not the only progress of historical criticism consists in the improvement of the instruments of research. Now first, as regards his conception of history, I have already pointed out that it was to him essentially a search for causes, a problem to be solved, not a picture to be painted, a scientific investigation into laws and tendencies, not a mere romantic account of startling incident and wondrous adventure.

Thucydides, in the opening of his great work, had sounded the first note of the scientific conception of history. 'The absence of romance in my pages,' he says, 'will, I fear, detract somewhat from its value, but I have written my work not to be the exploit of a passing hour but as the possession of all time.' Polybius follows with words almost entirely similar. If, he says, we banish from history the consideration of causes, methods and motives ([Greek text which cannot be reproduced]), and refuse to consider how far the result of anything is its rational consequent, what is left is a mere [Greek text which cannot be reproduced], not a [Greek text which cannot be reproduced], an oratorical essay which may give pleasure for the moment, but which is entirely without any scientific value for the explanation of the future.

Elsewhere he says that 'history robbed of the exposition of its causes and laws is a profitless thing, though it may allure a fool.' And all through his history the same point is put forward and exemplified in every fashion. So far for the conception of history. Now for the groundwork.

As regards the character of the phenomena to be selected by the scientific investigator, Aristotle had laid down the general formula that nature should be studied in her normal manifestations. Polybius, true to his character of applying explicitly the principles implicit in the work of others, follows out the doctrine of Aristotle, and lays particular stress on the rational and undisturbed character of the development of the Roman constitution as affording special facilities for the discovery of the laws of its progress. Political revolutions result from causes either external or internal. The former are mere disturbing forces which lie outside the sphere of scientific calculation. It is the latter which are important for the establishing of principles and the elucidation of the sequences of rational evolution.

He thus may be said to have anticipated one of the most important truths of the modern methods of investigation: I mean that principle which lays down that just as the study of physiology should precede the study of pathology, just as the laws of disease are best discovered by the phenomena presented in health, so the method of arriving at all great social and political truths is by the investigation of those cases where development has been normal, rational and undisturbed.

The critical canon that the more a people has been interfered with, the more difficult it becomes to generalise the laws of its progress and to analyse the separate forces of its civilisation, is one the validity of which is now generally recognised by those who pretend to a scientific treatment of all history: and while we have seen that Aristotle anticipated it in a general formula, to Polybius belongs the honour of being the first to apply it explicitly in the sphere of history. I have shown how to this great scientific historian the motive of his work was essentially the search for causes; and true to his analytical spirit he is careful to examine what a cause really is and in what part of the antecedents of any consequent it is to be looked for.

To give an illustration: As regards the origin of the war with Perseus, some assigned as causes the expulsion of Abrupolis by Perseus, the expedition of the latter to Delphi, the plot against Eumenes and the seizure of the ambassadors in Boeotia; of these incidents the two former, Polybius points out, were merely the pretexts, the two latter merely the occasions of the war. The war was really a legacy left to Perseus by his father, who was determined to fight it out with Rome.

Here as elsewhere he is not originating any new idea. Thucydides had pointed out the difference between the real and the alleged cause, and the Aristotelian dictum about revolutions, [Greek text which cannot be reproduced], draws the distinction between cause and occasion with the brilliancy of an epigram. But the explicit and rational investigation of the difference between [Greek text which cannot be reproduced], and [Greek text which cannot be reproduced] was reserved for Polybius.

No canon of historical criticism can be said to be of more real value than that involved in this distinction, and the overlooking of it has filled our histories with the contemptible accounts of the intrigues of courtiers and of kings and the petty plottings of backstairs influence - particulars interesting, no doubt, to those who would ascribe the Reformation to Anne Boleyn's pretty face, the Persian war to the influence of a doctor or a curtain-lecture from Atossa, or the French Revolution to Madame de Maintenon, but without any value for those who aim at any scientific treatment of history. But the question of method, to which I am compelled always to return, is not yet exhausted.

There is another aspect in which it may be regarded, and I shall now proceed to treat of it. One of the greatest difficulties with which the modern historian has to contend is the enormous complexity of the facts which come under his notice: D'Alembert's suggestion that at the end of every century a selection of facts should be made and the rest burned (if it was really intended seriously) could not, of course, be entertained for a moment.

A problem loses all its value when it becomes simplified, and the world would be all the poorer if the Sibyl of History burned her volumes. Besides, as Gibbon pointed out, 'a Montesquieu will detect in the most insignificant fact relations which the vulgar overlook.' Nor can the scientific investigator of history isolate the particular elements, which he desires to examine, from disturbing and extraneous causes, as the experimental chemist can do (though sometimes, as in the case of lunatic asylums and prisons, he is enabled to observe phenomena in a certain degree of isolation).

So he is compelled either to use the deductive mode of arguing from general laws or to employ the method of abstraction, which gives a fictitious isolation to phenomena never so isolated in actual existence. And this is exactly what Polybius has done as well as Thucydides.

For, as has been well remarked, there is in the works of these two writers a certain plastic unity of type and motive; whatever they write is penetrated through and through with a specific quality, a singleness and concentration of purpose, which we may contrast with the more comprehensive width as manifested not merely in the modern mind, but also in Herodotus.

Thucydides, regarding society as influenced entirely by political motives, took no account of forces of a different nature, and consequently his results, like those of most modern political economists, have to be modified largely before they come to correspond with what we know was the actual state of fact.

Similarly, Polybius will deal only with those forces which tended to bring the civilised world under the dominion of Rome (ix. 1), and in the Thucydidean spirit points out the want of picturesqueness and romance in his pages which is the result of the abstract method ([Greek text which cannot be reproduced]) being careful also to tell us that his rejection of all other forces is essentially deliberate and the result of a preconceived theory and by no means due to carelessness of any kind.

Now, of the general value of the abstract method and the legality of its employment in the sphere of history, this is perhaps not the suitable occasion for any discussion. It is, however, in all ways worthy of note that Polybius is not merely conscious of, but dwells with particular weight on, the fact which is usually urged as the strongest objection to the employment of the abstract method – I mean the conception of a society as a sort of human organism whose parts are indissolubly connected with one another and all affected when one member is in any way agitated.

This conception of the organic nature of society appears first in Plato and Aristotle, who apply it to cities. Polybius, as his wont is, expands it to be a general characteristic of all history. It is an idea of the very highest importance, especially to a man like Polybius whose thoughts are continually turned towards the essential unity of history and the impossibility of isolation.

Farther, as regards the particular method of investigating that group of phenomena obtained for him by the abstract method, he will adopt, he tells us, neither the purely deductive nor the purely inductive mode but the union of both.

In other words, he formally adopts that method of analysis upon the importance of which I have dwelt before. And lastly, while, without doubt, enormous simplicity in the elements under consideration is the result of the employment of the abstract method, even within the limit thus obtained a certain selection must be made, and a selection involves a theory.

For the facts of life cannot be tabulated with as great an ease as the colours of birds and insects can be tabulated. Now, Polybius points out that those phenomena particularly are to be dwelt on which may serve as a [Greek text which cannot be reproduced] or sample, and show the character of the tendencies of the age as clearly as 'a single drop from a full cask will be enough to disclose the nature of the whole contents.'

This recognition of the importance of single facts, not in themselves but because of the spirit they represent, is extremely scientific; for we know that from the single bone, or tooth even, the anatomist can recreate entirely the skeleton of the primeval horse, and the botanist tell the character of the flora and fauna of a district from a single specimen.

Regarding truth as 'the most divine thing in Nature,' the very 'eye and light of history without which it moves a blind thing,' Polybius spared no pains in the acquisition of historical materials or in the study of the sciences of politics and war, which he considered were so essential to the training of the scientific historian, and the labour he took is mirrored in the many ways in which he criticises other authorities.

There is something, as a rule, slightly contemptible about ancient criticism. The modern idea of the critic as the interpreter, the expounder of the beauty and excellence of the work he selects, seems quite unknown. Nothing can be more captious or unfair, for instance, than the method by which Aristotle criticised the ideal state of Plato in his ethical works, and the passages quoted by Polybius from Timaeus show that the latter historian fully deserved the punning name given to him.

But in Polybius there is, I think, little of that bitterness and pettiness of spirit which characterises most other writers, and an incidental story he tells of his relations with one of the historians whom he criticized shows that he was a man of great courtesy and refinement of taste - as, indeed, befitted one who had lived always in the society of those who were of great and noble birth.

Now, as regards the character of the canons by which he criticizes the works of other authors, in the majority of cases he employs simply his own geographical and military knowledge, showing, for instance, the impossibility in the accounts given of Nabis's march from Sparta simply by his acquaintance with the spots in question; or the inconsistency of those of the battle of Issus; or of the accounts given by Ephorus of the battles of Leuctra and Mantinea.

In the latter case he says, if any one will take the trouble to measure out the ground of the site of the battle and then test the manoeuvres given, he will find how inaccurate the accounts are. In other cases he appeals to public documents, the importance of which he was always foremost in recognising; showing, for instance, by a document in the public archives of Rhodes how inaccurate were the accounts given of the battle of Lade by Zeno and Antisthenes.

Or he appeals to psychological probability, rejecting, for instance, the scandalous stories told of Philip of Macedon, simply from the king's general greatness of character, and arguing that a boy so well educated and so respectably connected as Demochares (xii. 14) could never have been guilty of that of which evil rumour accused him. But the chief object of his literary censure is Timaeus, who had been unsparing of his strictures on others.

The general point which he makes against him, impugning his accuracy as a historian, is that he derived his knowledge of history not from the dangerous perils of a life of action but in the secure indolence of a narrow scholastic life.

There is, indeed, no point on which he is so vehement as this. 'A history,' he says, 'written in a library gives as lifeless and as inaccurate a picture of history as a painting which is copied not from a living animal but from a stuffed one.' There is more difference, he says in another place, between the history of an eye-witness and that of one whose knowledge comes from books, than there is between the scenes of real life and the fictitious landscapes of theatrical scenery.

Besides this, he enters into somewhat elaborate detailed criticism of passages where he thought Timaeus was following a wrong method and perverting truth, passages which it will be worth while to examine in detail. Timaeus, from the fact of there being a Roman custom to shoot a war-horse on a stated day, argued back to the Trojan origin of that people. Polybius, on the other hand, points out that the inference is quite unwarrantable, because horse-sacrifices are ordinary institutions common to all barbarous tribes.

Timaeus here, as was common with Greek writers, is arguing back from some custom of the present to an historical event in the past. Polybius really is employing the comparative method, showing how the custom was an ordinary step in the civilisation of every early people.

In another place, he shows how illogical is the scepticism of Timaeus as regards the existence of the Bull of Phalaris simply by appealing to the statue of the Bull, which was still to be seen in Carthage; pointing out how impossible it was, on any other theory except that it belonged to Phalaris, to account for the presence in Carthage of a bull of this peculiar character with a door between his shoulders.

But one of the great points which he uses against this Sicilian historian is in reference to the question of the origin of the Locrian colony. In accordance with the received tradition on the subject, Aristotle had represented the Locrian colony as founded by some Parthenidae or slaves' children, as they were called, a statement which seems to have roused the indignation of Timaeus, who went to a good deal of trouble to confute this theory.

He does so on the following grounds:- First of all, he points out that in the ancient days the Greeks had no slaves at all, so the mention of them in the matter is an anachronism; and next he declares that he was shown in the Greek city of Locris certain ancient inscriptions in which their relation to the Italian city was expressed in terms of the position between parent and child, which showed also that mutual rights of citizenship were accorded to each city.

Besides this, he appeals to various questions of improbability as regards their international relationship, on which Polybius takes diametrically opposite grounds which hardly call for discussion.

And in favour of his own view he urges two points more: first, that the Lacedaemonians being allowed furlough for the purpose of seeing their wives at home, it was unlikely that the Locrians should not have had the same privilege; and next, that the Italian Locrians knew nothing of the Aristotelian version and had, on the contrary, very severe laws against adulterers, runaway slaves and the like.

Now, most of these questions rest on mere probability, which is always such a subjective canon that an appeal to it is rarely conclusive. I would note, however, as regards the inscriptions which, if genuine, would of course have settled the matter, that Polybius looks on them as a mere invention on the part of Timaeus, who, he remarks, gives no details about them, though, as a rule, he is over-anxious to give chapter and verse for everything.

A somewhat more interesting point is that where he attacks Timaeus for the introduction of fictitious speeches into his narrative; for on this point Polybius seems to be far in advance of the opinions held by literary men on the subject not merely in his own day, but for centuries after. Herodotus had introduced speeches avowedly dramatic and fictitious. Thucydides states clearly that, where he was unable to find out what people really said, he put down what they ought to have said. Sallust alludes, it is true, to the fact of the speech he puts into the mouth of the tribune Memmius being essentially genuine, but the speeches given in the senate on the occasion of the Catilinarian conspiracy are very different from the same orations as they appear in Cicero.

Livy makes his ancient Romans wrangle and chop logic

with all the subtlety of a Hortensius or a Scaevola. And even in later days, when shorthand reporters attended the debates of the senate and a DAILY NEWS was published in Rome, we find that one of the most celebrated speeches in Tacitus (that in which the Emperor Claudius gives the Gauls their freedom) is shown, by an inscription discovered recently at Lugdunum, to be entirely fabulous.

Upon the other hand, it must be borne in mind that these speeches were not intended to deceive; they were regarded merely as a certain dramatic element which it was allowable to introduce into history for the purpose of giving more life and reality to the narration, and were to be criticised, not as we should, by arguing how in an age before shorthand was known such a report was possible or how, in the failure of written documents, tradition could bring down such an accurate verbal account, but by the higher test of their psychological probability as regards the persons in whose mouths they are placed.

An ancient historian in answer to modern criticism would say, probably, that these fictitious speeches were in reality more truthful than the actual ones, just as Aristotle claimed for poetry a higher degree of truth in comparison to history. The whole point is interesting as showing how far in advance of his age Polybius may be said to have been.

The last scientific historian, it is possible to gather from his writings what he considered were the characteristics of the ideal writer of history; and no small light will be thrown on the progress of historical criticism if we strive to collect and analyse what in Polybius are more or less scattered expressions.

The ideal historian must be contemporary with the events he describes, or removed from them by one generation only. Where it is possible, he is to be an eye-witness of what he writes of; where that is out of his power he is to test all traditions and stories carefully and not to be ready to accept what is plausible in place of what is true.

He is to be no bookworm living aloof from the experiences of the world in the artificial isolation of a university town, but a politician, a soldier, and a traveller, a man not merely of thought but of action, one who can do great things as well as write of them, who in the sphere of history could be what Byron and AEschylus were in the sphere of poetry, at once LE CHANTRE ET LE HEROS.

He is to keep before his eyes the fact that chance is merely a synonym for our ignorance; that the reign of law pervades the domain of history as much as it does that of political science. He is to accustom himself to look on all occasions for rational and natural causes.

And while he is to recognise the practical utility of the supernatural, in an educational point of view, he is not himself to indulge in such intellectual beating of the air as to admit the possibility of the violation of inviolable laws, or to argue in a sphere wherein argument is A PRIORI annihilated.

He is to be free from all bias towards friend and country; he is to be courteous and gentle in criticism; he is not to regard history as a mere opportunity for splendid and tragic writing; nor is he to falsify truth for the sake of a paradox or an epigram. While acknowledging the importance of particular facts as samples of higher truths, he is to take a broad and general view of humanity. He is to deal with the whole race and with the world, not with particular tribes or separate countries.

He is to bear in mind that the world is really an organism wherein no one part can be moved without the others being affected also. He is to distinguish between cause and occasion, between the influence of general laws and particular fancies, and he is to remember that the greatest lessons of the world are contained in history and that it is the historian's duty to manifest them so as to save nations from following those unwise policies which always lead to dishonour and ruin, and to teach individuals to apprehend by the intellectual culture of history those truths which else they would have to learn in the bitter school of experience, Now, as regards his theory of the necessity of the historian's being contemporary with the events he describes, so far as the historian is a mere narrator the remark is undoubtedly true.

But to appreciate the harmony and rational position of

the facts of a great epoch, to discover its laws, the causes which produced it and the effects which it generates, the scene must be viewed from a certain height and distance to be completely apprehended.

A thoroughly contemporary historian such as Lord Clarendon or Thucydides is in reality part of the history he criticises; and, in the case of such contemporary historians as Fabius and Philistus, Polybius in compelled to acknowledge that they are misled by patriotic and other considerations. Against Polybius himself no such accusation can be made. He indeed of all men is able, as from some lofty tower, to discern the whole tendency of the ancient world, the triumph of Roman institutions and of Greek thought which is the last message of the old world and, in a more spiritual sense, has become the Gospel of the new.

One thing indeed he did not see, or if he saw it, he thought but little of it - how from the East there was spreading over the world, as a wave spreads, a spiritual inroad of new religions from the time when the Pessinuntine mother of the gods, a shapeless mass of stone, was brought to the eternal city by her holiest citizen, to the day when the ship CASTOR AND POLLUX stood in at Puteoli, and St. Paul turned his face towards martyrdom and victory at Rome.

Polybius was able to predict, from his knowledge of the causes of revolutions and the tendencies of the various forms of governments, the uprising of that democratic tone of thought which, as soon as a seed is sown in the murder of the Gracchi and the exile of Marius, culminated as all democratic movements do culminate, in the supreme authority of one man, the lordship of the world under the world's rightful lord, Caius Julius Caesar. This, indeed, he saw in no uncertain way.

But the turning of all men's hearts to the East, the first glimmering of that splendid dawn which broke over the hills of Galilee and flooded the earth like wine, was hidden from his eyes. There are many points in the description of the ideal historian which one may compare to the picture which Plato has given us of the ideal philosopher. They are both 'spectators of all time and all existence.'

Nothing is contemptible in their eyes, for all things have a meaning, and they both walk in august reasonableness before all men, conscious of the workings of God yet free from all terror of mendicant priest or vagrant miracle-worker.

But the parallel ends here. For the one stands aloof from the world-storm of sleet and hail, his eyes fixed on distant and sunlit heights, loving knowledge for the sake of knowledge and wisdom for the joy of wisdom, while the other is an eager actor in the world ever seeking to apply his knowledge to useful things.

Both equally desire truth, but the one because of its utility, the other for its beauty. The historian regards it as the rational principle of all true history, and no more. To the other it comes as an all- pervading and mystic enthusiasm, 'like the desire of strong wine, the craving of ambition, the passionate love of what is beautiful.'

Still, though we miss in the historian those higher and more spiritual qualities which the philosopher of the Academe alone of all men possessed, we must not blind ourselves to the merits of that great rationalist who seems to have anticipated the very latest words of modern science.

Nor yet is he to be regarded merely in the narrow light in which he is estimated by most modern critics, as the explicit champion of rationalism and nothing more. For he is connected with another idea, the course of which is as the course of that great river of his native Arcadia which, springing from some arid and sun-bleached rock, gathers strength and beauty as it flows till it reaches the asphodel meadows of Olympia and the light and laughter of Ionian waters.

For in him we can discern the first notes of that great cult of the seven-hilled city which made Virgil write his epic and Livy his history, which found in Dante its highest exponent, which dreamed of an Empire where the Emperor would care for the bodies and the Pope for the souls of men, and so has passed into the conception of God's spiritual empire and the universal brotherhood of man and widened into the huge ocean of universal thought as the Peneus loses itself in the sea. Polybius is the last scientific historian of Greece.

The writer who seems fittingly to complete the progress of thought is a writer of biographies only. I will not here touch on Plutarch's employment of the inductive method as shown in his constant use of inscription and statue, of public document and building and the like, because it involves no new method.

It is his attitude towards miracles of which I desire to treat. Plutarch is philosophic enough to see that in the sense of a violation of the laws of nature a miracle is impossible. It is absurd, he says, to imagine that the statue of a saint can speak, and that an inanimate object not possessing the vocal organs should be able to utter an articulate sound.

Upon the other hand, he protests against science imagining that, by explaining the natural causes of things, it has explained away their transcendental meaning. 'When the tears on the cheek of some holy statue have been analysed into the moisture which certain temperatures produce on wood and marble, it yet by no means follows that they were not a sign of grief and mourning set there by God Himself.'

When Lampon saw in the prodigy of the one-horned ram the omen of the supreme rule of Pericles, and when Anaxagoras showed that the abnormal development was the rational resultant of the peculiar formation of the skull, the dreamer and the man of science were both right; it was the business of the latter to consider how the prodigy came about, of the former to show why it was so formed and what it so portended. The progression of thought is exemplified in all particulars. Herodotus had a glimmering sense of the impossibility of a violation of nature. Thucydides ignored the supernatural. Polybius rationalised it.

Plutarch raises it to its mystical heights again, though he bases it on law. In a word, Plutarch felt that while science brings the supernatural down to the natural, yet ultimately all that is natural is really supernatural. To him, as to many of our own day, religion was that transcendental attitude of the mind which, contemplating a world resting on inviolable law, is yet comforted and seeks to worship God not in the violation but in the fulfilment of nature.

It may seem paradoxical to quote in connection with the priest of Chaeronea such a pure rationalist as Mr. Herbert Spencer; yet when we read as the last message of modern science that 'when the equation of life has been reduced to its lowest terms the symbols are symbols still,' mere signs, that is, of that unknown reality which underlies all matter and all spirit, we may feel how over the wide strait of centuries thought calls to thought and how Plutarch has a higher position than is usually claimed for him in the progress of the Greek intellect.

And, indeed, it seems that not merely the importance of Plutarch himself but also that of the land of his birth in the evolution of Greek civilisation has been passed over by modern critics. To us, indeed, the bare rock to which the Parthenon serves as a crown, and which lies between Colonus and Attica's violet hills, will always be the holiest spot in the land of Greece: and Delphi will come next, and then the meadows of Eurotas where that noble people lived who represented in Hellenic thought the reaction of the law of duty against the law of beauty, the opposition of conduct to culture.

Yet, as one stands on the [Greek text which cannot be reproduced] of Cithaeron and looks out on the great double plain of Boeotia, the enormous importance of the division of Hellas comes to one's mind with great force.

To the north are Orchomenus and the Minyan treasure-house, seat of those merchant princes of Phoenicia who brought to Greece the knowledge of letters and the art of working in gold. Thebes is at our feet with the gloom of the terrible legends of Greek tragedy still lingering about it, the birthplace of Pindar, the nurse of Epaminondas and the Sacred Band.

And from out of the plain where 'Mars loved to dance,' rises the Muses' haunt, Helicon, by whose silver streams Corinna and Hesiod sang; while far away under the white aegis of those snow-capped mountains lies Chaeronea and the Lion plain where with vain chivalry the Greeks strove to check Macedon first and afterwards Rome; Chaeronea, where in the Martinmas summer of Greek civilisation Plutarch rose from the drear waste of a dying religion as the aftermath rises when the mowers think they have left the field bare. Greek philosophy began and ended in scepticism: the first and the last word of Greek history was Faith.

Splendid thus in its death, like winter sunsets, the Greek religion passed away into the horror of night. For the Cimmerian darkness was at hand, and when the schools of Athens were closed and the statue of Athena broken, the Greek spirit passed from the gods and the history of its own land to the subtleties of defining the doctrine of the Trinity and the mystical attempts to bring Plato into harmony with Christ and to reconcile Gethsemane and the Sermon on the Mount with the Athenian prison and the discussion in the woods of Colonus.

The Greek spirit slept for wellnigh a thousand years. When it woke again, like Antaeus it had gathered strength from the earth where it lay; like Apollo it had lost none of its divinity through its long servitude. In the history of Roman thought we nowhere find any of those characteristics of the Greek Illumination which I have pointed out are the necessary concomitants of the rise of historical criticism.

The conservative respect for tradition which made the Roman people delight in the ritual and formulas of law, and is as apparent in their politics as in their religion, was fatal to any rise of that spirit of revolt against authority the importance of which, as a factor in intellectual progress, we have already seen.

The whitened tables of the Pontifices preserved carefully the records of the eclipses and other atmospherical phenomena, and what we call the art of verifying dates was known to them at an early time; but there was no spontaneous rise of physical science to suggest by its analogies of law and order a new method of research, nor any natural springing up of the questioning spirit of philosophy with its unification of all phenomena and all knowledge. At the very time when the whole tide of Eastern superstition was sweeping into the heart of the Capital the Senate banished the Greek philosophers from Rome.

And of the three systems which did at length take some root in the city, those of Zeno and Epicurus were used merely as the rule for the ordering of life, while the dogmatic scepticism of Carneades, by its very principles, annihilated the possibility of argument and encouraged a perfect indifference to research. Nor were the Romans ever fortunate enough like the Greeks to have to face the incubus of any dogmatic system of legends and myths, the immoralities and absurdities of which might excite a revolutionary outbreak of sceptical criticism.

For the Roman religion became as it were crystallised and isolated from progress at an early period of its evolution. Their gods remained mere abstractions of commonplace virtues or uninteresting personifications of the useful things of life. The old primitive creed was indeed always upheld as a state institution on account of the enormous facilities it offered for cheating in politics, but as a spiritual system of belief it was unanimously rejected at a very early period both by the common people and the educated classes, for the sensible reason that it was so extremely dull. The former took refuge in the mystic sensualities of the worship of Isis, the latter in the Stoical rules of life.

The Romans classified their gods carefully in their order of precedence, analysed their genealogies in the laborious spirit of modern heraldry, fenced them round with a ritual as intricate as their law, but never quite cared enough about them to believe in them. So it was of no account with them when the philosophers announced that Minerva was merely memory. She had never been much else.

Nor did they protest when Lucretius dared to say of Ceres and of Liber that they were only the corn of the field and the fruit of the vine. For they had never mourned for the daughter of Demeter in the asphodel meadows of Sicily, nor traversed the glades of Cithaeron with fawn-skin and with spear.

This brief sketch of the condition of Roman thought will serve to prepare us for the almost total want of scientific historical criticism which we shall discern in their literature, and has, besides, afforded fresh corroboration of the conditions essential to the rise of this spirit, and of the modes of thought which it reflects and in which it is always to be found.

Roman historical composition had its origin in the pontifical college of ecclesiastical lawyers, and preserved to its close the uncritical spirit which characterised its fountain-head. It possessed from the outset a most voluminous collection of the materials of history, which, however, produced merely antiquarians, not historians. It is so hard to use facts, so easy to accumulate them.

Wearied of the dull monotony of the pontifical annals, which dwelt on little else but the rise and fall in provisions and the eclipses of the sun, Cato wrote out a history with his own hand for the instruction of his child, to which he gave the name of Origines, and before his time some aristocratic families had written histories in Greek much in the same spirit in which the Germans of the eighteenth century used French as the literary language. But the first regular Roman historian is Sallust.

Between the extravagant eulogies passed on this author by the French (such as De Closset), and Dr. Mommsen's view of him as merely a political pamphleteer, it is perhaps difficult to reach the VIA MEDIA of unbiassed appreciation. He has, at any rate, the credit of being a purely rationalistic historian, perhaps the only one in Roman literature.

Cicero had a good many qualifications for a scientific historian, and (as he usually did) thought very highly of his own powers. On passages of ancient legend, however, he is rather unsatisfactory, for while he is too sensible to believe them he is too patriotic to reject them.

And this is really the attitude of Livy, who claims for early Roman legend a certain uncritical homage from the rest of the subject world. His view in his history is that it is not worth while to examine the truth of these stories. In his hands the history of Rome unrolls before our eyes like some gorgeous tapestry, where victory succeeds victory, where triumph treads on the heels of triumph, and the line of heroes seems never to end.

It is not till we pass behind the canvas and see the slight

means by which the effect is produced that we apprehend the fact that like most picturesque writers Livy is an indifferent critic. As regards his attitude towards the credibility of early Roman history he is quite as conscious as we are of its mythical and unsound nature. He will not, for instance, decide whether the Horatii were Albans or Romans; who was the first dictator; how many tribunes there were, and the like.

His method, as a rule, is merely to mention all the accounts and sometimes to decide in favour of the most probable, but usually not to decide at all. No canons of historical criticism will ever discover whether the Roman women interviewed the mother of Coriolanus of their own accord or at the suggestion of the senate; whether Remus was killed for jumping over his brother's wall or because they quarrelled about birds; whether the ambassadors found Cincinnatus ploughing or only mending a hedge.

Livy suspends his judgment over these important facts and history when questioned on their truth is dumb. If he does select between two historians he chooses the one who is nearer to the facts he describes. But he is no critic, only a conscientious writer. It is mere vain waste to dwell on his critical powers, for they do not exist. In the case of Tacitus imagination has taken the place of history.

The past lives again in his pages, but through no laborious criticism; rather through a dramatic and psychological faculty which he specially possessed. In the philosophy of history he has no belief. He can never make up his mind what to believe as regards God's government of the world. There is no method in him and none elsewhere in Roman literature.

Nations may not have missions but they certainly have functions. And the function of ancient Italy was not merely to give us what is statical in our institutions and rational in our law, but to blend into one elemental creed the spiritual aspirations of Aryan and of Semite. Italy was not a pioneer in intellectual progress, nor a motive power in the evolution of thought. The owl of the goddess of Wisdom traversed over the whole land and found nowhere a resting-place. The dove, which is the bird of Christ, flew straight to the city of Rome and the new reign began. It was the fashion of early Italian painters to represent in mediaeval costume the soldiers who watched over the tomb of Christ, and this, which was the result of the frank anachronism of all true art, may serve to us as an allegory. For it was in vain that the Middle Ages strove to guard the buried spirit of progress. When the dawn of the Greek spirit arose, the sepulchre was empty, the grave-clothes laid aside.

Humanity had risen from the dead. The study of Greek, it has been well said, implies the birth of criticism, comparison and research. At the opening of that education of modern by ancient thought which we call the Renaissance, it was the words of Aristotle which sent Columbus sailing to the New World, while a fragment of Pythagorean astronomy set Copernicus thinking on that train of reasoning which has revolutionised the whole position of our planet in the universe. Then it was seen that the only meaning of progress is a return to Greek modes of thought.

The monkish hymns which obscured the pages of Greek manuscripts were blotted out, the splendours of a new method were unfolded to the world, and out of the melancholy sea of mediaevalism rose the free spirit of man in all that splendour of glad adolescence, when the bodily powers seem quickened by a new vitality, when the eye sees more clearly than its wont and the mind apprehends what was beforetime hidden from it.

To herald the opening of the sixteenth century, from the little Venetian printing press came forth all the great authors of antiquity, each bearing on the title-page the words [Greek text which cannot be reproduced]; words which may serve to remind us with what wondrous prescience Polybius saw the world's fate when he foretold the material sovereignty of Roman institutions and exemplified in himself the intellectual empire of Greece.

The course of the study of the spirit of historical criticism has not been a profitless investigation into modes and forms of thought now antiquated and of no account. The only spirit which is entirely removed from us is the mediaeval; the Greek spirit is essentially modern. The introduction of the comparative method of research which has forced history to disclose its secrets belongs in a measure to us.

Ours, too, is a more scientific knowledge of philology and the method of survival. Nor did the ancients know anything of the doctrine of averages or of crucial instances, both of which methods have proved of such importance in modern criticism, the one adding a most important proof of the statical elements of history, and exemplifying the influences of all physical surroundings on the life of man; the other, as in the single instance of the Moulin Quignon skull, serving to create a whole new science of prehistoric archaeology and to bring us back to a time when man was coeval with the stone age, the mammoth and the woolly rhinoceros.

But, except these, we have added no new canon or method to the science of historical criticism. Across the drear waste of a thousand years the Greek and the modern spirit join hands. In the torch race which the Greek boys ran from the Cerameician field of death to the home of the goddess of Wisdom, not merely he who first reached the goal but he also who first started with the torch aflame received a prize.

In the Lampadephoria of civilisation and free thought let us not forget to render due meed of honour to those who first lit that sacred flame, the increasing splendour of which lights our footsteps to the far-off divine event of the attainment of perfect truth.

Chapter 13

Comedy as Tragedy

George Meredith once described Oscar Fingal O'Flahertie Wills Wilde as "a mixture of Apollo and a monster."

And if Oscar Wilde was indeed a monstre sacre, he had all the right credentials. He was born in Dublin in 1854, the late child of an eccentric father and an equally eccentric mother, a nationalist poet who called herself Speranza; he went in easy stages to Trinity College, Dublin, and Magdalen College, Oxford, before arriving at his destined home in London. He was a poet but his youth was combined with cleverness, and he realized that self-publicity might count for more than mere achievement.

If he did not walk down Piccadilly with a lily in his hand, as the parody of him in Gilbert & Sullivan's "Patience" suggested, he did at least create the atmosphere in which such a floral parade might have been thought likely to occur. Wilde was an esthete only until he grew up, however, and it was in the late 1880's and 1890's that he began his serious work - his stories, his criticism, his one notorious novel and of course his plays.

Yet even as he composed those dramas, which will last as long as the English language itself, he was beset by rumors about his private life that eventually transformed him into what he described as "the pariah dog of the nineteenth century." It was a brilliant career: he went from poetry to prose, from prose to drama and then from drama to prison. He always did the unexpected so that, although he was not forgiven, he was certainly never forgotten.

But even before that fall which in some distant region of

his consciousness he seems positively to have longed for, he was something of a puzzle to his contemporaries. To some he was a savior (literally so, since on occasion he seemed to possess the gift of healing), whereas to others he was perilously close to becoming an Antichrist.

In appearance he was unmistakable - as one contemporary noted, he looked like a Roman emperor carved out of suet. But as soon as he opened his mouth, any unfavorable impression was dispelled - when he spoke, the delicately rounded sentences, the orotund expressions, the epigrammatic flashes of lightning, all worked together to render him a conversationalist unparalleled in his own country.

Those who knew him best also remarked on the sheer buoyancy of his spirits. Certainly his letters are unique, filled as they are with an exuberant and exhilarating wit; as Borges has said, "The fundamental spirit of his work is joy." But it was not just the bravura of his self-expression that gave him such a hold on his contemporaries. It was something much more profound and perhaps more dangerous, for, if he was a genius, he was one because he came to embody the obsessions of his own period.

He said of himself, "I was a man who stood in symbolic relations to the art and culture of my age," but it was both his blessing and his eventual tragedy that the age itself might most aptly be termed fin de siecle. Since we are now entering an equivalent period, perhaps we are in the best possible position to understand that joy in artifice and parody, that celebration of style and pastiche, that mockery of previous values, which such a time seems to encourage.

In Wilde's lifetime the end of "Victorianism" (and all that it had come to represent) was in sight, but nothing had come to take its place: it was a time of spiritual, moral, social and artistic chaos, when even the most formidable conventions and the firmest convictions began to crumble, to slide and eventually to dissolve.

In many ways it was a worn-out society, theatrical in its art, theatrical in its life, theatrical even in its devotions. It happened to be Wilde who defined both the conscience and the consciousness of the artist at a time when all other values were thrown into doubt. Indeed, it was from the wreck of those values that he tried to save the concepts of beauty and of pleasure. He knew Walter Pater just as he understood Ruskin, and he incorporated them into what he considered to be a finer philosophy of life.

Only the Puritans, whom he hated but whom he also understood, might call this "decadent." In fact, one has only to read his criticism - and essays like "The Critic as Artist" and "The Decay of Lying" are as fine in their way as the finest of his plays - to see how serious a critique of his age he actually provided.

His most inspired role, beyond that of dandy or Uranian (the 19th-century expression for those whom less sympathetic contemporaries called sodomites), was that of the esthetic philosopher: this was, you might say, a discipline he knew by heart, and in his deceptively simple and unarguably witty formulations he fashioned a vision of the world as subtle as that of Pater, as devastating as that of Schopenhauer.

"The truths of metaphysics," he said, "are the truths of masks." He was often (and wrongly) accused of insincerity, but he pre-empted this charge when he declared that "insincerity is a method by which we can multiply our personalities." In his disavowal of conventional ethics he is thoroughly Nietzschean.

"Those who see any difference between soul and body have neither," he remarked. "It is only shallow people who do not judge by appearances. The mystery of the world is the visible, not the invisible." Both art and conduct became the supreme reality, therefore, and there were times when he did not attempt to distinguish between the two.

There were even occasions when he declared that his only concern was to turn his own personality into a work of art - although, in a climate so hostile to the pursuit of personal perfection as that of England, such an art was bound to turn into one of open defiance. "I was a problem," he said with one eye on Victorian society and the other on the legal system, "for which there was no solution."

Essentially he remained an alien, and it was in this uncomfortable but necessary position that he was able to see English life very clearly. Shaw said that Wilde was a "very Irish Irishman," and although he told Yeats that "we are a nation of brilliant failures" Wilde himself belongs to a long line of successful Irish dramatists - among them Congreve, Sheridan and Goldsmith. Yet of all of them, perhaps, he was the one who was least at home in England.

Just as in his drama he exposed the hypocrisies of late Victorian life - and there is no more damning indictment of that society than "The Importance of Being Earnest" - so in his life his fondness for boys and drink scandalized those who believed themselves to represent public morality. No attitude could be more alien to the English "mind" than Wilde's comment that "I have never learned anything except from people younger than myself" and his belief in "that inordinate passion for pleasure which is the secret of remaining young."

But more importantly, it was a mistake for him to show the English in his dramas that their ideals were illusions, their understanding mere folly: it was only a matter of time before they turned on him. He had been their entertainer for a while but he soon became the figure in a fatal pantomime, to receive blows from the harlequin's wand and kicks from the clowns. He had dallied with them too long; he had grown too accustomed to "society" even as he mocked it.

It was thoroughly appropriate, therefore, that his splendid career should be ended by a Marquess and ruined by a visiting card. Lord John Sholto Douglas, the Marquess of Queensberry, dismayed by Wilde's association with his son, Lord Alfred Douglas, left his card with the message, "To Oscar Wilde posing somdomite" (sic).

Wilde sued Queensberry, lost, and was himself put on trial for consorting with minors. He longed for fame, but in the end he was destroyed by it. He ran willingly to his destiny, but he forgot that he could become its victim. He was the ox fattened with flowers, but only for the sacrifice.

Yet his fate is in some ways still the least interesting thing about him, just as his earlier poses did him a signal disservice.

At least he realized the latter: "To the world," he said, "I seem, by intention on my part, a dilettante and a dandy merely - it is not wise to show one's heart to the world." But there was one other paradox on which he rested his case, even in the well of the Old Bailey itself: "Art is the most serious thing in the world. And the artist is the only person who is never serious." So it is that although he turned conversation into an art, and his personality into a symbol, his real achievement lay elsewhere. Indeed there is a sense in which Oscar Wilde was the greatest artist of his time.

Some of his poems, most notably "The Ballad of Reading Gaol," have survived the work of more single-minded versifiers; he invented the art of modern criticism, just as he reinvented the art both of the parable and of the prose poem for a modern audience; as a letter-writer he is unequaled in his century, and no one can read "De Profundis," a letter he wrote to Alfred Douglas from his prison cell, without being almost as moved by it as he was; with "Salome" he created symbolic drama in English; "The Picture of Dorian Gray" has been described as the only French novel ever written in English; and of course he brought comedy back to the London stage.

The 19th century was on its deathbed and still he managed to make it laugh at itself.

And so he wrote drama for society, philosophy for his equals, epigrams for everyone. Above all he was a self-proclaimed "lord of language" - a master of style, and in every sense a modern master since many of his lessons have yet to be learned. But Oscar Wilde may be supposed to have the last word even here. "If one tells the truth," he once wrote, "one is sure, sooner or later, to be found out."

THE CRITIC AS ARTIST

A DIALOGUE. Part I. Persons: Gilbert and Ernest. Scene: the library of a house in Piccadilly, overlooking the Green Park.

GILBERT (at the Piano). My dear Ernest, what are you laughing at?

ERNEST (looking up). At a capital story that I have just

come across in this volume of Reminiscences that I have found on your table.

GILBERT. What is the book? Ah! I see. I have not read it yet. Is it good?

ERNEST. Well, while you have been playing, I have been turningover the pages with some amusement, though, as a rule, I dislike modern memoirs. They are generally written by people who have either entirely lost their memories, or have never done anything worth remembering; which, however, is, no doubt, the true explanation of their popularity, as the English public always feels perfectly at its ease when a mediocrity is talking to it.

GILBERT. Yes: the public is wonderfully tolerant. It forgives everything except genius. But I must confess that I like all memoirs. I like them for their form, just as much as for their matter. In literature mere egotism is delightful. It is what fascinates us in the letters of personalities so different as Cicero and Balzac, Flaubert and Berlioz, Byron and Madame de Sevigne. Whenever we come across it, and, strangely enough, it is rather rare, we cannot but welcome it, and do not easily forget it.

Humanity will always love Rousseau for having confessed his sins, not to a priest, but to the world, and the couchant nymphs that Cellini wrought in bronze for the castle of King Francis, the green and gold Perseus, even, that in the open Loggia at Florence shows the moon the dead terror that once turned life to stone, have not given it more pleasure than has that autobiography in which the supreme scoundrel of the Renaissance relates the story of his splendour and his shame.

The opinions, the character, the achievements of the man, matter very little. He may be a sceptic like the gentle Sieur de Montaigne, or a saint like the bitter son of Monica, but when he tells us his own secrets he can always charm our ears to listening and our lips to silence. The mode of thought that Cardinal Newman represented--if that can be called a mode of thought which seeks to solve intellectual problems by a denial of the supremacy of the intellect--may not, cannot, I think, survive. But the world will never weary of watching that troubled soul in its progress from darkness to darkness. The lonely church at Littlemore, where 'the breath of the morning is damp, and worshippers are few,' will always be dear to it, and whenever men see the yellow snapdragon blossoming on the wall of Trinity they will think of that gracious undergraduate who saw in the flower's sure recurrence a prophecy that he would abide for ever with the Benign Mother of his days--a prophecy that Faith, in her wisdom or her folly, suffered not to be fulfilled. Yes; autobiography is irresistible.

Poor, silly, conceited Mr. Secretary Pepys has chattered his way into the circle of the Immortals, and, conscious that indiscretion is the better part of valour, bustles about among them in that 'shaggy purple gown with gold buttons and looped lace' which he is so fond of describing to us, perfectly at his ease, and prattling, to his own and our infinite pleasure, of the Indian blue petticoat that he bought for his wife, of the 'good hog's hars-let,' and the 'pleasant French fricassee of veal' that he loved to eat, of his game of bowls with Will Joyce, and his 'gadding after beauties,' and his reciting of Hamlet on a Sunday, and his playing of the viol on week days, and other wicked or trivial things.

Even in actual life egotism is not without its attractions. When people talk to us about others they are usually dull. When they talk to us about themselves they are nearly always interesting, and if one could shut them up, when they become wearisome, as easily as one can shut up a book of which one has grown wearied, they would be perfect absolutely.

ERNEST. There is much virtue in that If, as Touchstone would say. But do you seriously propose that every man should become his own Boswell? What would become of our industrious compilers of Lives and Recollections in that case?

GILBERT. What has become of them? They are the pest of the age, nothing more and nothing less. Every great man nowadays has his disciples, and it is always Judas who writes the biography.

ERNEST. My dear fellow!

GILBERT. I am afraid it is true. Formerly we used to

canonise our heroes. The modern method is to vulgarise them. Cheap editions of great books may be delightful, but cheap editions of great men are absolutely detestable.

ERNEST. May I ask, Gilbert, to whom you allude?

GILBERT. Oh! to all our second-rate litterateurs. We are overrun by a set of people who, when poet or painter passes away, arrive at the house along with the undertaker, and forget that their one duty is to behave as mutes. But we won't talk about them. They are the mere body-snatchers of literature. The dust is given to one, and the ashes to another, and the soul is out of their reach. And now, let me play Chopin to you, or Dvorak? Shall I play you a fantasy by Dvorak? He writes passionate, curiously-coloured things.

ERNEST. No; I don't want music just at present. It is far too indefinite. Besides, I took the Baroness Bernstein down to dinner last night, and, though absolutely charming in every other respect, she insisted on discussing music as if it were actually written in the German language. Now, whatever music sounds like I am glad to say that it does not sound in the smallest degree like German. There are forms of patriotism that are really quite degrading. No; Gilbert, don't play any more. Turn round and talk to me. Talk to me till the white-horned day comes into the room. There is something in your voice that is wonderful.

GILBERT (rising from the piano). I am not in a mood for talking to-night. I really am not. How horrid of you to smile! Where are the cigarettes? Thanks. How exquisite these single daffodils are! They seem to be made of amber and cool ivory. They are like Greek things of the best period. What was the story in the confessions of the remorseful Academician that made you laugh? Tell it to me. After playing Chopin, I feel as if I had been weeping over sins that I had never committed, and mourning over tragedies that were not my own.

Music always seems to me to produce that effect. It creates for one a past of which one has been ignorant, and fills one with a sense of sorrows that have been hidden from one's tears. I can fancy a man who had led a perfectly commonplace life, hearing by chance some curious piece of music, and suddenly discovering that his soul, without his being conscious of it, had passed through terrible experiences, and known fearful joys, or wild romantic loves, or great renunciations. And so tell me this story, Ernest. I want to be amused.

ERNEST. Oh! I don't know that it is of any importance. But I thought it a really admirable illustration of the true value of ordinary art-criticism. It seems that a lady once gravely asked the remorseful Academician, as you call him, if his celebrated picture of 'A Spring-Day at Whiteley's,' or, 'Waiting for the Last Omnibus,' or some subject of that kind, was all painted by hand?

GILBERT. And was it?

ERNEST. You are quite incorrigible. But, seriously speaking, what is the use of art-criticism? Why cannot the artist be left alone, to create a new world if he wishes it, or, if not, to shadow forth the world which we already know, and of which, I fancy, we would each one of us be wearied if Art, with her fine spirit of choice and delicate instinct of selection, did not, as it were, purify it for us, and give to it a momentary perfection.

It seems to me that the imagination spreads, or should spread, a solitude around it, and works best in silence and in isolation. Why should the artist be troubled by the shrill clamour of criticism? Why should those who cannot create take upon themselves to estimate the value of creative work? What can they know about it? If a man's work is easy to understand, an explanation is unnecessary. . . .

GILBERT. And if his work is incomprehensible, an explanation is wicked.

ERNEST. I did not say that.

GILBERT. Ah! but you should have. Nowadays, we have so few mysteries left to us that we cannot afford to part with one of them. The members of the Browning Society, like the theologians of the Broad Church Party, or the authors of Mr. Walter Scott's Great Writers Series, seem to me to spend their time in trying to explain their divinity away. Where one had hoped that Browning was a mystic they have sought to show that he was simply inarticulate.

Where one had fancied that he had something to conceal, they have proved that he had but little to reveal. But I speak merely of his incoherent work. Taken as a whole the man was great. He did not belong to the Olympians, and had all the incompleteness of the Titan. He did not survey, and it was but rarely that he could sing. His work is marred by struggle, violence and effort, and he passed not from emotion to form, but from thought to chaos. Still, he was great. He has been called a thinker, and was certainly a man who was always thinking, and always thinking aloud; but it was not thought that fascinated him, but rather the processes by which thought moves.

It was the machine he loved, not what the machine makes. The method by which the fool arrives at his folly was as dear to him as the ultimate wisdom of the wise. So much, indeed, did the subtle mechanism of mind fascinate him that he despised language, or looked upon it as an incomplete instrument of expression. Rhyme, that exquisite echo which in the Muse's hollow hill creates and answers its own voice; rhyme, which in the hands of the real artist becomes not merely a material element of metrical beauty, but a spiritual element of thought and passion also, waking a new mood, it may be, or stirring a fresh train of ideas, or opening by mere sweetness and suggestion of sound some golden door at which the Imagination itself had knocked in vain; rhyme, which can turn man's utterance to the speech of gods; rhyme, the one chord we have added to the Greek lyre, became in Robert Browning's hands a grotesque, misshapen thing, which at times made him masquerade in poetry as a low comedian, and ride Pegasus too often with his tongue in his cheek.

There are moments when he wounds us by monstrous music. Nay, if he can only get his music by breaking the strings of his lute, he breaks them, and they snap in discord, and no Athenian tettix, making melody from tremulous wings, lights on the ivory horn to make the movement perfect, or the interval less harsh. Yet, he was great: and though he turned language into ignoble clay, he made from it men and women that live.

He is the most Shakespearian creature since Shakespeare. If Shakespeare could sing with myriad lips, Browning could stammer through a thousand mouths. Even now, as I am speaking, and speaking not against him but for him, there glides through the room the pageant of his persons. There, creeps Fra Lippo Lippi with his cheeks still burning from some girl's hot kiss. There, stands dread Saul with the lordly male-sapphires gleaming in his turban.

Mildred Tresham is there, and the Spanish monk, yellow with hatred, and Blougram, and Ben Ezra, and the Bishop of St. Praxed's. The spawn of Setebos gibbers in the corner, and Sebald, hearing Pippa pass by, looks on Ottima's haggard face, and loathes her and his own sin, and himself. Pale as the white satin of his doublet, the melancholy king watches with dreamy treacherous eyes too loyal Strafford pass forth to his doom, and Andrea shudders as he hears the cousins whistle in the garden, and bids his perfect wife go down.

Yes, Browning was great. And as what will he be remembered? As a poet? Ah, not as a poet! He will be remembered as a writer of fiction, as the most supreme writer of fiction, it may be, that we have ever had. His sense of dramatic situation was unrivalled, and, if he could not answer his own problems, he could at least put problems forth, and what more should an artist do? Considered from the point of view of a creator of character he ranks next to him who made Hamlet. Had he been articulate, he might have sat beside him.

The only man who can touch the hem of his garment is George Meredith. Meredith is a prose Browning, and so is Browning. He used poetry as a medium for writing in prose.

ERNEST. There is something in what you say, but there is not everything in what you say. In many points you are unjust.

GILBERT. It is difficult not to be unjust to what one loves. But let us return to the particular point at issue. What was it that you said?

ERNEST. Simply this: that in the best days of art there were no art-critics.

GILBERT. I seem to have heard that observation before,

Ernest. It has all the vitality of error and all the tediousness of an old friend.

ERNEST. It is true. Yes: there is no use your tossing your head in that petulant manner. It is quite true. In the best days of art there were no art-critics. The sculptor hewed from the marble block the great white-limbed Hermes that slept within it. The waxers and gilders of images gave tone and texture to the statue, and the world, when it saw it, worshipped and was dumb. He poured the glowing bronze into the mould of sand, and the river of red metal cooled into noble curves and took the impress of the body of a god. With enamel or polished jewels he gave sight to the sightless eyes.

The hyacinth-like curls grew crisp beneath his graver. And when, in some dim frescoed fane, or pillared sunlit portico, the child of Leto stood upon his pedestal, those who passed by, [Greek text which cannot be reproduced], became conscious of a new influence that had come across their lives, and dreamily, or with a sense of strange and quickening joy, went to their homes or daily labour, or wandered, it may be, through the city gates to that nymph-haunted meadow where young Phaedrus bathed his feet, and, lying there on the soft grass, beneath the tall wind--whispering planes and flowering agnus castus, began to think of the wonder of beauty, and grew silent with unaccustomed awe.

In those days the artist was free. From the river valley he took the fine clay in his fingers, and with a little tool of wood or bone, fashioned it into forms so exquisite that the people gave them to the dead as their playthings, and we find them still in the dusty tombs on the yellow hillside by Tanagra, with the faint gold and the fading crimson still lingering about hair and lips and raiment.

On a wall of fresh plaster, stained with bright sandyx or mixed with milk and saffron, he pictured one who trod with tired feet the purple white-starred fields of asphodel, one 'in whose eyelids lay the whole of the Trojan War,' Polyxena, the daughter of Priam; or figured Odysseus, the wise and cunning, bound by tight cords to the mast-step, that he might listen without hurt to the singing of the Sirens, or wandering by the clear river of Acheron, where the ghosts of fishes flitted over the pebbly bed; or showed the Persian in trews and mitre flying before the Greek at Marathon, or the galleys clashing their beaks of brass in the little Salaminian bay.

He drew with silver-point and charcoal upon parchment and prepared cedar. Upon ivory and rose-coloured terracotta he painted with wax, making the wax fluid with juice of olives, and with heated irons making it firm. Panel and marble and linen canvas became wonderful as his brush swept across them; and life seeing her own image, was still, and dared not speak.

All life, indeed, was his, from the merchants seated in the market-place to the cloaked shepherd lying on the hill; from the nymph hidden in the laurels and the faun that pipes at noon, to the king whom, in long green-curtained litter, slaves bore upon oil-bright shoulders, and fanned with peacock fans. Men and women, with pleasure or sorrow in their faces, passed before him. He watched them, and their secret became his. Through form and colour he re-created a world.

All subtle arts belonged to him also. He held the gem against the revolving disk, and the amethyst became the purple couch for Adonis, and across the veined sardonyx sped Artemis with her hounds. He beat out the gold into roses, and strung them together for necklace or armlet. He beat out the gold into wreaths for the conqueror's helmet, or into palmates for the Tyrian robe, or into masks for the royal dead. On the back of the silver mirror he graved Thetis borne by her Nereids, or love-sick Phaedra with her nurse, or Persephone, weary of memory, putting poppies in her hair.

The potter sat in his shed, and, flower-like from the silent wheel, the vase rose up beneath his hands. He decorated the base and stem and ears with pattern of dainty olive-leaf, or foliated acanthus, or curved and crested wave. Then in black or red he painted lads wrestling, or in the race: knights in full armour, with strange heraldic shields and curious visors, leaning from shell-shaped chariot over rearing steeds: the gods seated at the feast or working their miracles: the heroes in their victory or in their pain.

Sometimes he would etch in thin vermilion lines upon a ground of white the languid bridegroom and his bride, with Eros hovering round them--an Eros like one of Donatello's angels, a little laughing thing with gilded or with azure wings. On the curved side he would write the name of his friend. [Greek text which cannot be reproduced] or [Greek text which cannot be reproduced] tells us the story of his days.

Again, on the rim of the wide flat cup he would draw the stag browsing, or the lion at rest, as his fancy willed it. From the tiny perfume-bottle laughed Aphrodite at her toilet, and, with bare-limbed Maenads in his train, Dionysus danced round the wine-jar on naked must-stained feet, while, satyr-like, the old Silenus sprawled upon the bloated skins, or shook that magic spear which was tipped with a fretted fir-cone, and wreathed with dark ivy. And no one came to trouble the artist at his work. No irresponsible chatter disturbed him.

He was not worried by opinions. By the Ilyssus, says Arnold somewhere, there was no Higginbotham. By the Ilyssus, my dear Gilbert, there were no silly art congresses bringing provincialism to the provinces and teaching the mediocrity how to mouth. By the Ilyssus there were no tedious magazines about art, in which the industrious prattle of what they do not understand. On the reed-grown banks of that little stream strutted no ridiculous journalism monopolising the seat of judgment when it should be apologising in the dock. The Greeks had no art-critics.

GILBERT. Ernest, you are quite delightful, but your views are terribly unsound. I am afraid that you have been listening to the conversation of some one older than yourself. That is always a dangerous thing to do, and if you allow it to degenerate into a habit you will find it absolutely fatal to any intellectual development. As for modern journalism, it is not my business to defend it. It justifies its own existence by the great Darwinian principle of the survival of the vulgarest. I have merely to do with literature.

ERNEST. But what is the difference between literature and journalism?

GILBERT. Oh! journalism is unreadable, and literature is

not read. That is all. But with regard to your statement that the Greeks had no art-critics, I assure you that is quite absurd. It would be more just to say that the Greeks were a nation of art-critics.

ERNEST. Really?

GILBERT. Yes, a nation of art-critics. But I don't wish to destroy the delightfully unreal picture that you have drawn of the relation of the Hellenic artist to the intellectual spirit of his age. To give an accurate description of what has never occurred is not merely the proper occupation of the historian, but the inalienable privilege of any man of parts and culture. Still less do I desire to talk learnedly.

Learned conversation is either the affectation of the ignorant or the profession of the mentally unemployed. And, as for what is called improving conversation, that is merely the foolish method by which the still more foolish philanthropist feebly tries to disarm the just rancour of the criminal classes. No: let me play to you some mad scarlet thing by Dvorak. The pallid figures on the tapestry are smiling at us, and the heavy eyelids of my bronze Narcissus are folded in sleep. Don't let us discuss anything solemnly.

I am but too conscious of the fact that we are born in an age when only the dull are treated seriously, and I live in terror of not being misunderstood. Don't degrade me into the position of giving you useful information. Education is an admirable thing, but it is well to remember from time to time that nothing that is worth knowing can be taught. Through the parted curtains of the window I see the moon like a clipped piece of silver. Like gilded bees the stars cluster round her.

The sky is a hard hollow sapphire. Let us go out into the night. Thought is wonderful, but adventure is more wonderful still. Who knows but we may meet Prince Florizel of Bohemia, and hear the fair Cuban tell us that she is not what she seems?

ERNEST. You are horribly wilful. I insist on your discussing this matter with me. You have said that the Greeks were a nation of art-critics. What art-criticism have they left us?

GILBERT. My dear Ernest, even if not a single fragment

of art-criticism had come down to us from Hellenic or Hellenistic days, it would be none the less true that the Greeks were a nation of art-critics, and that they invented the criticism of art just as they invented the criticism of everything else. For, after all, what is our primary debt to the Greeks? Simply the critical spirit. And, this spirit, which they exercised on questions of religion and science, of ethics and metaphysics, of politics and education, they exercised on questions of art also, and, indeed, of the two supreme and highest arts, they have left us the most flawless system of criticism that the world has ever seen.

ERNEST. But what are the two supreme and highest arts?

GILBERT. Life and Literature, life and the perfect expression of life. The principles of the former, as laid down by the Greeks, we may not realise in an age so marred by false ideals as our own. The principles of the latter, as they laid them down, are, in many cases, so subtle that we can hardly understand them. Recognising that the most perfect art is that which most fully mirrors man in all his infinite variety, they elaborated the criticism of language, considered in the light of the mere material of that art, to a point to which we, with our accentual system of reasonable or emotional emphasis, can barely if at all attain; studying, for instance, the metrical movements of a prose as scientifically as a modern musician studies harmony and counterpoint, and, I need hardly say, with much keener aesthetic instinct. In this they were right, as they were right in all things.

Since the introduction of printing, and the fatal development of the habit of reading amongst the middle and lower classes of this country, there has been a tendency in literature to appeal more and more to the eye, and less and less to the ear which is really the sense which, from the standpoint of pure art, it should seek to please, and by whose canons of pleasure it should abide always. Even the work of Mr. Pater, who is, on the whole, the most perfect master of English prose now creating amongst us, is often far more like a piece of mosaic than a passage in music, and seems, here and there, to lack the true rhythmical life of words and the fine freedom and richness of effect that such rhythmical life produces. We, in fact, have made writing a definite mode of composition, and have treated it as a form of elaborate design. The Greeks, upon the other hand, regarded writing simply as a method of chronicling. Their test was always the spoken word in its musical and metrical relations.

The voice was the medium, and the ear the critic. I have sometimes thought that the story of Homer's blindness might be really an artistic myth, created in critical days, and serving to remind us, not merely that the great poet is always a seer, seeing less with the eyes of the body than he does with the eyes of the soul, but that he is a true singer also, building his song out of music, repeating each line over and over again to himself till he has caught the secret of its melody, chaunting in darkness the words that are winged with light. Certainly, whether this be so or not, it was to his blindness, as an occasion, if not as a cause, that England's great poet owed much of the majestic movement and sonorous splendour of his later verse.

When Milton could no longer write he began to sing. Who would match the measures of Comus with the measures of Samson Agonistes, or of Paradise Lost or Regained? When Milton became blind he composed, as every one should compose, with the voice purely, and so the pipe or reed of earlier days became that mighty many-stopped organ whose rich reverberant music has all the stateliness of Homeric verse, if it seeks not to have its swiftness, and is the one imperishable inheritance of English literature sweeping through all the ages, because above them, and abiding with us ever, being immortal in its form. Yes: writing has done much harm to writers. We must return to the voice. That must be our test, and perhaps then we shall be able to appreciate some of the subtleties of Greek art-criticism.

As it now is, we cannot do so. Sometimes, when I have written a piece of prose that I have been modest enough to consider absolutely free from fault, a dreadful thought comes over me that I may have been guilty of the immoral effeminacy of using trochaic and tribrachic movements, a crime for which a learned critic of the Augustan age censures with most just severity the brilliant if somewhat paradoxical Hegesias. I grow cold when I think of it, and wonder to myself if the admirable ethical effect of the prose of that charming writer, who once in a spirit of reckless generosity towards the uncultivated portion of our community proclaimed the monstrous doctrine that conduct is three-fourths of life, will not some day be entirely annihilated by the discovery that the paeons have been wrongly placed.

ERNEST. Ah! now you are flippant.

GILBERT. Who would not be flippant when he is gravely told that the Greeks had no art-critics? I can understand it being said that the constructive genius of the Greeks lost itself in criticism, but not that the race to whom we owe the critical spirit did not criticise. You will not ask me to give you a survey of Greek art criticism from Plato to Plotinus. The night is too lovely for that, and the moon, if she heard us, would put more ashes on her face than are there already. But think merely of one perfect little work of aesthetic criticism, Aristotle's Treatise on Poetry.

It is not perfect in form, for it is badly written, consisting perhaps of notes dotted down for an art lecture, or of isolated fragments destined for some larger book, but in temper and treatment it is perfect, absolutely. The ethical effect of art, its importance to culture, and its place in the formation of character, had been done once for all by Plato; but here we have art treated, not from the moral, but from the purely aesthetic point of view.

Plato had, of course, dealt with many definitely artistic subjects, such as the importance of unity in a work of art, the necessity for tone and harmony, the aesthetic value of appearances, the relation of the visible arts to the external world, and the relation of fiction to fact. He first perhaps stirred in the soul of man that desire that we have not yet satisfied, the desire to know the connection between Beauty and Truth, and the place of Beauty in the moral and intellectual order of the Kosmos.

The problems of idealism and realism, as he sets them forth, may seem to many to be somewhat barren of result in the metaphysical sphere of abstract being in which he places them, but transfer them to the sphere of art, and you will find that they are still vital and full of meaning. It may be that it is as a critic of Beauty that Plato is destined to live, and that by altering the name of the sphere of his speculation we shall find a new philosophy.

But Aristotle, like Goethe, deals with art primarily in its concrete manifestations, taking Tragedy, for instance, and investigating the material it uses, which is language, its subject-matter, which is life, the method by which it works, which is action, the conditions under which it reveals itself, which are those of theatric presentation, its logical structure, which is plot, and its final aesthetic appeal, which is to the sense of beauty realised through the passions of pity and awe. That purification and spiritualising of the nature which he calls [Greek text which cannot be reproduced] is, as Goethe saw, essentially aesthetic, and is not moral, as Lessing fancied. Concerning himself primarily with the impression that the work of art produces, Aristotle sets himself to analyse that impression, to investigate its source, to see how it is engendered. As a physiologist and psychologist, he knows that the health of a function resides in energy.

To have a capacity for a passion and not to realise it, is to make oneself incomplete and limited. The mimic spectacle of life that Tragedy affords cleanses the bosom of much 'perilous stuff,' and by presenting high and worthy objects for the exercise of the emotions purifies and spiritualises the man; nay, not merely does it spiritualise him, but it initiates him also into noble feelings of which he might else have known nothing, the word [Greek text which cannot be reproduced] having, it has sometimes seemed to me, a definite allusion to the rite of initiation, if indeed that be not, as I am occasionally tempted to fancy, its true and only meaning here. This is of course a mere outline of the book. But you see what a perfect piece of aesthetic criticism it is. Who indeed but a Greek could have analysed art so well?

After reading it, one does not wonder any longer that Alexandria devoted itself so largely to art-criticism, and that we find the artistic temperaments of the day investigating every question of style and manner, discussing the great Academic schools of painting, for instance, such as the school of Sicyon, that sought to preserve the dignified traditions of the antique mode, or the realistic and impressionist schools, that aimed at reproducing actual life, or the elements of ideality in portraiture, or the artistic value of the epic form in an age so modern as theirs, or the proper subject-matter for the artist.

Indeed, I fear that the inartistic temperaments of the day busied themselves also in matters of literature and art, for the accusations of plagiarism were endless, and such accusations proceed either from the thin colourless lips of impotence, or from the grotesque mouths of those who, possessing nothing of their own, fancy that they can gain a reputation for wealth by crying out that they have been robbed.

And I assure you, my dear Ernest, that the Greeks chattered about painters quite as much as people do nowadays, and had their private views, and shilling exhibitions, and Arts and Crafts guilds, and Pre-Raphaelite movements, and movements towards realism, and lectured about art, and wrote essays on art, and produced their art-historians, and their archaeologists, and all the rest of it. Why, even the theatrical managers of travelling companies brought their dramatic critics with them when they went on tour, and paid them very handsome salaries for writing laudatory notices.

Whatever, in fact, is modern in our life we owe to the Greeks. Whatever is an anachronism is due to mediaevalism. It is the Greeks who have given us the whole system of art-criticism, and how fine their critical instinct was, may be seen from the fact that the material they criticised with most care was, as I have already said, language.

For the material that painter or sculptor uses is meagre in comparison with that of words. Words have not merely music as sweet as that of viol and lute, colour as rich and vivid as any that makes lovely for us the canvas of the Venetian or the Spaniard, and plastic form no less sure and certain than that which reveals itself in marble or in bronze, but thought and passion and spirituality are theirs also, are theirs indeed alone.

If the Greeks had criticised nothing but language, they would still have been the great art-critics of the world. To know the principles of the highest art is to know the principles of all the arts.

But I see that the moon is hiding behind a sulphur-coloured cloud. Out of a tawny mane of drift she gleams like a lion's eye. She is afraid that I will talk to you of Lucian and Longinus, of Quinctilian and Dionysius, of Pliny and Fronto and Pausanias, of all those who in the antique world wrote or lectured upon art matters. She need not be afraid. I am tired of my expedition into the dim, dull abyss of facts. There is nothing left for me now but the divine [Greek text which cannot be reproduced] of another cigarette. Cigarettes have at least the charm of leaving one unsatisfied.

ERNEST. Try one of mine. They are rather good. I get them direct from Cairo. The only use of our attaches is that they supply their friends with excellent tobacco. And as the moon has hidden herself, let us talk a little longer. I am quite ready to admit that I was wrong in what I said about the Greeks. They were, as you have pointed out, a nation of art-critics. I acknowledge it, and I feel a little sorry for them. For the creative faculty is higher than the critical. There is really no comparison between them.

GILBERT. The antithesis between them is entirely arbitrary. Without the critical faculty, there is no artistic creation at all, worthy of the name. You spoke a little while ago of that fine spirit of choice and delicate instinct of selection by which the artist realises life for us, and gives to it a momentary perfection. Well, that spirit of choice, that subtle tact of omission, is really the critical faculty in one of its most characteristic moods, and no one who does not possess this critical faculty can create anything at all in art. Arnold's definition of literature as a criticism of life was not very felicitous in form, but it showed how keenly he recognised the importance of the critical element in all creative work.

ERNEST. I should have said that great artists work unconsciously, that they were 'wiser than they knew,' as, I think, Emerson remarks somewhere.

GILBERT. It is really not so, Ernest. All fine imaginative work is self-conscious and deliberate. No poet sings because he must sing. At least, no great poet does. A great poet sings because he chooses to sing. It is so now, and it has always been so. We are sometimes apt to think that the voices that sounded at the dawn of poetry were simpler, fresher, and more natural than ours, and that the world which the early poets looked at, and through which they walked, had a kind of poetical quality of its own, and almost without changing could pass into song.

The snow lies thick now upon Olympus, and its steep scarped sides are bleak and barren, but once, we fancy, the white feet of the Muses brushed the dew from the anemones in the morning, and at evening came Apollo to sing to the shepherds in the vale. But in this we are merely lending to other ages what we desire, or think we desire, for our own. Our historical sense is at fault.

Every century that produces poetry is, so far, an artificial century, and the work that seems to us to be the most natural and simple product of its time is always the result of the most self-conscious effort. Believe me, Ernest, there is no fine art without self-consciousness, and self-consciousness and the critical spirit are one.

ERNEST. I see what you mean, and there is much in it. But surely you would admit that the great poems of the early world, the primitive, anonymous collective poems, were the result of the imagination of races, rather than of the imagination of individuals?

GILBERT. Not when they became poetry. Not when they received a beautiful form. For there is no art where there is no style, and no style where there is no unity, and unity is of the individual. No doubt Homer had old ballads and stories to deal with, as Shakespeare had chronicles and plays and novels from which to work, but they were merely his rough material. He took them, and shaped them into song. They become his, because he made them lovely.

They were built out of music,
And so not built at all,
And therefore built for ever.

The longer one studies life and literature, the more strongly one feels that behind everything that is wonderful stands the individual, and that it is not the moment that makes the man, but the man who creates the age. Indeed, I am inclined to think that each myth and legend that seems to us to spring out of the wonder, or terror, or fancy of tribe and nation, was in its origin the invention of one single mind. The curiously limited number of the myths seems to me to point to this conclusion. But we must not go off into questions of comparative mythology. We must keep to criticism. And what I want to point out is this.

An age that has no criticism is either an age in which art is immobile, hieratic, and confined to the reproduction of formal types, or an age that possesses no art at all. There have been critical ages that have not been creative, in the ordinary sense of the word, ages in which the spirit of man has sought to set in order the treasures of his treasure-house, to separate the gold from the silver, and the silver from the lead, to count over the jewels, and to give names to the pearls. But there has never been a creative age that has not been critical also. For it is the critical faculty that invents fresh forms. The tendency of creation is to repeat itself.

It is to the critical instinct that we owe each new school that springs up, each new mould that art finds ready to its hand. There is really not a single form that art now uses that does not come to us from the critical spirit of Alexandria, where these forms were either stereotyped or invented or made perfect. I say Alexandria, not merely because it was there that the Greek spirit became most self-conscious, and indeed ultimately expired in scepticism and theology, but because it was to that city, and not to Athens, that Rome turned for her models, and it was through the survival, such as it was, of the Latin language that culture lived at all.

When, at the Renaissance, Greek literature dawned upon Europe, the soil had been in some measure prepared for it. But, to get rid of the details of history, which are always wearisome and usually inaccurate, let us say generally, that the forms of art have been due to the Greek critical spirit. To it we owe the epic, the lyric, the entire drama in every one of its developments, including burlesque, the idyll, the romantic novel, the novel of adventure, the essay, the dialogue, the oration, the lecture, for which perhaps we should not forgive them, and the epigram, in all the wide meaning of that word.

In fact, we owe it everything, except the sonnet, to which, however, some curious parallels of thought-movement may be traced in the Anthology, American journalism, to which no parallel can be found anywhere, and the ballad in sham Scotch dialect, which one of our most industrious writers has recently proposed should be made the basis for a final and unanimous effort on the part of our second-rate poets to make themselves really romantic.

Each new school, as it appears, cries out against criticism, but it is to the critical faculty in man that it owes its origin. The mere creative instinct does not innovate, but reproduces.

ERNEST. You have been talking of criticism as an essential part of the creative spirit, and I now fully accept your theory. But what of criticism outside creation? I have a foolish habit of reading periodicals, and it seems to me that most modern criticism is perfectly valueless.

GILBERT. So is most modern creative work also. Mediocrity weighing mediocrity in the balance, and incompetence applauding its brother--that is the spectacle which the artistic activity of England affords us from time to time. And yet, I feel I am a little unfair in this matter. As a rule, the critics--I speak, of course, of the higher class, of those in fact who write for the sixpenny papers--are far more cultured than the people whose work they are called upon to review. This is, indeed, only what one would expect, for criticism demands infinitely more cultivation than creation does.

ERNEST. Really?

GILBERT. Certainly. Anybody can write a three-volumed novel. It merely requires a complete ignorance of both life and literature. The difficulty that I should fancy the reviewer feels is the difficulty of sustaining any standard. Where there is no style a standard must be impossible. The poor reviewers are apparently reduced to be the reporters of the police-court of literature, the chroniclers of the doings of the habitual criminals of art. It is sometimes said of them that they do not read all through the works they are called upon to criticise.

They do not. Or at least they should not. If they did so, they would become confirmed misanthropes, or if I may borrow a phrase from one of the pretty Newnham graduates, confirmed womanthropes for the rest of their lives. Nor is it necessary. To know the vintage and quality of a wine one need not drink the whole cask. It must be perfectly easy in half an hour to say whether a book is worth anything or worth nothing.

Ten minutes are really sufficient, if one has the instinct for form. Who wants to wade through a dull volume? One tastes it, and that is quite enough--more than enough, I should imagine. I am aware that there are many honest workers in painting as well as in literature who object to criticism entirely. They are quite right. Their work stands in no intellectual relation to their age. It brings us no new element of pleasure. It suggests no fresh departure of thought, or passion, or beauty. It should not be spoken of. It should be left to the oblivion that it deserves.

ERNEST. But, my dear fellow--excuse me for interrupting you--you seem to me to be allowing your passion for criticism to lead you a great deal too far. For, after all, even you must admit that it is much more difficult to do a thing than to talk about it.

GILBERT. More difficult to do a thing than to talk about it? Not at all. That is a gross popular error. It is very much more difficult to talk about a thing than to do it. In the sphere of actual life that is of course obvious. Anybody can make history. Only a great man can write it. There is no mode of action, no form of emotion, that we do not share with the lower animals. It is only by language that we rise above them, or above each other--by language, which is the parent, and not the child, of thought. Action, indeed, is always easy, and when presented to us in its most aggravated, because most continuous form, which I take to be that of real industry, becomes simply the refuge of people who have nothing whatsoever to do. No, Ernest, don't talk about action. It is a blind thing dependent on external influences, and moved by an impulse of whose nature it is unconscious. It is a thing incomplete in its essence, because limited by accident, and ignorant of its direction, being always at variance with its aim. Its basis is the lack of imagination. It is the last resource of those who know not how to dream.

ERNEST. Gilbert, you treat the world as if it were a crystal ball. You hold it in your hand, and reverse it to please a wilful fancy. You do nothing but re-write history.

GILBERT. The one duty we owe to history is to re-write it. That is not the least of the tasks in store for the critical spirit. When we have fully discovered the scientific laws that govern life, we shall realise that the one person who has more illusions than the dreamer is the man of action. He, indeed, knows neither the origin of his deeds nor their results. From the field in which he thought that he had sown thorns, we have gathered our vintage, and the fig-tree that he planted for our pleasure is as barren as the thistle, and more bitter. It is because Humanity has never known where it was going that it has been able to find its way.

ERNEST. You think, then, that in the sphere of action a conscious aim is a delusion?

GILBERT. It is worse than a delusion. If we lived long enough to see the results of our actions it may be that those who call themselves good would be sickened with a dull remorse, and those whom the world calls evil stirred by a noble joy. Each little thing that we do passes into the great machine of life which may grind our virtues to powder and make them worthless, or transform our sins into elements of a new civilisation, more marvellous and more splendid than any that has gone before. But men are the slaves of words. They rage against Materialism, as they call it, forgetting that there has been no material improvement that has not spiritualised the world, and that there have been few, if any, spiritual awakenings that have not wasted the world's faculties in barren hopes, and fruitless aspirations, and empty or trammelling creeds. What is termed Sin is an essential element of progress.

Without it the world would stagnate, or grow old, or become colourless. By its curiosity Sin increases the experience of the race. Through its intensified assertion of individualism, it saves us from monotony of type. In its rejection of the current notions about morality, it is one with the higher ethics. And as for the virtues! What are the virtues? Nature, M. Renan tells us, cares little about chastity, and it may be that it is to the shame of the Magdalen, and not to their own purity, that the Lucretias of modern life owe their freedom from stain. Charity, as even those of whose religion it makes a formal part have been compelled to acknowledge, creates a multitude of evils.

The mere existence of conscience, that faculty of which people prate so much nowadays, and are so ignorantly proud, is a sign of our imperfect development. It must be merged in instinct before we become fine. Self-denial is simply a method by which man arrests his progress, and self-sacrifice a survival of the mutilation of the savage, part of that old worship of pain which is so terrible a factor in the history of the world, and which even now makes its victims day by day, and has its altars in the land. Virtues! Who knows what the virtues are? Not you. Not I. Not any one. It is well for our vanity that we slay the criminal, for if we suffered him to live he might show us what we had gained by his crime. It is well for his peace that the saint goes to his martyrdom. He is spared the sight of the horror of his harvest.

ERNEST. Gilbert, you sound too harsh a note. Let us go back to the more gracious fields of literature. What was it you said? That it was more difficult to talk about a thing than to do it?

GILBERT (after a pause). Yes: I believe I ventured upon that simple truth. Surely you see now that I am right? When man acts he is a puppet. When he describes he is a poet. The whole secret lies in that. It was easy enough on the sandy plains by windy Ilion to send the notched arrow from the painted bow, or to hurl against the shield of hide and flamelike brass the long ash-handled spear. It was easy for the adulterous queen to spread the Tyrian carpets for her lord, and then, as he lay couched in the marble bath, to throw over his head the purple net, and call to her smooth-faced lover to stab through the meshes at the heart that should have broken at Aulis.

For Antigone even, with Death waiting for her as her bridegroom, it was easy to pass through the tainted air at noon, and climb the hill, and strew with kindly earth the wretched naked corse that had no tomb. But what of those who wrote about these things? What of those who gave them reality, and made them live for ever? Are they not greater than the men and women they sing of? 'Hector that sweet knight is dead,' and Lucian tells us how in the dim under-world Menippus saw the bleaching skull of Helen, and marvelled that it was for so grim a favour that all those horned ships were launched, those beautiful mailed men laid low, those towered cities brought to dust.

Yet, every day the swanlike daughter of Leda comes out on the battlements, and looks down at the tide of war. The greybeards wonder at her loveliness, and she stands by the side of the king. In his chamber of stained ivory lies her leman. He is polishing his dainty armour, and combing the scarlet plume. With squire and page, her husband passes from tent to tent. She can see his bright hair, and hears, or fancies that she hears, that clear cold voice. In the courtyard below, the son of Priam is buckling on his brazen cuirass. The white arms of Andromache are around his neck. He sets his helmet on the ground, lest their babe should be frightened.

Behind the embroidered curtains of his pavilion sits Achilles, in perfumed raiment, while in harness of gilt and silver the friend of his soul arrays himself to go forth to the fight. From a curiously carven chest that his mother Thetis had brought to his ship-side, the Lord of the Myrmidons takes out that mystic chalice that the lip of man had never touched, and cleanses it with brimstone, and with fresh water cools it, and, having washed his hands, fills with black wine its burnished hollow, and spills the thick grape-blood upon the ground in honour of Him whom at Dodona barefooted prophets worshipped, and prays to Him, and knows not that he prays in vain, and that by the hands of two knights from Troy, Panthous' son, Euphorbus, whose love-locks were looped with gold, and the Priamid, the lion-hearted, Patroklus, the comrade of comrades, must meet his doom.

Phantoms, are they? Heroes of mist and mountain? Shadows in a song? No: they are real. Action! What is action? It dies at the moment of its energy. It is a base concession to fact. The world is made by the singer for the dreamer.

ERNEST. While you talk it seems to me to be so.

GILBERT. It is so in truth. On the mouldering citadel of Troy lies the lizard like a thing of green bronze. The owl has built her nest in the palace of Priam. Over the empty plain wander shepherd and goatherd with their flocks, and where, on the wine-surfaced, oily sea, [Greek text which cannot be reproduced], as Homer calls it, copper-prowed and streaked with vermilion, the great galleys of the Danaoi came in their gleaming crescent, the lonely tunny-fisher sits in his little boat and watches the bobbing corks of his net.

Yet, every morning the doors of the city are thrown open, and on foot, or in horse-drawn chariot, the warriors go forth to battle, and mock their enemies from behind their iron masks. All day long the fight rages, and when night comes the torches gleam by the tents, and the cresset burns in the hall.

Those who live in marble or on painted panel, know of life but a single exquisite instant, eternal indeed in its beauty, but limited to one note of passion or one mood of calm. Those whom the poet makes live have their myriad emotions of joy and terror, of courage and despair, of pleasure and of suffering. The seasons come and go in glad or saddening pageant, and with winged or leaden feet the years pass by before them. They have their youth and their manhood, they are children, and they grow old. It is always dawn for St. Helena, as Veronese saw her at the window. Through the still morning air the angels bring her the symbol of God's pain.

The cool breezes of the morning lift the gilt threads from her brow. On that little hill by the city of Florence, where the lovers of Giorgione are lying, it is always the solstice of noon, of noon made so languorous by summer suns that hardly can the slim naked girl dip into the marble tank the round bubble of clear glass, and the long fingers of the lute-player rest idly upon the chords.

It is twilight always for the dancing nymphs whom Corot set free among the silver poplars of France. In eternal twilight they move, those frail diaphanous figures, whose tremulous white feet seem not to touch the dew-drenched grass they tread on.

But those who walk in epos, drama, or romance, see through the labouring months the young moons wax and wane, and watch the night from evening unto morning star, and from sunrise unto sunsetting can note the shifting day with all its gold and shadow.

For them, as for us, the flowers bloom and wither, and the Earth, that Green-tressed Goddess as Coleridge calls her, alters her raiment for their pleasure. The statue is concentrated to one moment of perfection. The image stained upon the canvas possesses no spiritual element of growth or change. If they know nothing of death, it is because they know little of life, for the secrets of life and death belong to those, and those only, whom the sequence of time affects, and who possess not merely the present but the future, and can rise or fall from a past of glory or of shame.

Movement, that problem of the visible arts, can be truly realised by Literature alone. It is Literature that shows us the body in its swiftness and the soul in its unrest.

ERNEST. Yes; I see now what you mean. But, surely, the higher you place the creative artist, the lower must the critic rank.

GILBERT. Why so?

ERNEST. Because the best that he can give us will be but an echo of rich music, a dim shadow of clear-outlined form. It may, indeed, be that life is chaos, as you tell me that it is; that its martyrdoms are mean and its heroisms ignoble; and that it is the function of Literature to create, from the rough material of actual existence, a new world that will be more marvellous, more enduring, and more true than the world that common eyes look upon, and through which common natures seek to realise their perfection. But surely, if this new world has been made by the spirit and touch of a great artist, it will be a thing so complete and perfect that there will be nothing left for the critic to do.

I quite understand now, and indeed admit most readily, that it is far more difficult to talk about a thing than to do it. But it seems to me that this sound and sensible maxim, which is really extremely soothing to one's feelings, and should be adopted as its motto by every Academy of Literature all over the world, applies only to the relations that exist between Art and Life, and not to any relations that there may be between Art and Criticism.

Chapter 14

Oscar Wilde Chronology

1854 Born in Dublin. Son of Sir William Wilde, founder of the first eye and ear hospital in Great Britain, and Jane Francesca Elgee Wilde, a writer.

1864 Enters the Portora Royal School at Enniskillen.

1871 Enters Trinity College, Dublin.

1874-1879 Attends Magdalen College, Oxford. It is a time of conflict for him, conflict between the philosophies of Ruskin and Pater, between Roman Catholicism and Freemasonry, and between heterosexuality and homosexuality. He distinguishes himself for scholarship; also for dressing and acting eccentricly.

1878 Wins Newdigate Prize for his poem Ravenna.

1881 Publishes his first volume of verse, Poems. His manners and attire are satirized in Gilbert and Sullivan's comic opera Patience.

1882 A lecture tour of the United States is a great personal success. Produces his first play, in New York. Called Vera, it is unsuccessful.

1883-1884 Gives a successful lecture tour of the United Kingdom. Writes his second unsuccessful play, The Duchess of Padua.

1884 Marries Constance Lloyd the daughter of a Dublin barrister and a woman with financial resources. Takes a house in Chelsea, an artistic section of London. Makes and builds friendships with fellow artists.

1887-1889 Edits Woman's World, a popular magazine.

1888 Publishes The Happy Prince and Other Tales, a collection of original fairy tales.

1889 Publishes essay on Shakespeare's sonnets in Blackwood's Magazine, "The Portrait of Mr. W. H. " The theory of the essay is that many of the sonnets are addressed to a man. "The Decay of Lying" appears in The Nineteenth Century.

1890 Serializes The Picture of Dorian Gray in Lippincott's Magazine.

1891 Publishes several essays and three books exhibiting his far-ranging interests: Intentions, an important collection of dialogues containing Wilde's aesthetic philosophy; Lord Arthur Savile's Crime, and Other Stones, a collection of short stories; and The Picture of Dorian Gray, his only novel. The novel arouses a storm of controversy over its morality. Publishes another collection of stories, A House of Pomegranates. Produces The Duchess of Padua. Begins his friendship with Lord Alfred Douglas, a friendship that will prove disasterous.

1892 Enjoys great popular success for his production of Lady Windermere's Fan at the St. James's Theatre. Writes (in French) SalomŽ. It is not produced because of an old law forbidding theatrical depiction of biblical characters.

1893 Produces another success, A Woman of No Importance. Publishes Lady Windermere's Fan. Publishes SalomŽ in French.

1894 Renowned actress Sarah Bernhardt puts on SalomŽ in Paris. Wilde publishes SalomŽ in English translation. Writes The Importance of Being Earnest.

1895 Puts on An ldeal Husband at the Haymarket Theatre and The Importance of Being Earnest at the St. James's Theatre; it is his last and best dramatic work. This is the height of his theatrical success; both plays are popular and critical hits. Infatuated with Douglas, Wilde flaunts the friendship in public, drawing public criticism from Lord Douglas's father. Wilde sues for libel, but then abandons the case. Incriminating evidence that comes to light in cross-examination leads to Wilde's arrest for homosexual offenses. After a hung jury on his first trial, Wilde is found guilty of homosexuality in a second. The sentence is two years at hard labour. He is bankrupted, humiliated.

1897 In prison, writes De Profundis, a moving description of his spiritual progress to religious insight; it will be published in part in 1905 and in full in 1962. On his release from prison, goes in exile to the Continent, where he lives under an alias, Sebastian Melmoth.

1898 Publishes his best known poem, The Ballad of Reading Gaol. Also publishes two letters on prison reform. His wife dies.

1900 After being baptized into the Roman Catholic Church, he dies of cerebral meningitis at the Hotel D'Alsace. He is buried at Bagneaux.

Bibliography

Beckson, Karl. The Oscar Wilde Encyclopedia. (AMS, 1998)

Ellmann, Richard. Oscar Wilde. (Vintage, 1988) ISBN 0-521-47987-8

Holland, Merlin. The Wilde Album. (Fourth Estate, 1997) ISBN 1-85702-782-5

Igoe, Vivien. A Literary Guide to Dublin. (Methuen, 1994) ISBN 0-413-69120-9

Mason, Stuart [Christopher Millard]. Bibliography of Oscar Wilde. (Laurie, 1914; latest edition Oak Knoll Press, 1999) ISBN 1-578-98104-2

McKenna, Neil. The Secret Life of Oscar Wilde. (Random House, 2004) ISBN 0-09-941545-3

Raby, Peter (ed.). The Cambridge Companion to Oscar Wilde. (CUP, 1997) ISBN 0-521-47987-8

Tufescu, Florina. Oscar Wilde's Plagiarism: The Triumph of Art over Ego. (Irish Academic Press, 2008) ISBN 9780716529040

Wilde, Oscar. The Complete Works of Oscar Wilde. (Collins, 2003) ISBN 0-00-714436-9

Whittington-Egan, Molly. Such White Lillies: Frank Miles & Oscar Wilde, Rivendale 2008 ISBN 1904201091

Wood, Julia: The Resurrection of Oscar Wilde; The Lutterworth Press 2007, ISBN 9780718830717

Yates, Jim: Oh!Père Lachaise:Oscar's Wilde Purgatory, Édition d'Amèlie 2007: ISBN 9780955583605